**Matthew Collin** is a journalist who has been editor of *The Big Issue, i-D* and the *Time Out* website. He has written about popular culture, music, travel, technology and the politics of social justice for the *Observer*, the *Telegraph*, the *Guardian*, *Wired*, *Spin* and *Mojo*, amongst many others. He first reported from Belgrade for *The Face* in 1996. His last book, *Altered State: The Story of Ecstasy Culture and Acid House*, a history of the British drug and dance scene, was published by Serpent's Tail in 1997.

**Also by Matthew Collin and published by Serpent's Tail**

*Altered State: The Story of Ecstasy Culture and Acid House*

'At last somebody has written the *real* history of the last ten years, and written it with such wit, verve, empathy and profound intelligence. I can't recommend this marvellous piece of work enough' **Irvine Welsh**

'The first full history of the dance boom which, fuelled by Ecstasy, has transformed British culture over the past decade: here you will also find the drive to transcendence, or oblivion, that is at the heart of British pop' **Jon Savage**

'A tale as irresistible as the culture that inspired it' *Wired*

'*Altered State* is not just timely; it was crying out to be written' *Independent*

'This is the (as near as you can get it) definitive tale of E, acid house, 1988 and all that' *Loaded*

'Perhaps the most important document written about contemporary British society' *The Scotsman*

'Turns an admirably steeply investigative eye on the criminal takeover of the Ecstasy infrastructure' *Independent on Sunday*

'Sends all those imitation Irvines from the football-hooligan school of literary E-endeavours straight to the back of the class' *The Face*

# This is Serbia Calling

**Rock'n'roll radio and Belgrade's underground resistance**

**Matthew Collin**

Library of Congress Catalog Card Number: 00–108742

A complete catalogue record for this book can be obtained from the British Library on request

First published in 2001
by Serpent's Tail,
4 Blackstock Mews, London N4 2BT
website: www.serpentstail.com

Printed in Great Britain by Mackays of Chatham plc
10 9 8 7 6 5 4 3 2 1

# contents

# introduction

**'We are the generation which has ceased to exist'**
*Belgrade rock singer (2000)*

Welcome to the surreal life. A city where everything is permitted, and nothing is permitted. Where anything is possible, and everything is impossible. Where everything appears normal, but nothing is as it seems. Welcome to Belgrade, city of chaos.

In Serbia's capital, just over twelve months after the end of the Western bombing, few signs of airborne destruction remained – only the stacks of anti-NATO souvenir postcards on streetside stalls and a few collapsed state buildings, expertly gutted by the precision hits of smart bombs. War tourists and thrill-seekers looking for a holiday in someone else's misery would not have found much to delight them here. When the sun went down and the nocturnal parade began, cafés bustled with light and music as the city came out to play. People looked well-dressed, well-fed. This could, on first impressions, have been any central European capital.

It was, as so many things were here, just an illusion – one which quickly evaporated to reveal the truth beneath. In the designer bars of the Old Town, the soundtrack might have been the latest Western dance imports, but the babble of voices attested to very different circumstances. It was the peculiar quirks of language which gave the game away, words or phrases used in an unfamiliar manner. However a conversation began, it would inevitably drift towards a discussion of 'the situation', towards politics, what was happening 'inside' and 'outside', and towards the one over-riding, universal desire: to live a 'normal' life.

In the West, 'normality' is virtually taken for granted: it is the perennial, unchanging state of affairs. It is unremarkable, and thus rarely mentioned. Yet its meaning could not have been more different for the young people of Belgrade – for this was a generation whose normality had been snatched away, and replaced with uncertainty, poverty, war and violence. Those who grew up in Belgrade in the nineties were the dispossessed – a generation for whom time stood still. As one local record producer says: 'The years from twenty to thirty, these are the best years of your life. And they were stolen from me.'

Under the regime of Slobodan Milošević, normality was a dream, a distant and uncharted Utopia; it signified the opposite of everything that had happened to Belgrade's citizens over the past decade: four wars; a brutal police force running rampant; riots in the streets; a state of mass psychosis generated by the shrill propaganda of television; violent xenophobia; the militarisation of the urban landscape; all-pervasive deprivation; gangsters and war profiteers becoming the social elite, and murderers elected to parliament.

They had watched their lives collapse around them. Their country had shrunk – from mighty Yugoslavia to the tiny, wretched pariah state called Serbia, its name a byword for atrocity the world over. Their horizons had receded. Their social lives had been corroded by deprivation and the relentless silencing of alternatives. Their friends had emigrated in search of life and liberty. Some had been killed on the frontline. A few had killed themselves slowly, with heroin or alcohol. They had been discouraged from travelling outside the country, and information had been prohibited from coming in. Belgrade had become a prison cell, with its walls slowly closing in.

From a distance, the convulsions which ripped Yugoslavia apart inspired horror and disgust. But what did it feel like, from the inside, to have 'normality' stripped away and replaced with fear and misery?

Ten years previously, if you had asked someone of twenty-five what life would hold for them in Belgrade over the coming decade, they might have answered with a little trepidation, but still with some hope. They would not have predicted a series of dirty wars, a mass exodus of the brightest and most talented young people, the triumph of mafia overlords, and the effective establishment of a martial dictatorship, the last of its kind in Europe.

That young innocent of 1990 – if he or she existed – would most likely have left Belgrade long ago in search of peace and prosperity in America, Britain or Australia, as hundreds of thousands did during the nineties. This is not their story. Instead this is the story of those who stayed in the city, and struggled to survive, and tried their best to resist the whirlpool which dragged their lives relentlessly downwards into darkness. It is a tale of courage, foolhardiness, and a sheer bloody-minded refusal to give in, however high the odds were stacked.

It focuses on a small group of idealists who simply wanted to play rock'n'roll and tell the truth about what was really going on, and the coterie of like minds which coalesced around them, warming their hands at the flickering flame, keeping their dreams alive. They were few, thousands perhaps – in Milošević's Belgrade, the current was so strong that many couldn't help being swept along. They didn't always have the right answers. Sometimes the signal was too weak, or the transmission was fuzzy, or the interference got too strong. Sometimes there were, frankly, no answers that made any kind of sense at all in the face of the madness that reigned.

What they had was a small radio station – a student channel which evolved into one of the most powerful, dynamic and challenging broadcasters in the Balkans; one which compared favourably with the finest in Europe. This story revolves around that station, Radio B92, or B2-92 as it became known after state intervention usurped its premises, its frequency and its name. B92's tale mirrors the torrid contemporary history of Serbia – but, like all mirror images, it is an inversion, the complete opposite of Milošević's reality. Whatever happened in the city was reflected by B92; the political riots, the protests against the war in Bosnia, the vicious state crackdowns, the Draconian laws and the bully boys in their black leather jackets, the glory days of the winter of 1996–97, when it seemed the people would finally carry all before them – and the depression which came afterwards, when little really changed. Whenever political opposition flourished, they were right there, broadcasting it and amplifying it. Their voice could only be silenced by the crudest of interventions, and even then it returned, irrepressible, an energy which could not be destroyed.

But most importantly, what they tried to do was create a parallel world, one in which people still cherished human rights and justice, in which the world wasn't split into believers and heretics, good Serbs and delinquents, fighters for the heavenly kingdom and the evil forces of Western decadence. They dreamed of a world without borders, without xeno-phobia and hatred. They chose the international call-signs of techno and rock'n'roll over the parochial, folksy paeans to nationalism: the music of life over the music of death. They tried to tune into global progressive signals rather than the flatline monotone of isolation, while all around them Serbia looked inwards, gnawing on its own bones. In a country where politics and culture became one and the same – vehicles for unhappiness and oppression, orchestrated by the state and its lackeys – theirs was a vibrant cultural resistance, a unique fusion of pop culture and politics. They tried to keep alive some semblance of normal life, and of the spirit which thrived in the decade before the craziness took hold and turned them into marked men, citizens of one of the most hated nations on earth.

These were not typical young people. They did not, in many ways, represent their generation. They didn't vote for

Milošević, nor did most of them serve in the army, or emigrate. Although they attempted to reclaim the ordinary, they
were anything but. As Veran Matić, one of B92's founders
and still its central figure, says: 'We were selfish, because
through the station we came to create the things that we
lacked and those we wanted most. We created a world to live
in which was practically severed from the reality of repression
that surrounded us. It was perhaps the only way we could
survive.' This story takes place in that parallel world, and
attempts to trace its contours.

In a survey published in January 2000 by human resources
consultancy William M. Mercer, Belgrade was ranked the
twelfth worst city in the world to live in – below Sarajevo,
Lagos and Tripoli. Few who visited around that time would
argue. Reflecting the endemic feelings of paranoia, lawlessness
and uncertainty, the city itself seemed to be physically crumbling, as its bizarre mixture of survivalist capitalism, degraded
post-Communist bureaucracy and socially-sanctioned entrepreneurial criminality violated its urban soul. This was a city
which had almost lost its heart, and was fast losing its mind.

On a good day, looking north over town towards the slow
curl of the Sava river as it eased gently out of the Danube,
the tenements and towerblocks glinted silver, the colour of
promise and opportunity. When the sun hid itself, as it did so
often, behind stacked layers of dirty cloud, the eye was drawn
to the crumbling stucco, greasy windows and cracked paving
stones.

Yugoslavia's capital, with its population of around 1.5
million, has been the epicentre of Balkan power struggles for
many centuries. Since its founding, the city has been fought
over by successive waves of invaders – Celts, Romans, Huns,
Goths, Turks – and occupied by the Austrians during World
War One and the Germans during World War Two, when
heavy shelling obliterated much of its architectural heritage,
and the city was rebuilt in dour, Communist style. The latest

round of bombings, in 1999, left yet more of its buildings in ruins.

On a local tourist-information website, extravagant claims are made for the city's loveliness: 'Of all the cities I know, this one has the most beautiful position, the greatest amount of light and sunshine,' one writer opines expansively. 'It is indeed a White City, particularly from a distance. It is the whitest, the airiest of all the cities known to me, a white and sunny place, as if it had been chosen to be an image of freedom and the light in our flame.'

This is not a picture that is easily recognisable today. Although its name does mean 'white city', Belgrade is coated in every shade of grey – it is a concrete sprawl dominated by monolithic Communist structures, one of the ugliest towns in the world – an unreconstructed Cold War capital. As in most southern European cities, commercial and residential properties are not zoned off from each other, with apartment blocks in the central business district. Most of these are in various states of disrepair: plaster cracking, leaving buildings with flaked skins, paint in odd shades of bulk-bought lime and yellow, fading and scrofulous, stairwells dusty and lifts cranky and creaky.

Downtown is a jumble of tenements, kiosks, shops, offices, squares, alleys, mini-malls, dingy passageways and underpasses. The quality of light seems strained through a haze of exhaust fumes, cigarette smoke, pollution and neglect. Belgrade's landscape is a testament to the failure of Communist Party central planning. It goes on, sprawling, for miles. As you travel out of the city, the urban density dissolves into forests of utility housing, row upon row of grey municipal towers, the endless numbered 'bloks' of New Belgrade.

A few sectors of the downtown area still provoke the sense of awe they were originally intended to inspire – the grand boulevards, planned for opulent parades of Communist pomp, the Orthodox cathedral and the government buildings charged with the sternness and gravity of power – but the rest has merely been thrown up artlessly.

Nevertheless, Belgrade can be beautiful – when its concrete skeleton is swathed in a shroud of January snow amidst the first green shoots of a balmy spring or the final, glorious days of summer. Then its street life erupts into vibrant activity: a convivial pavement procession which endures whichever way the political winds blow – although those who live here insist that the daily parade is merely a pale and faded facsimile of that which existed a decade before.

Once proud and progressive, Belgrade became a city of money-changers and bootleg petrol-sellers, smuggled-chocolate vendors and streetside cigarette hawkers. Communism gave way to a vulgar survivalist capitalism: the brutal logic of market forces stripped naked, a patchwork system of entrepreneurial anarchy – heavily policed, yet essentially lawless.

For a year after the NATO bombing campaign of 1999, there were no air links into Belgrade from the West, only from 'friendly' countries like China. The easiest way to get in to the city was a six-hour minibus drive across the border from Budapest down the crumbling highway – a white-knuckle ride usually accompanied by the top-volume blare of folksy Balkan cover versions of Madonna and the gaudily galloping accordions of Bosnian rock from the driver's stereo. (The Lonely Planet guide to the region advised would-be visitors: 'Avoid.') Yugoslavia had once been a magnet for tourists – over nine million people visited the country in 1988. Belgrade itself was a regular stop-off on Western students' low-budget summer holiday Inter-Rail travel circuit. Now the city had been severed from the world physically as well as politically. Those left inside the wall were abandoned to their fate.

This book is a chronology of the Belgrade resistance, written from a Western perspective and seen through a partisan tourist's eye. Its focus is not the political intrigues and international power games played out by NATO, the United

Nations and the governments of the West, or the vile particulars of the wars in Croatia, Bosnia or Kosovo. The intricate details of the collapse of Yugoslavia have already been well documented elsewhere – although, of course, their influence leaves its mark on the people whose stories are told here. Instead it is the tale of another war, one which was fought beneath the surface of global politics; a ten-year battle for survival fought by the unarmed, those who dared to stand up and be counted against a dictator who held all the cards – economic, military and political – and whose words and deeds were backed up with riot-shields, tear-gas and automatic weapons. It is the story of those who chose to remain, locked 'inside', and spend their youth striving to invent another Belgrade and another Serbia – an oasis of sanity amidst the twisted surrealism of criminality and degradation. Music was their transport into this other world, a force not simply for escape, but for transcendence, while their attempts to overturn the suffocating censorship of Milošević's media – a quest for the truth, or as close to it as they could get – was a lifeline to reality from the universe of distortion which they were condemned to inhabit, a totem held up against the encroaching darkness.

# 1

# darkness falls
# 1989–90

'I once loved this city because my life here was a great party.
There were days when I regretted that Belgrade wasn't
Amsterdam, but there were many more when I was pleased that
it was not East Berlin. Today I understand that this was a great
place for life. And then darkness started to fall. At the very
beginning, seven, eight years ago, nobody knew what it was
all about. Nobody sensed that the devil himself was coming to
town. When it became clear, it was already too late. The city
was divided. They were on one side, and we were on the other.'

*Monologue from Mladen Matičević's Belgrade documentary*
*'Ghetto' (1995)*

It was the year of revolutions, the summer when hope
returned, when fear was finally banished and all those repressed
desires bubbled inexorably to the surface. History was being
rewritten: in Prague, Warsaw and East Berlin, autocratic
regimes were falling like dominoes as the triumph of 'people
power' sent a wave of collective euphoria rolling over Eastern
Europe. Freedom: you could feel it, smell it, almost taste it.

For a brief moment – twelve months, perhaps – you could
almost taste it in Belgrade too. The state here had never been
so suffocatingly oppressive as in Poland or East Germany; and
now people felt wealthy again, they had the money to travel,
and the electric waves of optimism made them feel that here
too freedom might rise like a whirlwind and lay waste to half

a century of history. In this moment, Belgrade was a fine place to live. The city's urban nightlife was exploding with creative energy; its football club, the mighty Red Star Belgrade, was riding high in Europe; a new wave of rock bands was pioneering sounds the country had never heard before; ideas which had been stifled for decades were being discussed openly. Belgrade was showing signs that it could one day become a truly cosmopolitan metropolis.

Or it could turn in on itself, swim against the currents flowing across Eastern Europe, and attempt to turn back the clock. Signposts towards this other route were easily visible, to those who hadn't averted their eyes from the horizon. All across the country, hundreds of thousands of followers of a Communist apparatchik named Slobodan Milošević were rallying – against 'bureaucracy', they said – but those who listened could hear the venomous undertones of Serbian nationalism, of racial supremacy: the ideology which would eventually pull Yugoslavia apart. But they did not, and could not at that time, know exactly how ruinous it would prove to be.

At the centre of it all was the Communist Party – as it had been the solid, immovable object casting its shadow over all public life in Yugoslavia since Josip Broz Tito took control during World War Two. Milošević wanted to control it, and use it to rule the country, to become the next Tito; others wanted to use its resources to establish a very different kind of society to the stagnant orthodoxy which had existed since Tito died.

1989: only a matter of months before the dramatic fall of the Berlin Wall and the glorious victory of Prague's Velvet Revolution. Refracted through the jarring realities of what happened afterwards, this one short year has become blurred and softened by nostalgia. Memories of these days, when optimism reigned briefly, are recounted now with the warm glow of longing, sometimes rendering them unreliable except as signifiers of otherness desired. But this much is true:

Belgrade was in the midst of an economic boom after a decade mired in financial crisis as debts to the West, run up by Tito, were called in after his death in 1980. Now, under the reforms of Ante Marković, the last prime minister of a united Yugoslavia, inflation was falling and wages were rising. The city began to feel good about itself for the first time in years.

The economic mood was reflected in a fertile urban renaissance. Belgrade, the capital of both Serbia and Yugoslavia, had never been a cultural backwater; these were not people who dreamed of tasting the forbidden fruits of Levi's jeans and Beatles albums, or would trade their entire wage packet for a box of Marlboros. Pop culture had been thriving for over two decades, since the first beat groups had risen to the clarion calls of the sixties youth rebellion. 'In any other Eastern European country, it's as if pop culture started in 1989 with the fall of the Berlin Wall,' says Dragan Ambrozić, who at that time was editor of rock magazine *Ritam* (*Rhythm*). 'In Hungary they really could not tell the difference between the Rolling Stones, the Sex Pistols and Jethro Tull – it was all rock'n'roll to them. But in Belgrade it was not only important which group you liked, but which records by that group.'

Indeed – and despite the exaggeration – Yugoslavs felt they had never been like *them*, those badly-dressed, ill-fed, wan-faced children of Bulgaria, Romania, Hungary, Poland, Czechoslovakia and East Germany in their enforced timewarp. Yugoslavs had money (although much of it was borrowed from the West), they could take holidays abroad – a result of wily Tito's policy of semi-liberal openness – they watched the latest Western films and bought the new rock records. Yes, their country was no paradise, but at the same time it was no prison. As the incisive Croat author Slavenka Drakulić explains, they viewed the other Eastern Bloc states as poor relations: sad, grey and dull. They looked down upon them. 'Travelling was important to people from Yugoslavia, because we could do it, while the others in Eastern Europe could not,' Drakulić writes in *Café Europa*, her tour of the capitals of the post-Communist East. 'It was enough to go to Prague or Budapest to feel superior.'[1]

For Belgrade's youth, affluent and carefree, life in 1989 seemed like one long party. It was, says Srdjan Andjelić, then a drama student, a cultural awakening in which long-dormant energies were liberated and ran wild in the city streets. 'The night was alive,' he remembers. 'In the clubs you had funk, acid house, punk, it was a great kind of confusion; every week you had something happening in town, either in rock'n'roll or art or football. It was an awakening for the whole of society.'

In the late seventies, punk rock had shocked and catalysed the Yugoslav cultural landscape. The new wave blew away the folk-rock and flares of the post-hippy mainstream and injected the environment with pure metropolitan adrenaline. Punk's anti-establishment slogans struck a deep chord with those young people who desired liberty from the rigid order of the Communist state, and gave them a medium to express their frustration and discontent. For many Western punk bands, the anarchist rhetoric was little more than posturing. In Yugoslavia, it was taken very seriously indeed: they had something very real to shout about, not simply an amorphous, ill-defined 'system'. Theirs was a raw, guttural, testosterone-laced garage thrash, indebted not only to the Sex Pistols but to the dark princes of distortion, the Velvet Underground.

Punk not only helped fuel the post-Tito questioning of Communist values which was going on in wider society – although it was often difficult to address the country's social situation without cloaking lyrics in allegory and metaphor – but also catapulted the country into the global pop moment. For those immersed in it, the experience was cathartic. 'It was like an explosion, a big bang, like punk in 1976 in the UK. It wasn't important if you could play or not, it was important what you were saying,' says Loka, who played in a series of minor Belgrade punk bands. 'We thought it was over with

Communism and we were really going forward. This is it! We're living in Europe now!'

Punk, which evolved into the more musically diverse 'new wave', would remain the dominant alternative current in Yugoslavia's pop life for almost a decade. The rock bands operating in 1989 were still in debt to its heritage – most of them were new wave veterans themselves – but were trying to take it one step further and engineer a new mutant fusion. These were adventurous players who believed in another kind of rock'n'roll; a collage of samples and symbols from past and present. Disciplina Kičme had two drummers and no guitarist – they thought the electric guitar had become an anachronism. Their sound was feral and primitive; warped James Brown funk crossed with the psychedelia of Jimi Hendrix and the blaring horns of a traditional Serbian brass band. (They would later relocate to London and experiment with drum'n'bass and techno under the name Disciplin A Kitschme.) The Partibrejkers mixed raucous post-punk energy with the classic bluesy riffs of the Rolling Stones, translating rock mythology into Belgrade street slang. They may not have been innovators, but their sheer passion was infectious: 'It was something I hadn't heard before – fast, loud and dangerous for sure,' remembers one fan on hearing them for the first time. 'The singer desperately yelled how even if he could live one thousand years he would fit his whole life into one day. To a young teenager, like myself then, that was the only and whole truth.'[2]

Culturally as well as politically, it seemed that transformation was imminent. 'Belgrade bands were always individualists who obeyed no rules and invented their own style – mixtures or mutations of different ideas, changing all the time,' Dragan Ambrozić explains. 'Sometimes it was just a pretentious mishmash; that was a Belgrade way: if you cannot produce something dangerous, pretend that you are doing so. But it was very important to stick out as completely different to the rest, so being original was like a holy quest.' For the first time since the sixties Yugoslav rock was receiving respect from overseas – although, apart from the folk crooners who earned their Deutschmarks playing to expat labourers in Germany, only Slovenian art-rockers Laibach ever managed to forge a genuine pop career outside Yugoslavia.

The epicentre of Belgrade's nocturnal underground was the Akademija (Academy) club. It was sited in the basement of the Faculty of Fine Arts and run by art students. This was an exclusive place; unless you were studying there, you couldn't get in, but those who really wanted to be part of it found a way. And it was worth it. The manager, Miomir Grujić, a charismatic bohemian better known by his nickname of Fleka, had spent time in London a decade earlier, hanging out with Clash acolyte Don Letts, one of the main movers who pioneered punk rock in 1976, and Akademija was his attempt to recreate the experience back home. Fleka was an artist himself, and so the club's decor, painted by the most talented young upstarts on the art circuit, changed regularly. One time it might be comicbook graphics, the next Keith Haring-style spraycan graffiti. It was like being part of a strange and relentlessly changing tableau.

'Bang! You were suddenly in the Underground,' exclaims Dragan Ambrozić, remembering Akademija's heady atmosphere. 'It was so dark, you couldn't breathe properly and the beer was warm, but the band would be playing real loud and you would be rubbing shoulders with all the genuine rock stars you had ever seen on TV.'

'We wanted to connect Belgrade with the main currents in art and music. We were trying to establish a new language, a new way of expression,' says Fleka. He organised parties, exhibitions, bizarre theatrical happenings which attracted the most radical, fantastic creatures of the night – and those who never wanted it to end. 'One thing is very important,' says Dragan Ambrozić. 'For years, Akademija was the only club open all night in Belgrade, so it evolved into a regular last stop for everybody. Some nights you would even find one or two homeless guys inside, early in the morning, sleeping the night away in the middle of the noise, behind the backs of the supposed Belgrade rock'n'roll jet set.'

These emerging cultural forces were documented by a cult student radio show, *Ritam Crca* (*Rhythm of the Heart*), which had been running each night since the early eighties. In its own anarchic, free-flowing, sometimes amateurish way, *Rhythm of the Heart* covered nightlife, experimental art, theatre and fashion; it translated and transmitted articles from British style and music magazines like *The Face*, it played the latest indie rock hits – but it also attempted to deal with the changes that were happening in the Communist system and provide a forum for alternative, dissident voices. The silencing of dissent under Tito's rule meant that many anti-Communist writers had fled abroad. So reporters were sent on clandestine missions to London to pick up banned books and make contact with political exiles. Sometimes these exiles were extremely scared, they lived in hiding, afraid of the long reach of Yugoslavia's secret police who had been known to assassinate opponents of Communism. Some insisted on hasty, cloak-and-dagger rendezvous, looking over their shoulder and talking in whispers.

*Rhythm of the Heart*'s editor, Veran Matić – then in his late twenties and the oldest and most politically astute among the crew – wanted to explore ideas and events that had been written out of Yugoslavia's official history. This was a difficult and potentially risky task, as the programme was nominally under the control of the local Communist youth organisation. Matić had been in trouble before and had been suspended twice, and caused his boss to be fired, for airing provocative and critical views. Although *Rhythm of the Heart*'s, journalists felt the time was right to push for a more open, democratic system, they sometimes had to disguise their opinions in coded language. If they went too far too often, the show might be over.

The overthrow of Communist regimes in other Eastern European countries encouraged them to be as daring as they could without arousing the wrath of the apparatchiks. If change was coming in Warsaw and Prague, why not here, too, in Belgrade? 'It was a time of great hope,' remembers one reporter. 'Communist regimes all over Europe were being torn down and we hoped ours would be too. We didn't know then how difficult it would be. We were naive.'

The disputes which would destroy Yugoslavia in the coming decade were already revealing themselves. *Rhythm of the Heart* regularly reported on the activities of the Communist youth organisations across the whole country, and the internal feuds between representatives of the different Yugoslav republics over human rights and the extension of democracy gave an insight into what was going on right at the top, amongst the senior party officials, beyond the public gaze. Each of the six Yugoslav republics – Serbia, Croatia, Bosnia, Slovenia, Montenegro and Macedonia – was by now pulling violently in different directions. Some were calling for increased liberalisation, while others wanted a back-to-basics return to hard-line Marxist principles. *Rhythm of the Heart*, naturally, sympathised with the liberal modernisers. The hard-liners were led by the chairman of the Serbian Communist Party, Slobodan Milošević, who had recently been involved in the sacking of the editors of a misfit youth magazine named *Student*.

By 1989, these conflicts had reached the top of the political agenda. Change was coming, but exactly what kind of change, no one could quite predict. For those who weren't looking over their shoulders, the summer of 1989 was the greatest party Belgrade had ever seen. But while the city's youth revelled in their new-found freedoms, their revels displayed distinct undertones of suppressed hysteria – as if this might be the last chance to live like this, and so these pleasures must be enjoyed as intensely as possible, before they disappeared forever.

'At that time, no one was really thinking about the future. Belgrade was a completely crazy town – parties, clubs, everything you could imagine, it was a fast life and we were riding on that wave of general optimism,' says Gordan Paunović, a DJ on *Rhythm of the Heart.* 'That was everyday life, but behind it this big dark wave was coming. It was a weird combination of feelings. You could feel that something bad was going to happen.'

Over the previous two years, millions of Serbs had taken part in a series of mass rallies all around the country which became known as the 'anti-bureaucratic revolution' or the 'happening of the people'. It was a populist outpouring of discontent with the bankrupt Communist bureaucracy, and it made a hero out of Milošević, the man who harnessed its energy and used it to fuel his rise to power. These 'meetings of truth', with their hostile slogans, uniforms and flags, paintings of saints and images of Milošević, had become explicitly nationalist, calling for Serbian unity against the threat of genocidal enemies at the republic's borders, and were increasingly characterised by naked xenophobia.

They came to a powerful climax on 28 June 1989, when hundreds of thousands of people (some say it was one million, although others consider this a laughable exaggeration) gathered to hear Milošević speak at Kosovo Polje – the site of a historic battle between Serbs and Turks 600 years previously and an emotionally-charged symbol in Serbian mythology. Perhaps not even fully understanding the power of the forces he was unleashing, Milošević reignited long-dormant fantasies about Serbia's legendary history and hopes that it could once again become a 'heavenly kingdom'. 'Six centuries later,' he declared, 'we are still in battles and quarrels. They are not armed battles, though such things should not be excluded yet . . .'[3] These words, a ferocious endorsement of nationalism, carried within them the seeds of the destruction of Yugoslavia.

By this time, Milošević was president of Serbia, and had ambitions to rule the entire Yugoslav state. Born in 1941 in the small industrial town of Požarevac, his upbringing was grim and bloody. Milošević's family was deeply dysfunctional: his father became mentally ill and blew his head off with a shotgun; ten years later, his mother hanged herself from a light fitting in the family living room, while his uncle also shot himself – a history which has led many to believe he inherited pathological self-destructive tendencies which he then imposed on his subjects. Nevertheless, the young Slobodan was a solid, straight-laced, chubby and unremarkable schoolboy. His childhood sweetheart, Mirjana ('Mira') Marković, would later become his wife. She came from a high-ranking Communist family; her aunt was Tito's lover, her mother a Communist partisan during World War Two who was tortured by the Nazis.

Milošević went to university in Belgrade to study law, became head of the college Communist Party's ideology section and later the chief of the entire Party (he was such a Party clone that he was nicknamed 'Little Lenin'). As Dragan Ambrozić commented later: 'He looked like a scarecrow – a real caricature of an apparatchik. It was obvious from the start he was not a guy who ever suspected he did anything wrong in his life. I am very afraid of that sort of idiot.' At university he also met Ivan Stambolić, who would become his mentor and act as best man at his wedding, and who took Milošević with him on his journey up through the ranks of the state institutions until, ultimately, Stambolić became president of Serbia.

Milošević developed a reputation as a dedicated if slightly dull loyalist, both modest and unambitious. The Communist boss demonstrated no interest in nationalist ideas although, after the watershed Memorandum of the Serbian Academy of Arts and Sciences – the explosive document which sparked the revival of Serbian nationalism – was published in 1986, he did not speak out in public against it.

In 1987, after he visited Kosovo – a region with enduring spiritual resonance in both the Serbian Orthodox religion and Serbian history – he grasped that the plight of the Kosovo Serb minority, which was outnumbered nine-to-one by ethnic Albanians, was an emotive issue upon which he could base a challenge for the leadership of the country. Setting aside his Communist beliefs, perhaps because he realised earlier than most that Communism's days were numbered in Eastern Europe, he invoked the spirit of nationalism enshrined in the controversial Memorandum and coldly ousted his friend Stambolić from the presidency, which he then grabbed for himself. 'He's willing to change ideology every day,' Stambolić said later. 'He'll change his beliefs, allies as well. He'll use anyone and then throw them away.'[4] Milošević had finally revealed himself as the most ruthless of operators: both ideology and friendship were nothing compared to what he desired most – power itself.

The nationalism which Milošević employed was far graver than simple patriotism. This was the mass psychology of hatred, aimed at perpetuating his own dominance of the country by blaming all its ills on a succession of enemies both outside and inside its borders. By defining other nationalities and political orientations as a threat, he managed to unite a large section of the population around him as the sole true defender of the Serbs.

Pondering his own recipe for success, Adolf Hitler once noted: 'The effectiveness of the truly national leader consists in preventing his people from dividing their attention, and keeping it fixed on a common enemy.'[5] This is exactly what Milošević succeeded in doing. He would dominate the country for the next decade, and to the outside world he would come to personify contemporary Serbia, while his own mental traits – passive aggression, manipulation, almost suicidal brinkmanship – would characterise the politics of the entire country.

Some thought that his nationalism was just a pose, another slick strategy of a ruling bureaucracy which was adept at hiding its true intentions behind a smokescreen of rhetoric, and didn't realise how dangerous Milošević might turn out to be. 'It was all meant to be a game,' says Dragan Ambrozić. 'Everybody was so sure that he was only saying those hard words, not meaning them, like any Communist in power.' Nevertheless, Milošević was never seen as a joke figure, even in the urban intellectual circles which despised him from the beginning. It was evident as soon as he reached the Party's higher ranks that he represented a serious threat to any hopes of further liberalisation in Yugoslavia. 'From the very beginning we took him seriously,' insists Veran Matić. 'He was the initiator of criminal proceedings against student and youth media outlets; he was the one to "deal with" liberal journalists; he was behind bans of certain books and trials of notable writers. What we couldn't possibly know was how far he could go with his project. And of course, we couldn't have known what the price would be that we all would have to pay.'

Each year, Yugoslavia celebrated Tito's birthday – usually with extravagant public displays of typically Communist, kitschy pomp and solemnity: thousands of children doing synchronised gymnastics, or bombastic parades and choreographed spectaculars. In 1989, Belgrade's Communist youth organisation, to show off how progressive Serbia was compared to the other Yugoslav republics, decided to found a youth radio and a television station to broadcast for two weeks only. It was decreed that *Rhythm of the Heart* would combine with another youth broadcaster, Index 202, a more conventional outfit which focused more closely on student issues, to create the radio station. Both groups rejected Communist orthodoxy; instead they were committed to democratic reform, and so the justification they gave in order to get the go-ahead was a remarkable piece of deception. According to Nenad Čekić, the station's first executive editor, who came from Index 202, it was couched in Party language and embellished with politically expedient jargon. 'We wrote things that we never intended to put into practice. It was just a façade for what we actually wanted to do,' he says.

It was also a fine piece of humour: Tito's disaffected

children creating a dissident institution in honour of the old master's name. On 15 May 1989, Youth Radio B92 was founded. Its slogan was: 'The radio you listen to, watch, read, touch . . . the radio that lives.' Some of its staff were rookie journalists, others were students obsessed with rock'n'roll, literature, or art. Some just wanted to be close to the primal energy of change, to run a little interference across the wires. Few really knew what they were doing, or understood its implications. They were simply enthusiastic and voracious for new sensations. Many of them had grown up in the midst of the new wave scene which gripped Yugoslavia's urban centres in the early eighties. They read the latest imported music magazines avidly. They had spent time abroad and soaked up the metropolitan aesthetics of London, Paris and Amsterdam. With the infectious zeal of youth, they believed they could transform the world around them.

They cleared the rubbish out of an old storage room which had once been used by the central committee of the Communist Party, and made it their headquarters. The local Communist youth organisation provided them with an ancient, low-powered state transmitter sited on a hill just outside town, and they began broadcasting.

Veran Matić, who secured the job of editor-in-chief, says B92 was founded on the principles of the United Nations Declaration of Human Rights: the right to personal liberty, justice, freedom from discrimination, freedom of movement, free elections and a free press. B92 appeared at the point when Milošević had begun to extend his influence over the Serbian media through a series of purges. Yet Matić's reporters and DJs imagined they could push the boundaries of what was possible in a one-party Communist state where most radio stations broadcast a safe, controlled mixture of official news and mainstream rock music. They wanted to deliver cutting-edge pop culture from the European fringes, connecting right to the source without mediation, to produce news bulletins which told the truth about what was really going on in their rapidly disintegrating country, and transmit interviews with people whose lives were concealed from the popular consciousness: junkies, AIDS patients, football hooligans escaped convicts, prostitutes and the downtown freaks who drank, took drugs and danced in nightclubs like Akademija. They would reveal to Belgrade another level of existence in all its terrible beauty.

'This was still a time of relative freedom of speech, and although Milošević's repressive policies were coming in, it was still a time when you hoped that by speaking your mind, you could actually make a difference,' says Jelena Subotić, who joined the station a few months after it was launched. She describes her new colleagues as 'fanatics' – 'young people who would not recognise fear if it was screaming in their face'.

At its inception, B92 was neither a public-service broadcaster in the BBC tradition or commercial radio driven by financial imperatives. Instead it was closer to non-profit community radio stations like those clustered around America's Pacifica foundation, a coalition which grew out of left-wing, pacifist currents in California in the forties with a remit to defend human rights and oppose discrimination, or to the ultra-radical socialist/surrealist 'free radio' stations of Italy in the seventies. The most famous of these, Radio Alice, was physically shut down by the police while on air. Its slogan could easily have been that of B92: 'Information is not just the repetition or the display of what is going on in reality, but it is a means of transforming reality.'[6] And while B92 was never exactly a pirate, although its official status was unclear for many years to come, its irreverent attitude recalled the daring stunts of Britain's outlaw broadcasters, who for three decades had played intricate cat-and-mouse games with the police to keep their stations on air and transmit music to the black inner-city communities which legal operators largely ignored. (Belgrade also had a thriving pirate scene in the eighties, when stations like Radio Phoenix would play Eurodisco using tiny transmitters and aerials mounted on the towerblock roofs of New Belgrade's estates.)

Like the British pirates, B92's music policy was defiant and uncompromising: the emerging grunge sound of Seattle and the vibrant new house beat of Chicago, bands like Public Enemy and the Pixies, spiky indie rock and hardcore hip hop. 'Rap music was a revolution for us – it was perfect for this time of political turmoil,' says music programmer Miško Bilbija. 'Someone once said that rap was CNN for black people – we used it as a soundtrack for what was happening in our heads.'

This focus on the leading edge of global alternative sounds was unique in a city whose airwaves were dominated by tepid Yugo-rock and bland Western pop (although, paradoxically, in its early days, B92 would switch over to MTV after-hours and relay the corporate music channel's output verbatim).

'B92 could never be just a wallpaper soundtrack in your home,' says one Belgrade writer, then a teenage listener living with her parents. 'It was very innovative and, for a radio station, unusually demanding. You had to listen and think, which didn't make it a very easy medium. But it was a pleasure, it was like giving and taking. It sounds like a love relationship, which for many people like me, it was.

'Throughout the news they were mocking the regime guys and making ironic, sarcastic remarks. You weren't supposed to do that in the news, but people liked it because they were relieved to hear someone say something like that so publicly and openly.'

While some of the station's staff simply wanted to create an alternative – whatever it might be – to project their own youthful exuberance, to shoot off some sparks, Veran Matić realised immediately that the station had a more serious mission. 'The depiction of genuine reality through professional news programmes came to be seen as subversion,' he explained later. 'True information became provocation, dialogue was labelled a sign of weakness, attempts at conflict resolution and compromise were tagged as cowardice, attempts to represent the interests of minorities were seen as a sign of genetic defects: to be normal meant to be subversive.'

Matić was born in a village near the small town of Šabac, west of Belgrade, and had studied literature at Belgrade University – although he quit after a year to pursue a career in journalism. He became literary critic, and then editor, at *Rhythm of the Heart*. In the eighties he was part of a circle of writers and intellectuals called the Free University, who gathered at each other's flats to discuss the possibility of political change, like the clandestine anti-Communist cell which clustered around Vaclav Havel in Czechoslovakia. The Free University was later raided by the police and some of its members put on trial.

Although some now see Matić as a future leader in waiting, he claims that party politics never really interested him. 'I didn't have a political line, I was more into individual justice, and journalism was one of the best professions to pursue that in, because through journalism you could say what was right and try to correct what was wrong in society,' he says. 'I wouldn't say that I was a dissident and the reason for this wasn't only the fact that I hadn't been imprisoned at all, but also because our radio station project was launched from within official youth organisations' structures. A very small number of people in Tito's Yugoslavia could rightfully be called "dissidents" in Eastern European terms.'

Most of B92's staff were urban youngsters, many were still at college. Born in 1962, Matić was more mature, he had vision, and he became what one of his colleagues calls the 'spirit leader' of the group. Alisa Stojanović, one of B92's arts reporters, believes that because Matić was something of an outsider, he drove himself harder: 'Veran really had to work hard, he *had* to succeed. He taught me so much – he had read more books, he knew more about politics. We were all playing and having fun. None of us knew what this station might become one day, the only person who perhaps knew a little was Veran, but I don't think even he really knew what could happen.'

Matić was an unpretentious, stocky character with a full beard and a thick brush of black hair, most comfortable in jeans and a casual shirt, who preferred to conduct his discussions in leisurely fashion over a beer or two. He became the linchpin around which everything revolved, the person everyone trusted. 'He had an image of being a very good manager, a good chief, someone who knows how to make people believe in him and think he's doing the right thing,' says one local radio analyst. If a journalist hatched a plan for a new innovation, he allowed them to get on with it with the minimum of interference – and thus he won their loyalty.

Although he didn't have a great radio voice, Matić's regular show, the keynote interview of the day, became required listening. His guests were diverse and occasionally disturbing thinkers – outcast ideologues like Kosovo Albanian leader Adem Demaci or right-wing nationalist Vojislav Šešelj. He was trying to open up debate, provoke the listeners, investigate the forbidden regions of Serbian consciousness and inspire a new kind of conversation about the country's history and future. 'Veran was a pioneer in this country because these things were still forbidden,' says Alisa Stojanović. 'He opened our eyes.'

Other shows were equally provocative. There was a campaign to legalise prostitution; another to abolish a piece of anti-homosexual law; a debate on legalising soft drugs which went all the way to the Serbian parliament (where it was rejected). This was radical radio unlike anything that had been heard in the city before. 'We were open to discuss anything that was happening around us – it sounds weird now but at that time no one was allowed to talk about these things,' says one staffer. Some of it was planned, some was improvised on the spot, and all of it was characterised by raw innocence and a refreshing absence of cynicism. 'It was a kind of hippy approach, it's true,' says Saša Mirković, who would later become B92's managing director. 'It was sometimes confused and anarchic, but we were dreamers who thought we could change the world.'

Amidst the serious programming were plenty of silly stunts, like the time the station pretended that the Yugoslav president had been kidnapped, or that Swedish pop stars Abba had been killed in a plane crash, and some shows which even their makers admit were 'a really serious abuse of decency on the airwaves', like the afternoon Matić invited his listeners to call the studio and shout obscenities at him. But there was also a lot of hard-edged, bitterly dark humour. This was the period when Milošević's mass rallies of nationalist Serbs all across Yugoslavia were reaching boiling point. A demonstration was organised in Ljubljana, the capital of Slovenia – a city noted for its lack of Serb inhabitants. A B92 presenter began randomly calling numbers in Ljubljana, introducing himself as 'Voja, your old friend from the army', and asking whether he could come and stay at their house that Saturday and bring twelve Serb friends with him. The recipients of the call, naturally, were horrified at the prospect of a dozen redneck nationalists descending upon them – but their reactions exposed what the rest of Yugoslavia thought of Serbia's populist frenzy.

This mixture of wilful pranksterism, political satire and left-field music didn't suit everyone. B92 was attacked as chaotic, unlistenable, or elitist. 'It was quite hermetic – they were into themselves,' says one critic. It was in direct conflict with the increasingly inward-looking and nationalistic mood of the country, attracting the chosen few and repulsing many others. 'B92 wasn't a reflection of the times, it was an exception,' says early listener Slobodan Brkić. 'The whole political and social climate in those days, when Milošević was coming to power, was really conservative. B92 was a conscious reaction to that; it was a window to the outside world, while the dominant trends in Serbia were seclusion, going back to old tribes, old values, a demagogical approach: very clear-cut ideas of good and bad.

'I really admire those people who gave up college to work there. I think they were stunned by the freedom they suddenly had – a whole radio station to play with! But there wasn't a plan of how it would develop and I don't think even in their wildest dreams they thought they would become so good or so important as they did. I could have been in a similar position, but I wasn't brave enough. It's a courageous decision to give up everything – but they were like cats in a fishmonger's shop: how could they resist the opportunity?'

After its allocated fifteen days of transmission were over, B92 cut a deal with the Communist youth organisation to continue broadcasting. It wasn't strictly legal, but neither was it exactly breaking the law. Like so many radio stations in post-Communist Yugoslavia, it operated in a grey area on the fringes of legality, its status continually uncertain. It would not secure an officially allocated frequency for many years.

Beneath its outward success, B92 was riven by arguments about exactly what kind of station it should be. The flash point was the extremist music policy. The people working on the news desk, most of whom had come from Index 202 and were predominantly professional journalists, couldn't quite grasp why the DJs loved to blast out distorted guitar feedback epics by Sonic Youth or the belligerent rants of Los Angeles gangsta MCs NWA rather than a more accessible soundtrack which would attract a wider audience for what they were doing. Sometimes there were on-air spats, when a DJ became so caught up in his set that he wouldn't let the newsreader get near the microphone until he had finished. 'They didn't want music that would disturb their focus on "more important things", so we had fights from the very beginning. It was immediately obvious that the combination wouldn't work very well,' says one DJ.

As 1989 progressed, executive editor Nenad Čekić grew angrier and angrier with the music department, which he felt was 'directly humiliating the listeners'. But Veran Matić had realised that if the station was going to offer a genuine alternative, it had to be radical to its core. There was no point in producing a different kind of news programme then broadcasting the same old pop pap you could hear everywhere else in town. This would just consolidate social inertia. They had to go further. An incendiary tirade from revolutionary rappers Public Enemy could prove as valid as a report on the machinations of the ruling elite, they imagined. A piece about the latest club or exhibition opening could have as much impact as an analysis of a Party boss's speech.

To establish a genuinely alternative social movement, politics and culture had to be synthesised to create a kind of feedback loop, each amplifying the other, each reinforcing the same message: question authority, think for yourself, don't swallow anyone's propaganda. Matić and the rest of the crew who had joined B92 from *Rhythm of the Heart* understood that their mission was wider than straightforward politics. They were going for total social pluralism, not simply democracy. They didn't just want to change the system – they wanted to transform society. Matić called it 'liberation through culture'.

'The argument of the music section was that their music was the counterpart in the subversive sense of the work that was being done in the news department,' he says. And it was also the inverted image of the retrograde fusion that the regime was assembling: 'The nationalist politicians had created this perpetual circle in which their culture helped them and supported them, and in turn they supported it, and both perpetuated the other's existence. Populist songs supported bad politicians, then eventually they began to support the killers. It turned into a business relationship. So we had to oppose not only their nationalist agenda but their populist culture. That's what gave us our strength – if our station had been founded on some political ideology, it would have been long gone by now. But because we used this idea of liberation through culture, we were able to survive.'

Nenad Čekić disagreed, and campaigned vigorously and vociferously for a more palatable music policy. 'I wanted to run a normal local radio station,' he says. 'I found theirs to be a very gloomy concept. They were offending the listeners with these radical attitudes. I didn't want to "enlighten" listeners with music that is hard to listen to. I didn't want to deliver sermons, I wanted to give people news.'

Some say it was a clash over cash – that a drift to the centre would attract advertisers and increase revenues. 'They were accusing us of not being able to get commercials because of the music we were playing,' says Alisa Stojanović. 'They were saying that nobody wanted to listen to it and the sponsors, the people who had money, didn't like it. Which was true – but we thought we were doing the right thing.' Others suggest it was a war of egos, that Čekić and Matić were wrestling for overall control, or that they simply despised each other. There is an element of truth in this too; the pair would square up to each other again more than once in years to come. Čekić admits that the atmosphere in the studio was charged with conflict: 'We hated each other very much, but we had a job to do. However, it was impossible to manage.'

But more than anything else it was a battle for the soul of the station. And by early 1990, Čekić couldn't even count on the support of all the journalists who had come with him from Index 202. 'For Čekić, B92 was too alternative, too crazy, he thought we weren't serious enough,' says one of them, news reporter Zoran Mamula. 'Matić thought it was good to be alternative, to be slightly unserious, to be the opposite of the state radio stations. Čekić was wrong then and he's wrong now.'

In June 1990, the final showdown erupted. Late one night, Fleka, the manager of the Akademija club who now had his own show on B92, was on the air. His slot, *Radio Bat*, which ran after midnight, was undoubtedly the weirdest programme on the B92 schedule. 'It was a brutal show – we would get so many angry listeners phoning us and asking: "How can you put this on the air?"' remembers Miško Bilbija. Fleka would play libidinous surf-punk and avant-garde oddities from surrealist Californian pop mutants The Residents, lashing it all together with apocalyptic, stream-of-consciousness psycho-babble. Nenad Čekić called the studio, infuriated, and ordered him to stop playing those awful records. Fleka fired back simply and angrily: 'Fuck off.'

'This was the end,' says Gordan Paunović. 'We didn't know what would happen but it couldn't go on any more. The next night when the signal was off, the station was locked, we were all at home asleep and no one was there, Čekić came in with a technician, cut off all the wires and took half the equipment away with him. The next morning when we came in, we couldn't believe it, there was nothing, no mixing desk, all the cables were cut, and half of the equipment was missing.'

The split was so acrimonious that those involved still get furious about it now, more than a decade later. Veran Matić says that Čekić wasn't expelled but that he 'burgled' B92 and stole some of its broadcasting equipment. Čekić, employing the caustic wit of the vanquished, insists that he only took his own gear – and that Matić had conspired with local Communist officials to oust him: 'They say I wanted to sabotage the station, to destroy it. It was said that I did it on the orders of the secret police. The people who are making these accusations don't know me. If I really wanted to prevent them from broadcasting, they wouldn't be able to put together a programme for two months! There is a gadget that can be used against every electronic device – it's called water. You switch them on and then pour it in. We only took what was ours, we said we didn't want to work with them any more and that we were going.'

Matić, usually calm and restrained, is almost speechless with anger at Čekić's allegations: 'I don't know how to respond,' he growls. 'This society is full of conspiracy theories and if you don't give names and motives then they should be dismissed altogether. He wasn't forced out – he ran.'

Back at B92, it was a race against time to get back on air. They worried that the forceful and bullish Čekić might start a public campaign against Matić to win back control of the station. A technician locked himself in a room with the equipment and a soldering iron, and set to work. Thirty hours later, he emerged sleepless but triumphant. B92 was ready for transmission again. What was more, a number of Čekić's old Index 202 colleagues decided to boycott their former boss and remain with B92, forming the core of the news department. Matić's ideas had prevailed, and now the station was ready for its next task: to track the urban resistance to the growing potency of Slobodan Milošević. It was a struggle which B92 would not only report on but participate in – and of which it would ultimately become the victim.

The month after Nenad Čekić departed from B92 in wrathful indignation, Serbia held a referendum on whether to become a democratic state. Demands for democracy, which had first emerged officially through the youth organisations the year before, had reached fever pitch in June 1990, when 70,000 people demonstrated in central Belgrade for multi-party elections. Later that day, fighting broke out with police at a smaller rally for press freedom outside the state TV station, and protesters were savagely beaten. It was a foretaste of the many more violent disturbances to come.

The referendum led to the adoption of a new constitution for Serbia, which enshrined democracy in law but also strengthened the powers of the president over the country's parliament. The civil institutions, media freedoms and legal checks and balances which are necessary for a functioning democratic system were never put in place. Vital elements of the Communist monolith remained, inimical to genuine multi-party, pluralist democracy. The new 'democratic' regime retained all the trappings of its predecessor – control of the election process, economic and political appointments, and the media – while the new opposition parties which blossomed that year were starved of media power and grew up fractious and naive. There had been no revolution; a new autocracy simply superseded the old.

'The Communist utopia was replaced by a mythologisation, one deception replaced another,' Veran Matić observed. 'The typical one-party system was replaced by pseudo-democracy, a system which mimicked democracy with a parliament, elections, political parties and a genuinely authoritarian regime which abhors democracy and has blocked the creation of democratic institutions.'[7]

The first multi-party elections were scheduled for December 1990. Some opposition parties believed that, as Communism had fallen elsewhere in Eastern Europe, so they too could overturn Milošević's Socialist Party of Serbia, which was little more than the Communist Party rebranded for the new democratic decade (while insisting that it represented a clean break with the follies of the past). During the election campaign, Milošević didn't employ the kind of nationalist rhetoric which had helped him seize power, and instead of blaming outside enemies for conspiring against Serbia, he preferred to emphasise his claim to possess the cure for the country's economic ills. As Yugoslavia trembled on the edge of collapse, he promised security and stability. Just prior to the elections, the regime printed large amounts of money to artificially inflate the economy. While generating a short-lived feel-good factor that benefited Milošević, it also set the country back on the road to financial ruin.

Milošević belonged to Yugoslavia's first TV generation; he had grown up with the medium and understood how efficiently it could shape public opinion. He knew how to use it, and he did so ruthlessly. Boosted by his almost total domination of the broadcast media, which relegated his opponents to minimal television coverage, he won a landslide victory at the polls, gaining over sixty-five per cent of the votes in the presidential election. His party secured over seventy-seven per cent of the seats in the new national assembly.

The sheer scale of the result was a shock, and it was hard to take in. A few months back, things had looked so hopeful – and now this. The demagogue triumphant; nationalism rampant; the country hurtling backwards, regressing towards . . . well, no one could really tell, but it was clear that it would be difficult now to avoid a depressing future. Belgrade would not be another Prague, or Berlin, or Warsaw. Those wondrous events would not happen here. The open door had been slammed shut.

'It looked beforehand like the opposition would win because they had huge rallies in city squares all over Serbia and it seemed that Milošević wasn't as popular as he was in the late eighties,' remembers Gordan Paunović. 'But it ended in the horror of this landslide – no one knows if it was a set-up. Television played a major role, they were really telling lies about the opposition, like saying Vuk Drašković [opposition party leader] had a villa on Lake Geneva, that kind of thing. It became obvious that television was under control from above and it was playing a role in projecting nationalism everywhere, supporting the most irrational ideas that Milošević had and preparing the country for war.'

For decades, the Yugoslav media had been less tightly controlled and more diverse than that of other Communist countries, despite the existence of a large state-controlled publishing and broadcasting network. Mirroring the other freedoms of which Yugoslavs were so proud, people could speak more freely, get away with more than in neighbouring countries, and after Tito's death, as one local journalist explains, there was 'a gradual acquisition of the freedom to write about things that had not been required by the guys upstairs. This in no way means that the desired level of autonomy had been achieved, but the demands were growing stronger.'[8] At the beginning of the nineties a whole range of new independent publishing outlets had been set up. However, once Milošević was installed as president, he began to tighten up control of the state media – particularly the mass-market daily newspaper *Politika* and the national TV network – by purging staff and installing puppets in key positions who would support the 'Serbian cause', rather than reporting objectively. One music editor was even sacked for playing a song by a Croatian rock star. These placemen would become the cheerleaders for nationalism and the prime instigators of the hysteria which within months would lead the country into war. The media would form the frontline artillery of Milošević's military machine.

'With us,' Milošević had promised in his election campaign slogan, 'there is no uncertainty.' He wasn't lying: it was now an absolute certainty that Yugoslavia was going straight to hell.

# 2

# fight the power
# 1991–92

**'Out of such evil no good can come'**
*Patriarch Pavle, head of the Serbian Orthodox Church (1991)*

Even in the last weeks, war in Yugoslavia still seemed impossible. Someone will stop it, everyone said. The world will do
something. They will come to their senses. It could never
happen here.

Slobodan Milošević's nationalist agitation had roused Serbia
from its soporific, post-Tito slumber to the brink of violence,
but in Belgrade at least, most young people were still deluding
themselves that somehow, perhaps through some late, dramatic
intervention from beyond the country's borders, bloodshed
would be averted.

'I don't think anybody really believed there was going to
be a war,' says one.

'Everyone was saying it was impossible,' a second declares.
'We didn't realise it was inevitable until the last minute.'

'I was really confused and didn't want to believe it was
actually happening,' remembers a third.

As they stood transfixed by a mixture of disbelief and denial,
war crept closer each day.

But before the doors swung open on the theatre of blood,
Milošević had one last piece of unfinished business to deal
with on his own doorstep. Since December 1990, rumours

had been circulating that he had somehow manipulated or massaged the election results to ensure his landslide win. There was smouldering resentment – particularly among the ranks of the Serbian Renewal Movement party, led by the iconic Vuk Drašković – that state media coverage in the period before the elections, which certainly was skewed in favour of Milošević and his cronies, had denied the opposition a fair hearing.

Drašković announced a mass demonstration for freedom of the media for 9 March 1991, in Belgrade. The state TV service, Belgrade Television (later renamed Radio Television Serbia) – nicknamed the 'Bastille' – immediately attacked him, accusing him of betraying Serbian interests. The government banned the protest. Drašković insisted it would go ahead regardless, and other parties came out in support. The government began bussing policemen in to Belgrade from the southern province of Kosovo, the crucible of its support. 'On the eve of the demonstration, the bloated police force spread its thick blue girth around the major entrances to Serbia's capital,' BBC correspondent Misha Glenny observed in his book *The Fall of Yugoslavia*. 'Their thick blue coats, which are cut so inelegantly that their owners appear restricted to slightly comic, robotic movements, would swing out of the darkness and into the murky light of orange phosphorous which demarcates the periphery of Belgrade. Cars were searched, drivers questioned. Some were turned back.'[1] The mood grew increasingly panicked as the stage was set for confrontation in the heart of the city.

The next morning, as the demonstrators began to gather and the police installed their armoury of night-sticks and riot shields all around the downtown area, Drašković's party issued an urgent warning of impending disaster. Some observers noticed armoured cars and water cannon parked surreptitiously in the back streets: this was not a police force preparing for a peaceful day on the job. Others realised that the demonstrators were hyped-up and nervy – and that these were not just the urban liberals who had been beaten up outside the Bastille the previous year, but that their ranks also included all kinds of others: hardcore nationalists, fashionable young things, criminals and football hooligans, all with their own diverse agendas. The soccer thugs had already shown their appetite for violence a year before, in May 1990, when the Delije (Warriors) fan club of Red Star Belgrade had fought viciously with the Bad Blue Boys of Dinamo Zagreb at a showpiece game in Croatia.

And there were hard men amongst the supporters of Drašković himself – some of whom would later be murdered in the gangland battles of the coming decade. Drašković was a former journalist and novelist, whose provocative writing had focused on the 'national question' – a taboo subject in the eighties when he forged his career – and who had long propagated a strident brand of Serbian nationalism, particularly the idea of a 'Greater Serbia'. His nationalism was so fierce that Milošević was often seen as a moderate in comparison. Drašković had helped to stir up anti-Albanian sentiment in Kosovo and anti-Muslim feeling in Bosnia (he would later drift to the centre and start to criticise Milošević's wars there).

Although his Serbian Renewal Movement supported the 'progressive' free market and privatisation, and Drašković became more excited by the concept of civil liberties once his own were threatened, his party remained strongly traditionalist in its ideology, and he often shifted between extreme nationalist, pro-royalist and 'modern' democratic positions in his public outbursts. A magnetic presence with dark eyes, long hair and a wild, unkempt beard, he saw himself as Serbia's leader in waiting, unequivocally superior to any other opposition politician. Few doubted that without Drašković's involvement and talent for mobilising his dedicated and determined followers to action, any resistance movement would be unlikely to succeed.

In its early days, the Serbian Renewal Movement was described as an 'eclectic combination of poets and gangsters'.

And Drašković himself was both poetic and streetwise. 'He was really a street person – he had really strong charisma and he knew how to deal with the masses,' according to one reluctant admirer of the figure they would come to call the 'king of the squares' in deference to his self-promoted reputation as the street-fighting man of the Serbian opposition.

The sun was shining but the wind was up, whipping along the boulevards. Just before the rally was due to start, demonstrators who had been cordoned off from the main body of the protest broke through police lines, and fighting erupted immediately. Tear-gas was fired, stones were thrown, punches landed. A police vehicle was captured and a Serbian flag raised above it in triumph. Despite their superior weaponry, the police retreated, but as soon as Drašković began to speak in Republic Square, they came back with exaggerated brutality. 'They started by hurling tear-gas canisters into the centre of the crowd, reinforcing this by driving water-cannon through the main body of the demonstrators,' Misha Glenny reported. 'Using horses and truncheons and firing automatic weapons into the air, they assaulted anybody who got in their way, launching Belgrade on a trajectory of uncontrollable violence.'[2]

Just off Republic Square were the offices of B92. Veran Matić, seeing the ruckus unfold beneath his window, grabbed a microphone, leaned out of the window and began describing the bloody scenes below as if he was commentating on a particularly confrontational football match, occasionally gasping for air as tear-gas spiralled upwards from the canisters police were firing straight at demonstrators' heads and limbs.

'I remember myself saying that the situation resembled the start of a civil war,' Matić recalls. 'Zoran Mamula, one of our reporters who was in the studio with me at the time, kept saying to me: "Slow down, slow down, don't provoke more violence." '

And a few floors below, the B92 staff who weren't working were out there, trading blows with the police. 'It was the greatest fight Belgrade has ever seen – and the only one that the demonstrators won,' says Gordan Paunović. 'They completely kicked the shit out of the police. Police were shooting tear-gas canisters and demonstrators were batting them back. It was kind of fun, in a way.

'By around three o'clock it was over – the fight ended and the whole centre was cleared of police. It was like a free territory. All the windows were broken, hooligans appeared and started stealing stuff from shops. There were serious numbers of wounded police because the Serbian Renewal Movement had lots of tough guys who knew how to fight.'

And two people lay dead – one policeman, and one teenage student who hadn't even been involved in the protest. He was a B92 listener and a Pogues fan, and he had only come into town to buy some tapes when he was shot in the head by one of Milošević's men. As Misha Glenny noted bitterly: 'For four years, Slobodan Milošević had been exciting Serbs with tales of the terror and discrimination that they faced. The first Serb to die in political terror since his rise to power was murdered by Serbian police working in the name of President Milošević.'[3]

Scared now, Milošević ordered the army to send its tanks on to the streets to flush the demonstrators out. It was a fearsome sight – more so because it was so unbelievable, the Yugoslav army invading its own capital, trying to win back territory occupied by the people of Belgrade themselves. As if signalling that there would be an internal war on dissidence to match the war outside Serbia's borders, Milošević was turning the guns on his own. It would not be the last time. 'I think Milošević was afraid that this was going to end in a coup,' says Gordan Paunović. 'He was afraid that Drašković would break into parliament and occupy it – but so what if he did? He still wouldn't have any access to television, and in this country it's more important to control television than parliament.'

As the tanks rolled into the centre, armed police kicked in

the doors of Radio B92 and burst into the studio. Veran Matić tried to stall them, asking them if they had a warrant. They looked confused for a moment. 'Warrant?' they asked. 'What warrant? Of course we have a warrant, yes, of course.' Matić asked them to show it to him. It didn't exist. So they called up their chief and, while waiting for the real document to arrive, B92 continued broadcasting as Matić attempted to reason with them, arguing that if the station was shut down, it would escalate the panic on the streets.

The warrant arrived and the police ordered Matić to stop transmitting immediately. As he went into the booth to announce the shutdown to the radio audience, a policeman followed him, threatening dire consequences if he said anything out of turn. With his voice trembling, Matić forced out his parting words to his listeners: 'Well guys, this is it. Our programme is banned.'

The policemen told Matić that B92 could go on broadcasting only if it played music and relayed reports from the state-run news agency Tanjug. He refused. The next morning, he was told by a neighbour that some men in uniform had been looking for him, but they had gone to the wrong address because the numbering system on his street was incorrect. 'They had come twice during the night, probably to arrest me, because they had already arrested Vuk Drašković and a number of other protesters. The state news said that criminal charges were brought against me and the chief editor of [TV station] Studio B, which was also banned, and that the charges were "provocation of unrest" and "calls to violent overthrow of the constitutional system". These were very grave accusations.'

When he arrived at the studio, the police were still there. They agreed that B92 could start broadcasting music from noon onwards. The DJs quickly came up with a plan to circumvent the information blackout. They hunted out any and every record they could find which described, in sound and lyrics, the violent clashes of the previous day and the state of high tension in the streets outside – rabble-rousing anthems like The Clash's punk war cry *White Riot* and Thin Lizzy's *The Boys Are Back In Town*. It was an amazing, defining moment – sound and action fused solid.

'We were able to say through music what we would have said in the news if it had been allowed, without the policemen who were sitting in the studios noticing anything wrong,' explains Matić. 'The policemen probably didn't speak English and the regime didn't understand music – but the listeners could understand the code. Our music section had always argued that their music was the counterpart, in the subversive sense, of what we were doing in news. This proved it.'

Before the station had been reporting events but now, as Matić says, it was also shaping them and magnifying them with its broadcasts. B92 had become a central component of the underground resistance movement – the voice of urban Belgrade under pressure. 'We never thought "we can't report this because it will get us in trouble",' says news reporter Zoran Mamula. 'We never thought about that. We knew that the police would probably stop our programmes. We expected that. It was not a surprise. After the police stopped us, we didn't change the way we worked. No, in fact we became more brave because we were angry. Before we were young, but during these demonstrations we grew up and became adults.'

One record they played over and again that day was Public Enemy's rap manifesto *Fight The Power*, with Chuck D's impassioned lyrics declaring: 'Our freedom of speech is freedom or death – we got to fight the powers that be.' Public Enemy had been the first rap band to bring militant black consciousness into hip hop and their influence had radicalised a whole generation of young black Americans. They, too, had run a student radio show in their native New York in the early eighties – a hip hop propaganda slot on Adelphi University's WBAU station, which succeeded in trouncing its white, conservative competition in the ratings table. Now their words were helping to catalyse another quest for freedom in another urban wasteland thousands of miles away.

That evening, groups of students began to gather in the 'Student City' district of the socialist-realist grid of tower-blocks that is New Belgrade, and decided to march across the Sava river into the city centre. They were met on the bridge by fully tooled-up riot police, and as tear-gas was fired, fighting broke out again. But once the students reached Tera-zije, one of the city's main thoroughfares, the police pulled back.

'At that time police were still reluctant to intervene against students,' suggests Gordan Paunović. 'In Yugoslavia, since the sixties students had this image as a really progressive part of society, so when they protest against something they must be right. There was this myth created around the 1968 student demonstrations in Belgrade when they were also beaten by the police, but then Tito had a meeting with them and said they had good intentions. So afterwards everyone glorified them – and a week later Tito arrested some of them. But this public myth about students having the right to protest about "irregularities" in society remained.'

The students also chanted for the return of B92 – and at around 8 p.m., the station started broadcasting news reports again. 'We were back on air because of the support we had from the streets,' believes Paunović. The police left the building and did not return. Veran Matić was not arrested or charged with any kind of incitement as he had feared.

The shutdown of B92 also proved that its power, as the electronic voice of the resistance, had rattled the regime. 'It was a panic act,' says Teofil Pančić, a journalist on the independent weekly magazine *Vreme*. 'What does it mean to shut down a small radio station? Imagine you are Slobodan Milo-šević, you have everything: the strongest police force, an army, a strong state media, whatever you want, then you destroy some small alternative radio station which is impossible to hear outside Belgrade. The only explanation is that this radio station had a really strong influence. Milošević was really shaken. He thought someone could go on B92 and call on everyone in Belgrade to join the demonstrations and throw out his government.'

There were still tanks swivelling their barrels in the city squares and uniformed men with guns patrolling the pavements. But the students remained on Terazije for the next ten days, joined by thousands of supporters, holding their own, open-air 'parliament', demanding the freeing of the jailed demonstrators and the sacking of the minister of police, an end to Milošević's media monopoly, freedom for B92 and other broadcasters and 'the uncovering of those responsible for all bloodshed and repressive measures'. The mood was electric, charged with youthful optimism and the ecstasy of resistance. 'We've seen them out,' one student told the BBC's Misha Glenny. 'This is now our country.'[4]

The 'Terazije parliament' was victorious – the interior minister and the head of Belgrade TV resigned, and Vuk Drašković and other protesters were released (although months later Drašković was threatened with prosecution and accused of attempting to stage a coup). Milošević, frightened now, agreed to meet some of the students, who confronted him bluntly and interrogated him with haughty disdain, visibly riling the president. And yet their apparent triumph proved superficial; the person they declared was 'responsible for all bloodshed and repressive measures' – Milošević himself – simply replaced the deposed TV boss and politician with other hard-line loyalists, and engineered the passing of a new Radio and Television Act which allowed him to get rid of anyone who opposed his policies. As the opposition went home clutching its empty victory, Milošević, the real winner, the man who had ridden the turbulent currents and survived with his power intact, prepared to go to war.

The fine threads which held Yugoslavia together were unravelling. After the riots of March, Milošević had reverted to a hardcore nationalist discourse, promoting the idea of a 'greater Serbia' encompassing all of Yugoslavia's Serbs in one state – which would include areas of Croatia and Bosnia. The other Yugoslav republics, calling for increased independence from Belgrade, moved inexorably towards secession. The Slovenians demanded autonomy and incurred economic boycotts from Belgrade. Croatia's belligerent new leader Franjo Tudjman fanned the flames of nationalism in his territory. Skirmishes broke out between Croatian policemen and the Yugoslav army, which Milošević had taken over and was using to back up his grand project. Serb minorities within Croatia and Croat minorities in Serb-dominated regions began to stockpile weapons for 'self-defence'. Milošević and Tudjman began to map out strategies for grabbing parts of multi-ethnic Bosnia for themselves. As each republic pursued a conflicting agenda, mutual enmity and intolerance escalated to the point where hostilities were certain.

The atmosphere in Belgrade was growing increasingly nervous as the nationalist propaganda pumped out by the state media became more raucous. Encouraged by high-ranking officials and senior policemen, groups of nationalists and regime loyalists began to arm themselves, creating battalions of fighting men who were prepared to defend the country they were told daily was under threat from violent outsiders who would destroy Yugoslavia and annihilate the Serbs. The environment was becoming militarised, and the streets of the city were colonised by aggressive characters in fighting colours.

Some of these groups of 'volunteers', as they were known, were paramilitary wings of established political parties. The right-wing firebrand Vojislav Šešelj, leader of the Serbian Radical Party, set up his Serbian Chetnik Movement, named after the nationalists who fought Tito's Communist partisans in World War Two. Vuk Drašković established the Serbian Guard, declaring: 'Serbia must punish those who threaten Serbs.' The Serbian Guard's leader, himself a former convict, stated: 'In all liberation and resistance movements across the

world a place will always be found for patriotic "criminals".'
The nucleus of the Guard had acted as 'security' to Drašković
at the 9 March demonstrations. There were also a plethora
of other, smaller paramilitary groupings with names like the
Chetnik Avengers and the Serbian Falcons.

The Belgrade independent weekly *Borba* estimated that a
fifth had been convicted of some crime: 'Some went to the
frontlines directly from prison. According to unverified
sources, some of the prisoners who were about to finish their
sentence were able to reduce it if they agreed to join the
volunteers.' The most notorious of the paramilitaries was
the Serbian Volunteer Guard, better known as the Tigers,
masterminded by former bank robber Željko Ražnatović, alias
Arkan, who was the leader of Red Star's soccer hooligans, the
Delije, and who drew many of his recruits from their ranks.

Nationalist paraphernalia had also begun to displace the
trinkets hawked by street vendors on Belgrade's main ped-
estrianised shopping area, Knez Mihailova – T-shirts and
memorabilia commemorating the Chetniks of World War
Two, and tapes of militant Serbian songs. Belgrade, which had
seemed a year before to be almost cosmopolitan, a southern
European capital dotted with terrace bars, cafés and locally-
run concessions of international fashion chains like any other,
had turned warlike – a transformation which struck fear into
those who had almost succeeded in convincing themselves
that Serbia would pull back from the brink of self-immolation.
And for its urban youth, those for whom nationalism was
incomprehensible, barbaric, despicable, it seemed like the
onset of a particularly unpleasant nightmare from which, try
as they might, they could not stir themselves.

'For me personally, the darkest period of the nineties was
the build-up to the war, and the awakening of nationalistic
hysteria that was needed to mobilise support for the military
adventures of the regime,' says B92 presenter Jelena Subotić.
'Hate speech was coming from everywhere – TV, newspapers,
people talking in bars. It was all of a sudden legitimate to

engage in war-mongering, to be racist, to hate, while feeling different and being tolerant was extremely isolating.

'Violence was all around us, if only in the rhetoric on state TV and in the newspapers. The regime was preparing its followers, recruiting supporters and mobilising forces for its sickening adventure. It was probably the lowest point of Serbia's public consciousness.'

Many still suspect that Milošević only decided to lead the country to war because the mass protests showed how vulnerable his position was and he therefore needed to create conflict to distract the population from examining his failings and ejecting him from the presidency. His position was, naturally, consolidated by the shrill voice of state television, where he made a rare appearance to declare: 'Yugoslavia has entered into the final phase of its agony.' He ordered the mobilisation of reservists in the police service and the formation of additional militia forces. The opposition parties could not agree a common strategy and fell into disarray.

The first shots had already been fired in armed disputes between the Yugoslav republics. But when Slovenia and Croatia declared independence from Yugoslavia on 25 June 1991, war began in earnest. 'This was not how any of us had imagined the future eighteen months before, when the great wave of change swept across Eastern Europe,' wrote Slavenka Drakulić. 'This was not how it was supposed to be. I felt cheated.'[5] As Milošević had predicted, the long, final phase of Yugoslavia's agony had indeed begun.

In the liberal circles of urban Belgrade, it hardly seemed real. And of course it wasn't, yet: war was something that Belgrade's youth, like people across the rest of the world, were only watching on TV. 'It was very strange because it looked completely virtual from here,' remembers Gordan Paunović. 'Seeing the war in Croatia on telly was just like seeing any other war on telly – it was far away from you. The only things you could actually see in Belgrade were military convoys.'

To swell the numbers of the regular army fighting alongside

the nationalist volunteer militias, a draft was announced: all men of fighting age were ordered to join up. This was when the real consequences of nationalist agitation came home to the Serbian capital: now you too, young man, must put on the uniform, go to the frontline and die for Milošević.

Belgrade immediately became the centre of practical opposition to the military programme. Men started living with their friends, their relatives − anywhere but at their registered home address, where the recruiters might come calling. In the northern city of Novi Sad, it was reported, people even went as far as unscrewing street signs and switching them around to confuse the recruiters. Radio B92 began to broadcast a checklist of ways to avoid the call-up, passing on rumours about which area the recruiters might be operating in that night. 'Looking back on it now, it seems strange there was no action taken against us, because this was a free and open appeal to young people not to participate in this mess,' says Veran Matić. Nonetheless, some of B92's presenters took the precaution of hiding their identities behind phoney names while on air.

Suspicion reigned. 'During the peak of the call-up, almost nobody opened their doors at night unless there was some sort of a secret code you shared only with your closest friends and family,' says Jelena Subotić. 'And it got worse once the police started drafting people on the streets, in bars or clubs. For a few months, men of drafting age could hardly be seen outside − everybody was hiding somewhere.'

The ones who were served their call-up papers did everything they could to escape transportation to the frontline. Some went to psychiatrists to get themselves signed off, feigning mental illness. Others simply went AWOL.

'I was drafted in May 1991 when the war started,' says Gordan Paunović. 'I was in the army for two weeks and then they let me go home, they told me to be on standby and they'd call me back in a month. And of course they did, because that's when they wanted to go to Croatia.' His unit was sent to Vukovar, where one of the most vicious sieges of the war took place. Many of his comrades were killed – but Paunović himself had already gone into hiding, far away on the Montenegrin coast. When he finally returned to Belgrade a couple of months later, everything seemed different somehow. It had become a militarised zone. 'All I can remember was this incredible darkness in the city. It was full of strange faces; rural, primitive faces – refugees and people who had been in battle around Vukovar, looting villages then coming back to the city in their camouflage uniforms. It was a dark time.'

Paunović was one of tens of thousands of young Belgraders who never went to war. Only an estimated thirteen per cent of those eligible for mobilisation in the city actually made it to the army – a clear indication that huge numbers of young Serbs rejected Milošević's war-mongering. Some wanted nothing to do with ethnic cleansing, mass murder, torture and looting; many simply hoped to save their own skins. Within a year, there were around 6,000 cases pending against deserters and draft-dodgers in the Belgrade military court.

But this was not a message you could see on state TV. As one wit joked: 'War is a continuation of prime time news using other media.'[6] The regime propaganda portrayed a homogenised nation, rising as one to defend itself and repel the evil hordes from Serbia's hearth – a message which many Western journalists would also embrace. The film *Vukovar 1991*, made by Radio B92 in an attempt to show the other side of the war, documented how Radio Television Serbia depicted the total destruction – or in its own words, 'liberation' – of the wretched, besieged town of Vukovar in Croatia. According to RTS, there were no 'unnecessary casualties' in this 'operation house-cleaning'. The Croats were 'inhuman fascists' who 'used children as shields' against bullets. Croat Catholic churches were 'fortresses' and 'arms caches'. And the Serbs of Vukovar? RTS pictured them as either 'tortured citizens' or, in the case of the paramilitary volunteers, patriotic heroes wielding the sword of justice to defend their brethren.

In the film, as Vukovar is pulverised to a stony skeleton, one volunteer declares: 'Freedom has arrived.'

Then follows a weird tableau of a Serbian army commander appealing for the Croats' final surrender through a set of loudspeakers mounted on a tank. Martial music blares over the tinny sound system as he urges his men: 'Boldly, boldly, indestructible heroes, let us deliver the final blow . . . Show them how tough you are . . .'

Captured Croats were labelled deviants and drug addicts, committed to the genocide of the Serbian population. RTS broadcast lingering shots of mutilated bodies and 'mass graves', tales of teeth prised from the mouths of the living, allegations that Croats disembowelled men, chopped off youngsters' fingers and even wanted to roast children on a spit. No hard evidence to support this was produced, but it wasn't necessary: RTS was employing the barbaric, irrational rhetoric of war. Label your opponent subhuman so it is more acceptable to kill him. Manufacture fear, intensify the dread. Convince people there is an international conspiracy against them. Damn anyone who disagrees as a traitor or a foreign agent, a servant of the murderous enemy.

And all across Serbia, it seemed to be working. In the film's most telling scene, its simple words more chilling than any of the butchery, a woman stares intently into the lens and says: 'When I see what's going on on TV, I want to help, and it's worth sacrificing my life for this Serbia of ours.'[7]

'Without the role played by television, war would perhaps not even have happened, or at least it would not have been so bloody,' novelist Filip David told B92's cameras. And Milošević, who had learned the tricks of the propaganda trade as chief of Belgrade city council's information department in the sixties and had planned his original strategy to seize power in collaboration with four of the country's top media magnates, realised that the guarantor of his power was the electronic media. Within eighteen months of the war starting, he had purged thousands of workers at Radio Television Serbia, placing them on 'compulsory leave'. Many were members of independent trade unions not controlled by Milošević's Socialist Party; masses of policemen prevented them coming in to work. 'RTS has become a loophole through which guns are being fired – at our own people this time,' said sports commentator Dragan Nikitović. 'TV Bastille is now complete – the guillotine has been put in place.'[8]

Over the coming years, Milošević also installed loyal appointees in key posts in the administration of Belgrade University, to ensure political compliance after the student demonstrations, and on the governing boards of the National Theatre, the National Library, the Institute for Protection of Cultural Monuments and the Museum of Contemporary Art. The regime began to extend its tentacles, exerting control over all spheres of public life, from the media to the judiciary and the education system, from the army to the arts. A Socialist Party official declared that no one could work in a state institution 'unless they think like we do'.[9] Again and again, critical thought was purged.

The ultimate symbol and last line of defence of Milošević's government was the police force – and he invested heavily in it to make sure he had, in the words of one opposition politician, his own 'praetorian guard' to consolidate his power. The events of 9 March had shown they could be beaten in a hand-to-hand street fight. So Milošević poured increasing amounts of money into the force; within a few years, police spending would outstrip investment in healthcare, education and even the army. Over the decade, numbers were increased to 100,000, nearly twice as many officers per citizen as New York City, and they were equipped with high-tech personnel carriers, helicopters and other gizmos of internal repression. New secret service units were established. Milošević was constructing a domestic war machine, a private army to deal with the 'enemy within' – his own people. 'The goal is to let them know that any attempt at change is futile and doomed to fail in advance,' an anonymous police officer told Belgrade reporter Daniel Sunter.[10]

In early 1992, fighting broke out in Bosnia between Bosnian Serbs, who wanted to remain part of Yugoslavia, Muslims, who desired their own sovereignty, and Bosnian Croats loyal to Franjo Tudjman's secessionist regime in Zagreb. But as the war took hold, so did the anti-war resistance in Belgrade. When the first barricades between Serbs and Muslims were erected in Sarajevo in March, a prelude to the three-year, four-month siege of the city, B92 staged a stunt in central Belgrade, setting up barriers and blocking a street in an attempt to bring the reality of ethnic division home. Traffic was gridlocked and Veran Matić lampooned the war-mongers, patrolling the barricade in a military uniform topped with a beret and dark glasses.

Unrest against the regime was spreading. A petition calling on Milošević to resign attracted 840,000 signatures. In March 1992, the opposition parties rallied 50,000 people outside St Sava's cathedral in downtown Belgrade. Students returned to Terazije to continue their protests. The Centre for Anti-War Action urged: 'We are on the verge of complete catastrophe. Let us save ourselves from death, shame before the entire world, isolation and poverty. Let us do away with the political adventurers and false patriots, this is our last chance!'[11]

Another B92 prank, aimed at thwarting a tax hike on baby goods, called on mothers to bring their children to Milošević's house in the affluent suburb of Dedinje and offer them up to the president to take care of. 'During the war there was always a sense that words were not enough and real action should be taken out in the streets. All the babies were crying, which we thought meant that they wanted to be nowhere near Milošević,' laughs Veran Matić. This small protest, at least, was successful: the taxes were revoked two days later.

At the height of the killing in Vukovar, where Serb forces

were besieging the Croats, B92 and the Centre for Anti-War
Action brought together three of the city's top rock bands,
Partibrejkers, Električni Orgazam (Electric Orgasm) and Ekat-
erina Velika (Catherine The Great), to form a 'supergroup'
named Rimtukituki and record a pacifist anthem. *Slušaj 'Vamo
(Mir, Brate, Mir) – Listen Here (Peace, Brother, Peace)* – was
pressed up on a seven-inch single and distributed free. 'We
rented a truck, put all the musicians on it, and cruised all
around town throwing away the records to the people who
were running along behind us,' says Gordan Paunović. The
rock'n'roll tour of the city concluded on 8 March 1992 with
a huge anti-war concert for 50,000 people in Republic Square
under the slogan 'Don't Count on Us'. Yet despite this and
other rallies, the peace movement, already relatively small
and starved of media coverage, became marginalised and never
managed to capture the mainstream imagination.

No effective resistance could be mounted without information, and the regime was doing its best to ration the supply,
distorting it through the prism of its own nationalist ideology.
'One thing that very few people from outside the country
can understand is that Milošević claimed from the beginning
that Serbia was not at war – that was the biggest victory of his
politics, convincing people we were not at war,' says Gordan
Paunović.

This was confirmed by the only interview that any of the
Milošević family ever granted to Belgrade's independent radio.
Mira Marković, Milošević's wife, the despised 'Lady Macbeth
of the Balkans' who was seen by many as the sinister power
behind the throne, came to B92's studios and spoke to Veran
Matić, telling him that she and her husband were no nationalists. 'She shocked the listeners – she was all for peace,' says
Matić. 'She actually condemned nationalism and the leaders
who had taken us into the war, and said there wouldn't be
peace until all of them were no longer in power. One listener's
reaction was: "Excuse me, but why don't you tell your

husband that?" It was a clear indication that she wasn't living in the same space and time as the rest of us.'

B92 wanted to drag the war into Belgrade's living rooms, to expose the bloody truth about what Milošević and his cronies were really doing. It established links with like-minded radio stations such as Studio 99 in Sarajevo, Radio 101 in Zagreb and Radio Student in Ljubljana to transmit collaborative programmes and on-the-spot reports from the other (now former) Yugoslav republics. The bulletins from Sarajevo, where street battles broke out in April 1992, were particularly distressing. The multi-ethnic Bosnian capital was being pounded by the relentless shelling of Serb artillery and strafed by sniper fire, but few in Belgrade really knew how desperate the situation was. Almost a decade later, some listeners still have the broadcasts on tape, treasured reminders of the true meaning of war.

Veran Matić also wanted to spotlight the real war heroes – the people who said no. 'There were mass desertions from the frontline, whole units laid down their arms and just left the battlefield,' he says. 'Once a whole unit rebelled and said they wouldn't go to the front. The commander of the unit said: "OK, those who want to go to war step this side, and those who don't go that side." There was one guy who kept changing sides and at the end stood between them and shot himself. This story became symbolic of the anti-war movement.

'There was another example in the early days of the Bosnian war when the Serbs killed a local Serb actor who tried to protect Muslims from being attacked in the streets. There were many events like this, but these people have been forgotten, although they should have monuments erected to them. Pinpointing these events was a way to fight against the homogenisation of nationalist feeling, although it was very difficult to fight it because it had progressed so far. We wanted to give people as much direct experience of the war as possible to show them how gruesome it was.'

As the Serb-controlled Yugoslav army advanced on Više-
grad in Bosnia, one Muslim unit was holding out against
them. Its leader realised he was doomed to failure and in
desperation threatened to blow up a dam over the River Drina
and flood the entire area. Matić managed to find his phone
number and on dialling, to his surprise, was connected straight
away.

'I was in the middle of my show and didn't expect to get
through, and I was like: "God, what do I do now?" So I just
said: "Hi, what's up?" He said: "Tell the army to withdraw
or else I'll blow the dam up." The interview became a kind
of psychotherapeutic negotiation with me saying: "Don't do
it, there are people living in the valley, you'll kill them as
well." I tried the argument that there were Muslims and their
children living there, but he just responded: "If we can't live
together, we'll *swim* together." '

Just after Matić's call, the commander set off his explosives,
but the blast failed to burst the dam.

It became increasingly difficult to report from the war zones
accurately. The phone lines to the other republics were cut
off, and journalists had to try other means to get through,
like routing their calls via London or Amsterdam. A plea to
international media groups for funding for satellite telephones
was ignored. But B92 still endeavoured to give as many view-
points on events as possible, quoting local sources and Western
media reports as well as the state news agency. 'That was very
irritating for the regime because they wanted the media to
just have one version, the Serbian version: we are the victims,
we are defending ourselves, and everyone else is bad,' says
Teofil Pančić of the independent magazine *Vreme*. 'It was very
important to make people realise that Serbs are not better or
worse than other people and we can also do bad things.

'B92 was very anarchic – sometimes it sounded like there
were three or four punks just hanging around in the studio
making jokes, but this was very charming because the environment was so depressing. It was a sort of therapy for the

listeners. At that time, what could you see? Your country splitting apart, war starting. A year before, you couldn't have imagined anything like that; war was in the past, ancient history – but now you had military police all around who could send you straight to the frontline. You had less and less money and less and less opportunities to do anything. So the station was a light in the darkness for people who didn't want to become a part of all that.'

The entire cultural life of Belgrade, now dominated by the dead hand of Milošević's ideology, fell under the shadow of the war. Warfare became culture, culture became warfare. The two were inseparably intermingled, driving each other forward in a grotesque symbiosis of spiralling hatred.

'This dominant culture was a culture of death; it celebrated death,' says Teofil Pančić. 'If you turned on the TV, what you saw was someone in a uniform trying to say to you that it's great to be a soldier and go to Vukovar and die. Then you had so-called folk singers singing songs about Greater Serbia and Serbian soldiers and how we all love our motherland and how we should all be willing to kill and be killed for it, to liberate our Serbian brothers and sisters in Croatia and Bosnia. It was so morbid and it was all around you: all those songs and people in uniform everywhere.

'What B92 and others did was celebrate life; that's the difference. They tried to remain normal and say that there is the possibility of another kind of life, a totally different society than the one that actually existed here. The only other alternative was Radio Belgrade, which you just couldn't listen to because it was in a timewarp – it sounded like Radio Moscow in 1945.'

Refuting the official version of events inevitably aroused the wrath of the nationalist majority – even in relatively progressive Belgrade. 'Sometimes it was very hard to listen to B92's phone-in programmes because it was a time of mass propaganda so almost every day you could hear some listeners calling and saying: "You are traitors, you should be killed, you should be sent to jail, you should be sent to the frontline, you are supporting Croats, Muslims, Americans . . ." ' recalls Pančić.

It was obvious that B92 had become much more than a little student radio station playing noisy rock records. It was now the centre of a social movement: anti-war, anti-nationalism; pro-democracy, pro-human rights. It had made links with peace activists, not only in Belgrade but all across disintegrating Yugoslavia. It began to support minority rights, independent trade unions, the women's movement, freedom of speech. It was making films, publishing books of anti-war stories, releasing records by local bands; trying to keep alive the creative spirit of the young, urban Belgrade which had flourished in the eighties, and attempting to stop Serbia being isolated from the rest of Europe, left behind to stagnate into cultural torpor and the state-sponsored cult of death.

'When the borders were closed and war started, if we hadn't had B92 we would have been locked in a kind of prison,' one listener explains. 'We stopped travelling – we stopped living, actually – so the only contact we had with the outside world was through B92. It became a cultural phenomenon and it was stronger, unfortunately, than any political movement here.'

The shutdown of March 1991 had demonstrated exactly what the regime thought of them; now they had gone further, questioning the nationalist militarism on which Milošević's support was founded. 'The opposition parties were saying nothing about Bosnia, the government was acting as if it wasn't going on. It was all being swept under the carpet,' says another listener. 'This was what turned B92 into a serious political force. Nobody reacted against the war in Bosnia, only B92 created this huge manifestation against it. The government may not have understood what they were doing, but they certainly didn't like it.'

But by 1992, Veran Matić had begun to worry that the authorities, angered by B92's anti-war campaign, would shut down the station again. He decided to attempt a daring experiment: before B92 could be banned, it banned itself. 'There was a rumour that we would be closed down, so what we did was pretend that it had actually happened,' says Matić. 'We put different presenters in the studio and a sweet bimbo on the phone saying: "Oh, they've all gone on holiday, we can't help you." Nobody knew what we were doing, not even fellow journalists. Reuters published the story that B92 was banned and the listeners were freaking out; we were told that some of them actually smashed their radios.'

Duška Anastasijević, a long-time admirer of B92, was tuned in that day. 'For a whole day they converted into a Socialist Party programme, with horrible music, domestic Yugo-pop and folk, and these terrible news bulletins.' It had the same impact, she says, as when in 1938 US radio broadcast a drama-tisation of Orson Welles' tale of Martian invasion, *War of the Worlds*. On hearing it, thousands of Americans started to panic that warrior aliens had actually landed on Earth. Of the 600 people who phoned in to B92 that day, only one didn't accept that the station had been taken over: it was all too believable.

'People were calling and saying: "What's happening? What are you doing to us?" And the girl on the switchboard was very calm and professional, she would just reply: "No, I don't see any problem, this is B92, maybe it's different, but so what?" ' Anastasijević recalls: 'Listeners were asking for Veran Matić and she was saying: "Oh, I don't know, who's he?" People were really disturbed about it, and then you realised how much this radio station meant to people who were desperate and couldn't find out what was going on.'

As the day progressed, Matić began to realise that his experi-ment was seriously upsetting the listeners, and he called a halt. The following day, he aired the tapes of all the complaining calls: 'That was the point when both us and the listeners realised how much the station meant to both of us – and it also averted the ban, because we showed how strong we were.'

But it made Matić worry that B92 had set itself up as

infallible and that, instead of questioning what the station told them, its listeners were blindly accepting everything it broadcast as truth – in exactly the same way as the rest of the population was swallowing state TV propaganda whole: 'The experiment proved that if you said that you were the only trustworthy voice enough times, people would start to believe you.'

Matić began to wrestle with his conscience – what gave him the right to be the sole true voice, he asked himself. 'Who am I to persuade people that my idea of justice is the correct one? Why can't people open their minds and think for themselves?' he says. 'These suspicions made me reluctant to go into the studio and speak into the microphone on a regular basis, so gradually I stopped doing my shows and finally I felt that I should stop being on the programme at all.'

And B92 had a new slogan: 'Trust no one, even us.'

There was one question which every young man in Belgrade was asking himself, again and again: should I stay or should I go? Should I remain here and perhaps be called up to fight and die in some hole in Bosnia for someone whose cause I care nothing about? Or should I leave my family, my friends, leave this country and emigrate into the uncertainty of a foreign land, where I know nobody and everyone I meet will think that I, as a Serb, am just another one of those bestial murderers they have seen on their television, ethnically cleansing Bosnia?

In the year that passed between the summers of 1991 and 1992, thousands of people emigrated – perhaps as many as 300,000, most of them young and impatient to live a normal life without the constant fear of war and the threat of the army draft. Every other day, it seemed, some friend was packing his bags and saying goodbye to Belgrade. 'During these months, society changed a lot,' says Uroš Djurić, a former rock musician turned conceptual artist who also had a show on B92. 'These people who left were the critical mass. They had the quality which would have helped us to keep things together here.'

It was a brain drain of enormous, catastrophic proportions. These were the 'brightest and the best', the young, the educated and the independently-minded. Their reasons for fleeing weren't hard to understand. As one later émigré explained: 'I felt there wasn't much I could do any more in my field of work, that avenues for expression were becoming increasingly limited, that society was becoming less and less tolerant and day-to-day living was reduced to mere subsistence, without any prospect for achieving anything significant, either for myself or for society. Right now, I don't think I will ever return to live there.'

And sooner or later, says Veran Matić, the émigrés would turn around and ask those who remained: what are you still doing in that sorry country? Are you insane? And those who remained would think: am I? 'Then you feel that something has seriously changed, that your friend of yesterday has begun to see you as an insect,' says Matić. 'And you become angry and sad because of that.'

Their exodus both weakened the opposition and bolstered the power of the regime, because these were the ones least likely to vote for Milošević. And those who remained felt increasingly isolated, culturally, politically and psychologically, and wondered again whether they too should go.

In East Germany before the fall of the Berlin Wall, author Timothy Garton Ash was told by one of his local acquaintances that leaving the country was the only sensible choice: '"Soon," he added bitterly, "there'll be nobody left in this country but a mass of stupid philistines and a few crazy idealists."'[12] And it's hard to describe the courage of those who decided, whatever might happen, to stay in Belgrade and fight for their generation's future. Because, as artist Uroš Djurić says, refusing to emigrate was no grand, romantic sacrifice. It didn't make you feel good. It was harsh and very real.

'I don't feel angry with the people who left. Why should

I? I can understand their way of seeing things. But my identity is here and I want to struggle for the right kind of society here. I know it would be much easier to go and live somewhere else, but it's high time that we start to live here properly. Why should I always have to go abroad to find what I need? I want to get it here. I want to emancipate my own surroundings.

'I don't want to go to the US to wash dishes. Here I'm an artist, but when I go outside, I'm nobody. Most of our friends who have left are living like peasants, they are fighting to survive every day and they always feel like they are guests in these countries.'

People in Belgrade had begun to adopt the language of the prisoner. Travelling abroad was now referred to as going 'outside'. Serbia was 'inside' – a huge jail full of unhappy inmates, many of whom had become so institutionalised they didn't realise that their country was being ripped to shreds around them.

'I always wanted to live outside,' says Djurić. 'I used to go to Berlin for two or three months each year. But when the war started, most of the people who never thought about living somewhere else were emigrating. And myself, who always wanted to live outside the country, came back home.

'This society was something worth fighting for, and anyway, I didn't have much choice any more, because from 1992, I was marked as a Serb – and fuck it, I am a Serb! It's not easy for Serbs going outside because of this mark on their heads, this new trademark; people read you in a totally different way to before. I didn't want to be part of that. It's humiliating and it also created a wall around this country which practically gave Milošević the power to do anything he wanted inside the wall. And of course, he didn't miss his chance!'

Despite the suffocating embrace of media conformity, the military campaign didn't entirely stifle political resistance. At an opposition rally in March 1992, the head of the Serbian Orthodox Church, Patriarch Pavle, blasted the president for his involvement in 'the madness of this fratricidal war'. In a deeply religious country, his words had real impact. Vuk Drašković's Serbian Renewal Movement, despite the virulent nationalism of its early days, declared its support for the draft-dodgers and deserters and denounced the conflict as 'dirty, senseless and fatal'.

And in June 1992, students started camping out in front of parliament, demanding immediate elections and the replace-ment of the government. They staged a series of satirical, theatrical al fresco spectaculars, like a public walk past the state TV headquarters with eyes closed (titled 'The Strolling of the Blind'), and a mass offering of bars of soap to members of the Serbian parliament ('to wash their dirty tongues'). Despite all that was going on around them, people had not yet lost their notoriously dark Belgrade humour.

In December, it was election time again. Despite painting himself as a wartime statesman, despite his control of the political system and the state bureaucracy, despite his domi-nance of the mass media and despite the perennial in-fighting amongst the opposition parties, this time Milošević looked as if he was under serious threat of losing the Serbian presidency to Milan Panić, a pharmaceuticals magnate who had defected from Yugoslavia in the fifties while competing for his country as part of the national cycling team and become an American citizen. Panić, who had returned to Belgrade, had held high office in the Yugoslav administration, and was initially seen as a Milošević stooge, but went on to criticise some of the worst excesses of the war in Bosnia. Vuk Drašković, the most popular opposition figure, stood down from the election race to give Panić a clear run at his goal.

Panić wanted Serbia to seek a peaceful solution in Bosnia, get rid of its pariah status and rejoin the international com-munity. 'Now or never' was his campaign slogan. He asked the United Nations to lift the sanctions it had imposed on Serbia to show its support for an anti-Milošević candidate. (The West refused — an act which, some say, would cause Serbs to suffer for years to come, and cause many to ponder on exactly how much the rest of the world really wanted democratic change in their country. It was, says Veran Matić, 'the first of a number of lost opportunities'.)

Milošević, on the other hand, labelled Panić a CIA stooge and celebrated the country's isolation. 'Serbia is not for sale,' declared his running slogan. Socialist Party propaganda divided Serbs into two simple categories: 'patriots' and 'traitors', those who were for Serbia and therefore for Milošević, and those who gave succour to the wanton aggression of 'Muslim fundamentalists' and 'Croat fascists' by opposing him. The Socialists' official platform claimed to uphold the basic values of freedom, social justice, solidarity and peace, but this was sounding increasingly like a hollow joke.

Exit polls suggested that the final count would be extremely close. But when the results were announced, Milošević had won by a huge margin. His support swelled by the hundreds of thousands of Serb refugees who had fled Bosnia, and the opposition undermined by the loss of support of those who had emigrated, Milošević secured fifty-three per cent of the vote, with Panić coming in second on thirty-two per cent. International observers said the elections were 'seriously flawed', while Vuk Drašković insisted they had been 'rigged to the last degree'. There was no way of finding out; Milošević ran both the police and the election machine. The paramilitary leader Arkan, who had formed his own political party, won five seats in parliament.

Central Belgrade, as usual, had rejected Milošević outright. And the city's rock community, shrunken by emigration and the draft, did its best to fight back with the only weapons it had – vicious satire and distorted guitars, thrashed hard in anger. Antonije Pušić was a cult singer with a conceptual art background (he had been a member of eighties avant-garde group KPGS – an acronym for 'Dick, Pussy, Shit, Tits'). He created a character called Rambo Amadeus, who relentlessly scoffed at the national mentality that underpinned the regime. Rambo Amadeus was comic, ironic and obscene by turns, sending up the folk singers who crooned their disgusting war lullabies. 'He borrowed from a cultural type which, akin to Shakespeare's "divine fool", was the confused and ignorant simple man who inadvertently or with a special comic license reveals the truth,' says American writer Eric D. Gordy.[13]

During the December 1992 election campaign, Rambo Amadeus appeared at a concert that was shown live on national television. For his first few songs the singer, clad in an old shepherd's fur coat, performed without comment. Then midway into his set, he stopped the band and launched into a tirade of abuse directed at the TV audience. 'I don't want to play for you stupid brainless motherfuckers who will vote for Milošević tomorrow. Fuck you all and suck my dick,' he ranted – and walked off the stage.

Before the war, many young Belgraders had been blind to what was going on in their country's political circles – 'people of my generation were distinctively anti-political – it was a statement to be anti-political', says one. They found it stupid and irrelevant, the province of careerists and dull Party officials. Now politics had colonised every aspect of ordinary life, creeping up and imposing itself on every idea, every move, every decision they made. As Slobodan Brkić, one of Belgrade's best house music DJs, who works under the name DJ Brka, explains: 'Politics came into it for me in the early nineties when the whole thing visibly collapsed in front of my eyes. It was only later I learned it had all been brewing for some time!'

The walls were closing in. Within two short years, Yugoslavia, once a country of twenty-two million people, relatively wealthy, its people free to travel abroad, had become Serbia, internationally renowned criminal renegade, with little opportunity for fun, work or travel. The world had shrunk to the local, the provincial.

'Those miserable bastards, they took away so much of my life!' exclaims Brkić. 'Ljubljana [in Slovenia] was a part of my life, Dubrovnik [in Croatia] was a part of my life, Sarajevo [in Bosnia] was a part of my life. What do I have in common with some guy in rural Serbia? We live in different worlds, you know. I would have so much more in common with a guy in Zagreb [Croatia's capital] who had similar interests and shared the same culture. And the whole nation was forced to opt for those kinds of allegiances. What could I get out of a guy from rural Serbia? Fucking nothing! I could get much more out of an urban guy from Zagreb.'

Prague and Budapest, formerly the impoverished, pallid-faced cities that Belgraders visited with disdain, were now being groomed for entry to the affluent cocoon of the European Union, while Serbia was hurtling backwards in time. 'They were liberated and going up, while we were falling down fast,' says Teofil Pančić. 'We had become the last remaining Eastern Europeans.'

All that the regime had to offer young Serbs was traditional values and the poisoned dream of racial unity. Milošević had stolen their freedom, their culture and their youth.

'It was a narrowing of possibilities, a narrowing of horizons, for the sake of a weird idea of security and commonality,' says Slobodan Brkić. 'These limitations were imposed by this collective "we", thinking it would be better, that we would feel happier. It's an absurd concept: somebody's promising you more happiness from less. It's pathetic.'

At least, they told themselves, this is as bad as things can get. It can't get much worse here now. Can it?

# 3

# it's almost midnight
# 1993–95

'Belgrade epitomised the Chicago of the Twenties, the economic
crisis of the Berlin of the Thirties, the intelligence intrigues of
the Casablanca of the Forties and the cataclysmic hedonism
of the Vietnam of the Sixties'

*Aleksandar Knežević and Vojislav Tufegdžić,*
*The Crime That Changed Serbia (1995)*

Despite the turbulent events of the previous two years, nothing
could have prepared the city for what was to happen in 1993.

Inflation had been rising steadily since the election of Milošević in 1990. The punitive sanctions imposed in the middle
of 1992 by the United Nations Security Council, backed up
later by a naval blockade to prevent fuel coming in, accelerated
the economic crisis. Serbia had already been in a parlous
financial state before the war, and its economy was decimated
by the loss of trade with the former Yugoslav republics, the
cost of its support of the Bosnian Serb military campaign, and
the impact of the war on domestic consumers. Despite this, the
government continued to print money to cover salaries and
pensions in what one observer called 'the effective equivalent
of writing massive numbers of bad cheques'.[1]

Things were spinning wildly out of control as the economy
careered into a state of hyperinflation. By February 1993, the
monthly rate of inflation had reached 200 per cent. By August,
it was 1,880 per cent per month; by November, 20,190 per

cent. In January 1994, the rate peaked at a mind-bending 313,563,558 per cent – one of the highest in history.

Prices rose by the hour. Wages paid in the morning could be worthless by dinnertime. Banknotes of tens of thousands of dinars wouldn't even cover a bottle of beer. On 2 November 1993, a loaf of bread cost 12,500 dinars. A month and a half later, it cost 4,000,000,000 dinars. According to one Serbian economist, 'the dinar objectively lost the meaning and all the functions of money'. The only functioning currency was the Deutschmark, and those who had no Deutschmarks had nothing. People couldn't tell what they earned or what they'd spent. They were lost in a vortex of uncertainty.

In Belgrade, an almost nihilist hedonism, which recalled the decadence of inter-war Germany's Weimar Republic, gripped the city. Money was meaningless, the future was a black hole, and people were living hard and fast, obliterating any thoughts of tomorrow. 'It was a really wild time, but it wasn't the joyful fun of 1989 and 1990,' says B92 presenter Srdjan Andjelić. 'There were no moral limits; there were so many drugs. We were living in a closed community, so people had to find a way out.

'It was the first time we really saw the abyss we were going into, the first time we felt that things would only get worse and worse. You might go to a barbecue and there would be drugs and girls and beer, like a scene from some movie, and the next day you could only afford to have one yoghurt to eat. And all they had in the shops was light bulbs – rows of red, green and blue light bulbs.'

Hyperinflation thrust the majority of the population into instant, punishing deprivation. 'Universal compulsory poverty', as American sociologist Eric D. Gordy called it, brought the country even further into the grasp of Milošević. 'The repeated efforts to secure the means of everyday life made conditions of "normality" inaccessible to most people and encouraged further isolation, resignation and passivity,' commented Gordy. 'Psychologically, the impossibility of meeting everyday needs fostered a sense of defeat.'[2] The president was shutting down the options, narrowing the horizons, undermining any remaining will for autonomous activity.

The average salary had dropped to around 100 Deutschmarks per month – hardly enough to buy the basic necessities for living. In 1989, many had been earning ten to twenty times that amount. This economic destabilisation worked in Milošević's favour; turning people's thoughts away from political change towards simple survival, wiping out the middle class by forcing them to spend all of their hard currency savings, accelerating the emigration of urban youth, and bolstering the economic strength of an emerging criminal elite which was profiting from the war and sanctions-busting.

For most young people, there was simply nothing to do except wait, and hope, for it all to end. Time effectively stood still as society was petrified. 'It was a one-year gap when nothing happened. We would just go to each other's flats and have parties,' says rock journalist Dragan Ambrozić. 'Someone would buy one box of cigarettes and we would all share it. We didn't have anything to do, just talk to friends and play the old records again and again.

'It was both a comedy and a tragedy. That experience of money losing its value is hard to explain. You are holding a piece of paper and you can't buy anything with it, or if you can buy something, it's something that you don't need. It shook our whole world and afterwards it was hard to pick up the pieces of any kind of normal life.'

In the months before hyperinflation took hold, two huge pyramid schemes, which had vacuumed up enormous amounts of ordinary Serbs' hard currency savings, collapsed in spectacular fashion, fuelling the inflationary tornado. Both pyramids called themselves 'banks' and offered unusually high rates of interest on people's investment; both seemed to be legitimate, and both could lay claim to connections with the regime. Dafina Milanović's Dafiment bank made contributions to the national pension fund, turning her into what journalist

Tim Judah called a 'Serbian Queen of Hearts' – although she had a history of fraud and corruption, and had helped fund some of the paramilitary warlord Arkan's cross-border smuggling operations. The Jugoskandik bank was run by Jezdimir Vasiljević, alias Gazda Jezda (Jezda The Boss), an equally colourful figure who achieved fame when he brought the veteran chess player Bobby Fischer to Serbia. Vasiljević had given money to both the Socialist Party and to paramilitary groups, and he too was close to Arkan.

Some analysts suggest that the brief adventures of both Dafiment and Jugoskandik were supported by Milošević – at the very least as a diversion from the prevailing hardship. Pyramid schemes like these were rife in the pauperised states of the post-Communist East during the mid-nineties and their perpetrators were often rumoured to be state puppets, surreptitiously encouraged to continue their business in order to (at least temporarily) mollify the population.

While Romania was the first to be damaged by such unorthodox investment predators, the most notorious pyramid schemes were established in Albania later that decade, where almost a sixth of the population invested around $1.5 billion in get-rich-quick capers, selling their houses and land to join the gold rush. As one observer noted later: 'The schemes became so massively popular that anyone who said a word against them would appear opposed to the entire nation.'[3] The ruling party both endorsed and profited by the collective euphoria of this manic speculation. As the schemes failed, Albania erupted into armed unrest, with riots in the streets and demonstrators burning government buildings, ultimately resulting in an all-out civil war.

Just as in Albania and Romania, Serbia's Dafiment and Jugoskandik banks could only keep on paying out interest as long as people kept pumping money in. Once the deposits dried up, inevitably, the pyramids imploded, causing anarchy as investors rushed to try to withdraw what they could. Both left ordinary investors millions of Deutschmarks out of pocket.

Serbian hyperinflation came to an abrupt end in January 1994, when the old dinar was abolished and the ravaged economy began to return to relative stability – although it would never really recover its pre-war robustness. The electricity shortages which followed that winter, causing lengthy and unpredictable power cuts, compounded the mood. These were dark times, and Belgrade was in dark spirits, physically and psychologically. At least this was a city with a cruel sense of humour. One opposition politician joked that 'the only good thing about not having electricity is that then there is no television to tell us that we have electricity'. But it was hard not to equate the blackouts on information and the descending gloom of warfare with the blackouts caused by power failures, as the opposition Democratic Party did at its 'rally against darkness' that December.

The combination of wartime smuggling and sanctions-busting created a new social class in Serbia, a wealthy criminal cabal which was intimately linked to the political, military and economic elite. They were known as the 'nouveau riche' – although, in practice, nouveau riche simply meant rich from crime. As one sarcastic commentator puts it: 'Today's nouveau riche are yesterday's criminals and tomorrow's "businessmen".'

Sanctions turned smuggling into a big business. Trade could not be conducted legitimately, so illicit import–export outfits replaced legal ones as the criminals seized control of the financial centre ground. Hence the West unwittingly aided the new criminal aristocracy in its rise to influence.

Dealing in smuggled arms, petrol, cigarettes, drugs and stolen cars was fantastically lucrative. The regime, too, was dependent on the smugglers to ensure the flow of goods into the country; goods that ordinary people also desired. It was almost impossible not to be complicit, and inevitably the criminals' wealth and power grew at incredible speed.

'Serbian leaders conducted the wars in Croatia and Bosnia with such cynicism that it is hardly surprising that, for many, "defending Serbdom" was indistinguishable from making money,' suggested Tim Judah. Many got rich by doing business with their supposed enemies. 'Hundreds of millions of Deutschmarks' worth of weaponry, ammunition, fuel and goods were traded across the frontlines and even more was looted by Serbs, not just from their enemies but from their own people as well,' Judah wrote.[4]

Flushed with smugglers' loot, Belgrade became a gangster's paradise: the downtown casinos with their flashing lights and spinning roulette wheels, the expensive restaurants, the discos blasting out kitschy Yugo-dance hits, the smoky snooker halls, the glitzy summer terrace bars on the waterfront of the Sava river. These were floating follies decorated with neon, chrome, mirrors and promotional posters for the corporate luxuries of Marlboro, with televisions screening cable TV football, and 'classy' names like Amsterdam or Monza Racing.

Then there were the pricey bars of upscale hotels like the Hyatt and the Intercontinental across the river in New Belgrade, where the hard-faced, crop-headed men in leather jackets would park their shiny Jeeps with their dark tinted windows and flaunt their thick gold rope-chains and peroxide molls in Lycra micro-miniskirts. These were the hustlers' temples: shrines to Belgrade's easy-come, easy-go, screw-you materialism.

Young Belgraders knew which bars and cafés to avoid – not that they could afford to drink there anyway. However, the nouveau riche, the only ones with money to binge on imported liquor and Western designer trinkets from high-fashion boutiques which remained open despite the crushing recession, inevitably transformed the cultural landscape.

'The "mafiasation" of the city was becoming really obvious,' Jelena Subotić remembers. 'There were more and more black sports cars running around with tyres squeaking in the middle of the night. The Belgrade we cherished was gone, replaced by the culture of guns and BMWs. The fact that the police turned a blind eye to the mafia and actually allowed it to prosper and permeate every segment of society contributed to the general feeling of uneasiness, anxiety and disillusionment.'

The rise of Belgrade's criminal elite was another step towards the total decivilisation of the country, believes Dragan Ambrozić. Young people saw the gangsters getting rich as their parents became poor, and made the logical deduction: crime and only crime pays. The gangsters became renegade heroes for Belgrade teenagers – glamorous pirate marauders living the very highest of lives. 'It was only by corruption and smuggling that you could survive here,' says Ambrozić. 'No wonder gangsta rap is popular now with the younger generation, because they were brought up in this situation and they learned you can only make money by some illegal activity – by just taking what you want. It's that ghetto attitude, rappers like Snoop Doggy Dogg really appeal to them because they deliver the same message: be tough, because that's the only way you can survive. All moral values were just destroyed.'

Many criminals who had been operating in exile for years returned to their native country, dazzled by the spoils of war. 'Some became involved with Serbian paramilitaries, which under the cover of patriotism became rapacious looting machines,' wrote Tim Judah. 'After they had stolen all the cars and other goods from frontline towns, they turned their attention to the home front.'[5]

This is confirmed by *The Crime That Changed Serbia*, a remarkable video made by B92's film unit. Produced at the height of the first explosion of wartime gangsterism, its directors secured remarkable access to the main players in the Serbian underworld. The cocky gangsters addressed the camera while lolling in jacuzzis, carousing in riverside bars, caressing their semi-automatic pistols, and posing in swanky cafés with pouting, scantily-clad girls on their knees, boasting openly of their exploits. Most of them blamed the upsurge in organised crime on the UN sanctions, Serbia's corrupt legal system and the war.

A state security official who had once commanded a special unit for international operations was also interviewed. Before the war, he suggested, criminals were dealt with in an unorthodox way – they were given false papers by his unit then kicked out of the country, and only came back to Belgrade to spend the proceeds of their illicit activities abroad. But in 1991, many of them returned home and helped inspire the emergence of a new breed of criminals.

These brawny young thugs in their shell suits with colossal gold name-plate necklaces – a Balkan parody of Run-DMC-style eighties hip-hop chic – seemed proud of their status as the only role models in town. 'People can't live on 100 Deutschmarks a month,' said one. 'More and more young people are making up their minds: death or glory.'

Another likely lad, his head shaven to the bone and his tight black designer clothes bulging with muscles, bragged: '"Mortals" are ordinary people who live ordinary lives. There's no way they can experience the excitement, beauty, disappointment, bad and good things in life that we get through in a day.

'Every single young man would like to be a criminal, if only for five minutes. He would like to ride in a fancy car with a fancy girl and some gold around his neck.'[6]

Many of them established 'legitimate' businesses to launder their loot: nightclubs, casinos or restaurants. The war in Bosnia ensured a ready supply of weapons, and internecine feuds and turf wars resulted in an increasing number of shoot-outs between young men full of testosterone with something to prove. They would crow about their exploits in the local press, exaggerating their heroism for a fascinated readership. They had the swaggering confidence of kings of Serbia's wild frontier, caring little for the law or for death.

The criminal class benefited the Milošević regime in a host of ways: it evaded UN sanctions and got essential goods across borders and frontlines, and it provided manpower for some of the war's murkier episodes. The two fed on and nourished each other, and the entire economy of Serbia became reliant on illegal trading. As one local analyst claimed later: 'There is no mafia outside the power structure. The mafia is Milošević and his coterie. You either belong to the power structure and you have license to do whatever you want – or you don't.'[7]

The mafia's impact wasn't hard to quantify. In the first two years of the war, the number of murders in Belgrade doubled. The B92 film ends poignantly with a succession of funerals of the same men who had earlier boasted to the camera of their immortality; their fast life on the edge brutally cut short. 'It was a unique film which couldn't be shot now, because only two of the interviewees are still alive,' says Veran Matić of B92. 'One is serving fourteen years in prison in Greece and the other one has just had a warrant issued for his arrest.' Fittingly, the film also goes by the title of *See You In The Obituaries*.

The most notorious of Belgrade's criminals was Željko Ražnatović, better known as Arkan; his alias taken from one of the many false passports he possessed while on the run in Europe. It was Arkan – celebrity killer, comic-book goon, murderous superman – who best symbolised the links between the gangster clans, the Milošević regime and the war.

Through his battlefield profiteering, ethnic cleansing, and links with soccer thugs, the political establishment and the tawdry social elite of nouveau riche Belgrade, Arkan personified the ultimate model of the new Serbian businessman, a pirate entrepreneur and renegade anti-hero whose life became a metaphor for the tragic drama of Belgrade's culture of death.

Although many details of his life have become blurred as his spectacular career was mythologised by allies and enemies alike, it is known that he carried out his first petty crimes at the age of fourteen, in 1966, and was sentenced to three years in juvenile jail. Soon he was an accomplished and persistent bank robber, pulling off jobs all over Europe. In 1974, he was arrested in Belgium and sentenced to ten years in prison, although he managed to escape. In 1979, he was sentenced to seven years in a Dutch jail, but escaped again. In 1981, he was arrested during an armed robbery in Germany; although wounded, he escaped for a third time, from the prison hospital. On a fourth occasion, he busted his partner-in-crime out of a Swedish courtroom, storming the building, threatening the judge and then escaping through the window – 'like in a low-budget thriller', said one observer. Simultaneously, he was also working for Yugoslav state security – reputedly as a 'liquidator' responsible for assassinating dissident émigrés. Right up to his death, he was still wanted by Interpol.

In the eighties, Ražnatović returned to Belgrade, where he worked in nightclub security and then became the leader of the Delije (Warriors), Red Star Belgrade's fan club. These were the glory days of Red Star – in 1991, they won the European Cup. Arkan was brought in to calm anti-Communist agitation among the hardcore supporters, who had begun to chant nationalist slogans ('We are the warriors from proud Serbia/Come on to the terraces, greet the Serbian race'). Serbian football thugs, who modelled their flamboyant displays of banners and flares on Italian fans and their taste for violence on the English, had been some of the first to embrace hatred against Serbia's former 'brother republics'. One supporter demanded: 'One should give the fans true recognition, because they were the first to support Serbia in these changes. I think that it all began in the stadium.'[8]

As a 'special adviser' to the club, Arkan was also spotted sitting on the bench with the coach and it was rumoured his influence was so great that he was even involved in team selection. In 1990, as war loomed, he founded his own param-ilitary unit, the Serbian Volunteer Guard – better known as the Tigers – with Warrior hooligans forming the nucleus of his fighters. Their exploits at away fixtures had prepared them well, Arkan insisted: 'Remember that, as supporters, we had trained first without weapons . . .' The club newspaper would go on to cover the Warriors' exploits on the battlefield as if they were a series of important international fixtures, calling them 'fearless fighters, heroes to a man'.[9] In turn, the hooligans adapted their terrace chants, turning them into battlefield anthems.

While running the fan club, Arkan briefly had his own show on Radio B92 as part of a slot leased from the station by the Red Star fan club. Each Friday, Arkan and his entourage of hooligans would come down to the studio and chat to the listeners about the upcoming match – and their marauding exploits of the previous weekend. 'It was really extreme,' recalls B92 DJ Gordan Paunović. 'They would describe how they had been smashing up Zagreb, or talking about who could break the biggest shop window with a concrete block.' (Arkan later commented: 'I could see war coming because of that match in Zagreb, I foresaw everything.')[10]

In November 1990, Arkan was arrested for arms offences in Croatia, but when freed on appeal he fled to Belgrade, taunting his captors: 'You will never catch me alive!' After that, the Warriors' radio programme came to an abrupt end – so abrupt that the fledgling warlord still owed B92 money for the lease of the airtime. Three years later, he wanted to hire another slot to promote the political party he had founded. Veran Matić refused, but asked him to come in for an interview. After the show ended, Matić asked him: 'OK Arkan, what happened to our 300 Deutschmarks?' Arkan retorted coolly: 'It's your contribution to the defence of our mother country.'

During the wars in Croatia and Bosnia, his Tigers carried out some of the most brutal ethnic cleansing, backed with hardware supplied by the regime. Arkan revelled in the role. He posed arrogantly for Western cameras in front of a tank with his balaclava-clad cronies, holding a tiger cub in one hand and a machine gun in the other, and even produced a promotional video for his exploits.

Arkan was an essential part of the Belgrade war machine – the one who did the regime's dirty work while Milošević looked the other way. His controller, the interior minister

Radovan Stojičić, alias Badža, provided the link to the man known as the 'puppet master' of the paramilitaries, Milošević himself. A few years later, Badža was executed, shot in the head in a Belgrade pizzeria, after famously insisting that organised crime didn't exist in Serbia. Arkan and Milošević both mourned at his funeral.

Arkan had grown rich by running illicit petrol and cigarettes across the borders, and when he returned home, attempted to buy the football team he loved, Red Star. Rejected outright, he tried again with FC Priština of Kosovo. But it was only on the third attempt that he grasped the sporting glory he so desired. In 1996, he bought a lowly third-division Belgrade team, FC Obilić. He upped their wages, brought in new players and enforced a rigorous regime of discipline – but also used his paralegal skills to 'persuade' referees and opposing players that his team should win. Obilić were accused of bribing officials and intimidating other teams into losing while their skull-cropped fans chanted death threats from the terraces. One journalist declared him 'the patron saint of football thugs the world over'.[11]

'He blackmailed everyone,' says one Red Star fan. 'His players played the most important games obviously doped. His gunmen called key players of rival teams in the middle of the night before the match offering "protection" for their families and kids. They even started a fire once in a hotel where a rival team was based a night before a match.' As Red Star striker Perica Ognjenović said after playing against Obilić in one particularly fractious fixture: 'This is not soccer, this is a war.'[12] Knowing Arkan's reputation, few dared beat them and Obilić hurtled up the league, and in 1998 won the Yugoslav championship in their first season in the top division. (In a bizarre epilogue, one of Arkan's business partners, Giovanni di Stefano, would later attempt to buy the Scottish football club Dundee – boasting of his links with Saddam Hussein, Gerry Adams and Yasser Arafat.)

Arkan had consolidated his business empire in Belgrade.

He owned shops (including a patisserie near the Red Star stadium selling notoriously good ice-cream), exported fruit to Western Europe, dealt in currency exchange, ran nightclubs and a casino in the upmarket Hotel Jugoslavija, and headed a security firm which bore the same name as his paramilitary unit.

With his chubby, cheeky face, Arkan saw himself as a smooth operator, a showman with a keen sense of occasion. He would appear, expensively besuited, at film premieres, big football matches and top restaurants, and happily held court in fluent English to Western journalists in the opulent Hyatt Hotel, insisting that all he had ever done was defend his beloved country, despite the indictment of the International War Crimes Tribunal. His audience always found him charming, if not a little scary.

Arkan's villa in the affluent Dedinje area – opposite the Red Star stadium and not far from the Milošević residence – was a landmark to nouveau riche post-Communist criminal chic: all pastel marble and mirrored windows, piled high like a wedding cake, opulent and arrogant, expensive yet irredeemably tacky. A guard stood in the street outside the gate, peering threateningly into the windows of passing cars.

In the end, this protection was to no avail. Just after 5 p.m. on 15 January 2000, Arkan was approached by four men in tracksuits and trainers in the marble-tiled lobby of the Intercontinental Hotel in New Belgrade. One asked him casually if the fitness club was open. Then they pulled guns and started firing, and the 47-year-old gangster took a bullet from a Heckler-Koch machine gun through the left eye. He was dead on arrival at hospital. The warlord who had graduated in hotel management and spent much of his social life in hotel bars, ended his life, fittingly, as he had lived it.

The rumours multiplied. Was this the result of a simple gangland disagreement, settled in the traditional Belgrade style with a bullet in the face, or was there some deeper, darker implication – did Arkan, once Milošević's puppet killer but now superfluous to requirements, know too much? Some speculated that he was shot because he was cutting a deal with the War Crimes Tribunal in The Hague to escape prosecution by supplying damning testimony on Milošević's connections to ethnic terror in Bosnia; such a powerful man could never be attacked without getting the approval of the authorities. Others suggested he had become embroiled in a turf war with Milošević's son Marko over the spoils of the smuggled gasoline trade, or that he was about to come out in support of the political opposition.

The wildest rumour held that he was not dead at all, but had staged the shooting and skipped town to avoid his impending demise at the hands of a regime which no longer wanted him around. One reporter was even asked by her editor if she had actually seen the corpse inside his casket.

Shortly before his death, Arkan had told the press: 'My whole life has been one mega thriller movie.' The screenplay had come to a dramatic end – although no-one was quite sure why. Facts were hard to come by, and speculation went into overdrive. The local press devoted huge special issues to his funeral, wallowing in gruesome titillation over page after page of graveside photographs. Two of Arkan's associates had also been murdered in Belgrade in the preceding months, and people wondered whether this was a start of a gang war in the city – or were all the killings politically motivated? In a city where power and crime were interchangeable, it was hard to judge. One opposition politician warned: 'The denouement among the strongmen has begun.' Not long afterwards, defence minister Pavle Bulatović was also assassinated.

War had its heroes and its villains; its look and its smell. And it had its own sound, too: a local electro-ethnic hybrid called turbo-folk. Turbo-folk was indigenous Balkan disco, a gloopy melange of chirpy techno-pop and traditional folk melodies; a naive re-creation of an imagined West gleaned from MTV, mixed with resynthesised relics of village life. It was optimistic and patriotic, modern yet nostalgic, tugging at the heartstrings of rural folk who left Serbia's farmlands in search of big-city prosperity, poor, wistful refugees arriving in Belgrade on the run from Bosnia, and soldiers caught up in the conflicting emotions of wartime. It was a music which nourished, and was nourished by, Slobodan Milošević. As one Belgrade journalist says: 'Turbo-folk was the state soundtrack of the regime, and Milošević was its star.'

At the end of the eighties, Serbia was already in the throes of a folk revival. *Novokomponovana narodna muzika* ('newly-composed folk music'), as it was known, was a modernised roots style blending age-old themes with new lyrics of love, loss and infidelity; a kind of Slavic country-and-western. Milošević's rise to power had been supported by patriotic singers who wailed eulogies to their conquering hero on cassettes of agit-prop songs (sample lyric: 'They can hate us or not love us, but nobody can do anything to a Serb').[13]

These ditties would become increasingly strident and militaristic as the prospect of war loomed, with the singers dressing in combat fatigues and praising the fighting prowess of Serbian manhood. But this archaic revival was superseded by the phenomenal popularity of turbo-folk, which reconstituted the traditional peasant values of rural Serbia in a contemporary setting.

'Turbo-folk represented this quest for social stability,' explains Dragan Ambrozić. 'It sounded modern but it promoted a very conservative mind-set; basic family values and distinctive roles for male and female: he is a strong man, very successful, and she is sexy and beautiful, but she stays at home. It's all about social and family stability.

'Ninety per cent of it was love songs. There were a few patriotic songs but they were less important. Most of it was just glamour, putting some shiny moments into an otherwise depressing life. State television promoted it because it banished thoughts of bad things, of hyperinflation. The nouveau riche was listening to it – the guys who made a fortune out of smuggling petrol or whatever was needed during the sanctions.'

And turbo-folk, in turn, portrayed the nouveau riche as fabulous, enviable creatures, wearing Versace and sipping imported liquor, living a charmed life, role models of a fantasy Serbia. It created an imaginary world, suggested American writer Eric D. Gordy, full of 'images of glamour, luxury and the "good life" – a world populated by young women in miniskirts who drive luxury automobiles, live in fantastically spacious homes, and spend their time in fashionable hotel bars'.[14] Or as one Belgrader puts it, less politely: 'Turbo-folk said work less, earn more, cheat and steal, fuck a lot, drive a stolen Golf GTi, enjoy life!'

For Belgrade's young urbanites, driven further and further into an underground, bunker mentality, turbo-folk meant war, isolation and the shrill hysteria of nationalism. It was the deathly rattle of Milošević, of the paramilitaries and the profiteers – the new ruling class who had ruined their city, their culture and their lives. 'Like nationalism, it appealed to the need for identification and belonging – it was a perfect channel for disseminating the poisonous seeds of hatred,' says B92 presenter Jelena Subotić. Listening to turbo-folk poppets like Ceca or Goca meant saying yes to the regime; listening to rock, soul or techno was a defiant no. And because turbo-folk was so strongly identified with nationalism, rock'n'roll became an even more powerful symbol of opposition.

In the Eastern European imagination, wrote Slavenka Drakulić, Europe had always represented freedom – both political and material. It meant democracy, but also consumer gratification: 'It is something distant, something to be attained, to be deserved. It is also something expensive and fine: food, cars, light, everything – a kind of festival of colours, diversity, opulence, beauty. It offers choice: from shampoo to political parties. It represents freedom of expression. It is a promised land, a new Utopia, a lollipop.'[15]

But in Belgrade, the idea of Europe, so close in 1989, had

receded beyond the horizon. Superficially at least, Milošević's Serbia represented one of the last pockets of resistance to the globalised popular culture of MTV, Sony, Time-Warner and McDonald's. It celebrated indigenous popular art forms and shunned the embrace of Western corporate mediocrity. Despite being physically inside Europe, it rejected the new European cultural-economic hegemony.

Nevertheless, despite all their hatred of the West, Serbian politicians and 'businessmen' did not forgo the trappings of Western affluence. 'People appear on TV and criticise the New World Order, but they are wearing Armani suits and driving BMWs,' says the passionate and emotional Borka Pavičević, director of the Centre For Cultural Decontamination arts foundation. 'Are they drinking Bulgarian whisky? Are they wearing Chinese shoes? No, they are wearing Italian shoes and Versace clothes and driving a Mercedes Benz!'

Turbo-folk became a metaphor for the colonisation of everyday life by the symbols of xenophobia and backward-looking Serbian traditionalism. As Jelena Subotić says: 'Serbia became turbo-folk.' Its ideology, the twisted mentality of the regime, permeated films, fashion and literature. 'The cutting of all ties made our culture provincial,' says Dragoljub Mićunović of the Belgrade Institute of Social Studies. 'In the publishing business, only romanticism or non-critical traditionalism remains.'[16]

It even manifested itself in architecture; in the high kitsch abodes of war profiteers and gangsters like Arkan, their tacky combinations of expensive stone and mirrored glass shameless signifiers of ill-gotten gains. Borka Pavičević calls them 'turbo houses' – built with bloody cash and designed to flaunt it.

'They are like tombs,' she says. 'You can see the death culture of nationalism in them. If you analyse the aesthetics of these turbo houses, which are built on money from war, the windows are small, you can never see the door and you never see the children playing outside, because they are afraid.

Something is wrong and they know it is dangerous, somebody is being protected.'

The popularity of turbo-folk was boosted by the launch of a series of new television entertainment channels: relentlessly upbeat stations with names like TV Pink and TV Palma, their sets a riot of day-glo colours, their presenters flashily-attired and irrepressibly jolly. 'It was a crazy eruption of bad taste – "times are bad but let's have fun",' says Duška Anastasijević. 'You had a complete contrast – grey reality on one side, and on the other this flashy Versace thing. It was so obnoxious but you felt compelled to watch it because it was so amazing at the same time.'

The owners of the new channels were inevitably linked to the regime (Milošević's daughter Marija also operated her own TV and radio stations, both named Košava). They fed their depressed public a constant diet of trivia, glitz, lightweight pop and live appearances from the new turbo-folk celebrities. 'All you needed to be a turbo-folk star was big tits, a nice ass and a well-connected boyfriend,' says one Belgrade music writer. 'And of course, you needed to be on TV Pink.'

The shiniest star in the firmament was Svetlana Veličković, who adopted the stage name Ceca. The small-town girl from southern Serbia started her career at fifteen with a hit called *The Nagging Flower*. The country went crazy for her smouldering looks, voluptuous figure and dark, glossy hair, and she rapidly developed into the glamour queen of Serbian pop. Before the war, when the economy was thriving, the teenage diva symbolised the new prosperity, mixing traditional sentiments of village life with the innocently provocative sexuality of the girl-woman in a style similar to Kylie Minogue during her years on the Australian soap opera *Neighbours*.

Ceca also won herself a reputation as a femme fatale. Her early boyfriends, according to local rumours, included a FC Partizan footballer and a Belgrade mafia boss who was later murdered. Rumour also has it that she was once spotted in Geneva dating a Muslim – a heretical relationship. Her father appealed to Arkan to rescue her, and he travelled to Switzerland and brought her home. Later she played a gig for his Tigers, and they fell in love, although the affair was kept secret until Arkan divorced his wife.

The wedding of Arkan and Ceca in February 1995 spotlighted the umbilical link between war and pop culture in the most dramatic fashion. It was the defining ritual that consummated Serbian culture's flirtation with death.

Arkan arrived in a stretch limousine in a forty-strong cavalcade of expensive automobiles. He played the part of the military hero in a vintage officer's uniform with shiny leather boots, epaulettes, a pill-box hat and a machine gun; she was swathed in layers of diaphanous white – part Scarlett O'Hara, part Serbian farmyard sweetheart. Two thousand well-wishers lined the street outside as the sound of a gypsy brass band was drowned out by a fusillade of automatic weapons fired by Arkan's entourage. Locals compared the occasion to the marriage of Prince Charles and Lady Diana Spencer. 'They're such a beautiful pair, so much in love, a role model for the rest of the Serbs,' one bystander insisted.

Their marriage would not even reach its fifth anniversary before Arkan was executed in Belgrade. The week before he was shot dead in January 2000, Ceca appeared on the popular chat show, *Maksovizija* (*Maxovision*), on Pink TV. This had been the forum where she had announced her impending wedding to the warlord. Now she was promoting her new CD, *Ceca 2000* – but the show was marred by what could, with hindsight, be interpreted as either bizarre premonitions or blatant threats. One viewer phoned in to say: 'Ceca, you look like Goca.' Goca was another turbo-folk starlet, and her lover, a suspected drug dealer, had just been killed. Another called with some words of advice for Arkan, who was sitting in the front row with his leather jacket on his lap. 'Arkan,' the caller warned. 'Put your jacket on, it's going to get fucking cold here.'

In another strange coincidence, Ceca had just issued a

promotional video clip for her latest single, *Evidence*. In the promo, her husband cheats on her and she kills his lover. It was a brutal little performance – and one which was filmed in the Intercontinental Hotel, where her real-life husband was shot dead.

Despite the fact that the former Yugoslav republics were at war with each other, turbo-folk succeeded in crossing the frontlines and became popular all over the region. Many Serbian hits were actually recorded in Croatia, ostensibly an enemy state, including the greatest of them all, *It's Almost Midnight* – its title if nothing else a succinct summation of the apocalyptic feeling of the times. And yet the genre's reign was brief; it came and went with the war itself. Within a couple of years it had evolved into a kind of satellite TV-influenced, Balkanised dance-pop, the tiniest flourish of squealing, synthesised accordion the only remnant of its traditional roots.

The dominance of turbo-folk and nationalist art consigned urban culture and rock'n'roll – its audience devastated by mass emigration and universal compulsory poverty – to the margins. United Nations sanctions had cast Serbia into the cultural wilderness. Foreign travel was difficult to negotiate, international media impossible to obtain, overseas contacts frowned upon; the world was shrinking, perceptions narrowing. Serbia was talking to itself alone, enabling the regime to control the dissemination of information even more effectively. Economic, political, cultural and social alternatives to Milošević's vision were suppressed. The country became increasingly inward-looking – punishing for those who valued outside connections, but perfect for the nationalists who were pushing their message of 'Serbs against the world'.

'The "solid peasant" from rural areas came to define the idea of national identity,' author Eric D. Gordy writes. 'In contrast, a view of urban life and culture as unnatural and dishonest came to be promoted.' Because Belgrade had repeatedly rejected Milošević in elections and become the centre of the anti-war movement, its urban culture was despised as a refuge for degenerates and quislings. One rabid nationalist identified the entire city as a treacherous cell: 'Belgrade is Tito's whore. It sees itself as Yugoslav, cosmopolitan, democratic. The only thing it doesn't want to be is what it is: Serbian.'[17] And yet Belgrade embraced its status as the last bastion of progressive thought in Serbia, to the enduring disgust of the regime. Mira Marković would later call it 'an architectural, cultural and moral garbage dump'.[18]

A few older rock stars, entranced by nationalism, became enthusiastic proponents of the political establishment. Those who did switch sides to support the state were often rewarded with better production, distribution and marketing facilities: the wages of collaboration, as many opposition musicians saw it. 'A lot of people agreed – for money, for influence, for flats, for whatever – to be part of this,' says Belgrade rock writer turned political columnist Petar Luković. 'Even some of my friends, for the sake of money, decided to silently be part of this regime's culture. They say it doesn't change the nature of what they do, but of course it does. It's a pact with the devil. You are a part of the establishment and they will use you whenever they want. Very few people in rock'n'roll stayed clean.'

The satirical bard Rambo Amadeus once stated: 'Rock'n'roll in Serbia died the moment Slobodan Milošević appeared.' Although this was not entirely true, those who refused to play the regime's game did so in the knowledge that there was now no way back, and all they would have to subsist on was their principles.

But despite the economic impossibility of making a career out of music without selling out to the state, a new generation of bands did emerge as the nineties progressed. Their music was often dense and noisy, sometimes confrontational, influenced by avant-garde post-punk and reggae and, for the first time in Serbia, it revelled in cutting and mixing genres – an imaginative counterblast to the suffocating cultural conformism. The most original new voice was Darkwood Dub. Inspired by Sonic Youth, Can, Captain Beefheart, the Velvet Underground and, as their name suggests, dub reggae, they began to assemble a loose-limbed, fractured, spindly jazz-punk-funk layered with cryptic poetry.

Like most rock musicians, they resented being seen as part of a movement – in this case a post-Communist Belgrade new wave, the inheritors of the underground current of the eighties – and preferred to stress their individualism. 'The only thing we have in common is that we're still here, still alive and still making music,' says guitarist Vladimir Jerić.

But they shared the disillusionment of the generation who grew up thinking things were about to get better and suffered the pain of seeing them get much, much worse. As Dragan Ambrozić says: 'They were the voice of a generation which had a lot of ideals but saw them crash and didn't know what to do about it, although they still believed. This generation was thinking, "should I stay or get out of here?", but decided to remain and participate in the street protests. They were the poetical voice of this generation which was betrayed from all sides – by the government, the opposition and the international community.'

They believe that remaining in Belgrade gave their music an urgency and power it wouldn't have possessed had they emigrated. 'There are no words that make sense to explain why we live in Belgrade rather than anywhere else,' says Jerić. 'It's unwise to devote your life to music here, but for some strange reason we decided to stay and waste our lives together!'

'You can't live in Belgrade and not be aware of everything that's happening around you. If I decided to stay in my apartment and watch satellite television and surf the Internet, it would be like Disneyland, no problem. But once you leave the house you have to deal with it.'

Being a rock musician in such an environment, Jerić suggests, was to cut yourself loose from mainstream society and its values. This was no great career move. No one would view you as a hero. 'There are two models for a young man here: one is a bald-headed guy wearing gold, driving a Mercedes with lots of ammo in his pockets, the other is a person who finished brilliantly in his university faculty and immediately moved to Canada or Australia to get a job there. No other models exist.'

Theirs was the sound of darkness falling, of a city cracking under the strain. It wasn't overtly political – most Belgrade bands eschewed the banner-waving crassness of agit-prop rock – but it conveyed the desperation immaculately; the frustration of the dispossessed, turning inwards on themselves because the outside world no longer made sense; alone in their own city, in their own apartments, in their own heads. 'Ever since I remember this country has been declining – except for one year, 1990,' explains B92's Gordan Paunović. 'So if you're young and you're growing up in Belgrade, you build this mechanism of detaching yourself from reality as much as you can. So you had a kind of anger against the system, but it was more a means of escape than direct action. It was introverted rather than extrovert.'

It was, inevitably, both marginalised and marginal, employing a kind of psychic defence mechanism which was often incomprehensible to outsiders. Serbian rock was cut adrift from global trends and trapped in time by political circumstances. The indigenous mainstream had all but disappeared, leaving a music scene polarised between turbo-folk on the one side and the avant-garde on the other. Few bands remained, and very few good ones. One local newspaper commentator headlined a piece on the Belgrade rock of the mid-nineties: 'Harmless, depressive, minority-oriented.'[19]

The B92 film *Geto* [*Ghetto*] was a walk on the wilder side of pop life in Belgrade during the war years. Goran Čavajda, the drummer from seminal eighties post-punk band Električni Orgazam, hair dyed raging orange, long coat flapping in a hard wind, traversed the city streets, unfurling a lengthy prose poem which contrasted the conformity of the general population with the exuberance of his beloved yet embattled 'underground'. Simultaneously an exotic freak show and an elegy for a lost life, it was set to a suitably crepuscular sound-track by Darkwood Dub.

Belgrade, Čavajda insisted, had become a 'concentration camp'. He bemoaned the loss of his exiled friends, who ran away in search of a better life but ended up 'washing dishes in LA or cleaning cars in London'. 'They left desperate and humiliated. For me, they were the most beautiful people in the world and I'll never come to terms with the fact that they're gone,' he said. 'There were times when their decision seemed OK to me, and times when I thought leaving town was treason. Now I know it simply had to be like that.

'As time goes by, I see that in spite of nostalgia, my friends believe less and less that they'll ever return. They know they'll only find bad shit and decay here. What turns them off more than anything is that the city they left no longer exists, except in their memories.'

Passing stalls piled with trash and hawkers touting bootleg sportswear and smuggled tat, he sighed: 'This was never a pretty street but in recent years it has turned into a pigsty. Those who can't afford anything decent any more buy junk from those who lost their jobs, houses and towns. It depresses me to see how low we have sunk.'

He wondered what still kept him in the city: 'When fear creeps in, I want to go away. The next moment I feel I might be needed here, because someone has to remember all this. There are moments I wish I could sleep it all off and wake up in another time.'

Emigration and desperation, he speculated, would ulti-mately combine to make Belgrade 'an ethnically cleansed city of creeps and mutants'. Nothing good remained but a few last outposts of hedonism, people who were simply 'barking in a ghetto', allowed to carry on because no one was interested in what they were saying: noisy punks thrashing in a basement, a surreal artist with rotten teeth and a black leather jacket, some pretty girls dancing around the front room of their flat, a few beers at a rare rock gig. Hope had been strictly rationed.

'I belong to a generation which has ceased to exist,' Čavajda stated blankly. He later moved to Australia, where he died in the late nineties.[20]

For some, the only sensible response to what everyone, by now, simply referred to as 'the situation' was the most vicious of gallows humour. Many young Belgraders had grown up watching *Monty Python's Flying Circus* on television, and surreal satire was already second nature. The city had a strong tradition of absurdist theatre and art – during the inter-war years, the Dadaist art movement Zenit, with its headquarters in Belgrade, had published a series of pamphlets promoting a pacifist, cosmopolitan spirit and at the same time imagining the birth of a 'barbarogenius', throbbing with the primitive energies of the Balkans, who would shake the foundations of the morally bankrupt West. Perhaps his day had now come.

The strangest public manifestations of all were Fleka's broadcasts on Radio B92. Fleka was an old friend of B92's editor-in-chief Veran Matić; they had grown up together in the same small town and attended the same school. 'He knew me when I was a teenage rebel, a schoolboy with long hair, no school uniform and Jefferson Airplane records in my bag instead of school books,' Fleka says.

By this time, the former manager of the seminal Akademija club was suffering from a wasting disease and slowly going blind, his hands palsied, his unseeing eyes hidden behind dark glasses. Encouraged by Matić, Fleka's *Radio Bat* show mirrored the simultaneous psychological disintegration of the city around him. 'In the show I am some kind of transformer, some kind of idiot, some kind of madman,' he explains. 'I try to make contact with the listeners, to make some provocation, to awake their subconscious. I am trying to make them ask themselves questions. I let them show their ugly faces.'

During the summer of 1995, in a grand satire on hyperinflation, B92 invited pop-art pranksters the K Foundation to show the film of their money-burning stunt, *See The K Foundation Burn A Million Quid*, in Belgrade's central Republic Square, and take calls from listeners during Fleka's programme.

The K Foundation, Bill Drummond and Jimmy Cauty, began their peculiar career as the Justified Ancients of MuMu and then the KLF (Kopyright Liberation Front). They became notorious after they were sued by Abba for sampling the Swedish group's music on the album *1987 – What The Fuck Is Going On?* They had a couple of underground hits on the rave circuit, then collaborated with ageing pop veterans like Gary Glitter and Tammy Wynette on a series of chart smashes which would make them very rich men. Perversely, commercial success also made them extremely unhappy, and they decided to get rid of their spoils in the most spectacular manner possible. They withdrew £1 million from the bank in cash, took it to the remote Scottish island of Jura, and burnt it – 'to keep warm', according to Drummond – in a bizarre Situationist art statement.

It was the kind of bitter madness that made perfect sense in a country where money had ceased to have any meaning. Before they flew to Belgrade, Drummond and Cauty recorded a drum-and-bass version of the theme from Western movie *The Magnificent Seven*. They had initially wanted ex-Take That star Robbie Williams to sing on it, but instead rang Fleka in Belgrade and asked him to free-associate a few lines over the telephone. The presenter croaked: 'Serbia calling . . . This is Radio B92 . . . Humans against killing, that sounds like junkies against dope . . .'

Fleka was speaking hurriedly because one of B92's news reporters was hassling him to get off the phone as he was waiting for a call from a contact in Bosnia. Nevertheless, Drummond and Cauty thought it was perfect: 'He had this wildly charismatic, Beefheartian rumble of a voice that tore through you like some Slavic Howlin' Wolf,' Drummond later recalled. 'Some voices, as soon as you hear them, whatever words they're saying, have that instant sound of authority, of being the real thing. Fleka had it.'[21]

The K Foundation's appearance on *Radio Bat* was a bafflingly strange, challenging yet remarkable piece of avant-garde broadcasting. It was a perfect metaphor for the psychosis which permeated the city; the ultimate in uneasy listening. The show began with squeaking bat noises, electronic call signs and distorted fruit machine bleeps, then burst into Wayne County's foul-mouthed punk-rock party piece *If You Don't Want To Fuck Me, Baby Fuck Off*.

A taped voice droned: 'No thoughts, no feelings, no emotions, no desires, nothing . . . no mind, no thoughts, no feelings, no emotions . . . nothing . . . nothing . . . nothing . . .'

Fleka screamed: 'Zombie zone! Zombie town! Zombie land!'

The taped voice interjected: 'It's time to kick ass and chew bubblegum.'

Wayne County leered: 'If you don't want to fuck me, baby baby baby fuck off!'

Fleka screamed again: 'Madness, madness, madness!'

Then he introduced Bill Drummond and Jimmy Cauty, offering them a hyperinflation-era, multi-million dinar note with its seemingly endless string of zeroes. ('They were quite surprised, they never saw notes with so many zeroes, it was ten times more than they burned in Britain, but just with one note,' Fleka commented later.) He asked them to rip it up live on air. 'This is a public transmission of crime on frequency B92,' he said. 'Half for Bill, half for Jim.'

'Thank you very much,' Jimmy Cauty replied.

'We're the K Foundation, we're in Belgrade and we urgently need to know the answer to the following question: "We burned a million pounds and we need to know if that's a crime against reality",' Bill Drummond announced.

The first caller, a woman, ordered Cauty and Drummond

to fuck off. 'That's right, a lot of people have told us to fuck off actually,' responded Cauty. 'A lot of people don't like it.'

Fleka: 'She's complaining about the amount.'

Cauty: 'It's not enough. She's right.'

Drummond: 'How much should we have burned then?'

Fleka: 'Maybe ten million. I suggest a zillion pounds.' He played Arthur Brown's *Fire*, then The Ruts' punk classic *Babylon's Burning*, shouting: 'Mental bomb! Art of provocation!'

When the music ended, he declared: 'Stay with us, die with us. We are the worst radio show in town, as you can see.'

Another man called in, and, to the tune of *Singing In The Rain*, crooned: 'You're burning up my money, just burning up my money, what a glorious feeling, I'm poor again . . . Welcome to Serbia.'

'Burn Zombie Town down!' Fleka screamed, cueing up the K Foundation's pompous, orchestrated version of *Que Sera Sera* (actually titled *K Cera Cera* and credited to The One World Orchestra Featuring The Massed Pipes And Drums Of The Children's Free Revolutionary Volunteer Guard). After it had finished, he hummed, to the tune of *Que Sera Sera*: 'When I was just a little boy, I asked Big Brother, what should I be? Should I be penniless, should I be rich, this is what he said to me: "Que sera sera, future is now, just now, so close your eyes and try to see your future, zombie!"'

The show ended.

The track Drummond and Cauty recorded with Fleka's voice, *The Magnificent*, became a regular jingle on B92 during the street protests which followed in 1996. In his brilliant, self-deprecating autobiography, *45*, Drummond was bemused but proud that he managed to create, albeit unwittingly, an anthem for an underground resistance movement on the other side of Europe. 'You spend your pop life longing for one of your three and a half minute slices of radio fodder to rise above being mere pop music, to enter the social fabric of the nation and times we live through, like *Give Peace A Chance* or

*Anarchy In The UK* or *Three Lions*,' he wrote. 'And this morning I learn that a track we recorded in a day, never released as a single, thought was crap and had forgotten about has taken on a meaning, an importance in a "far off land" for a struggle I hardly understood. Strange.'[22]

At around the same time, Belgrade's urban nightlife received a much-needed injection of new energy. Techno music – a primal current coursing through the clubs and raves of Europe – exploded into life, a flaming beacon amidst the gloom of poverty and war. It was, says Dragan Ambrozić, not before time: 'As lots of young, bright people left the country, the rock audience became tiny. But for the younger generation, going out to a rave was their own way of showing that they didn't belong to this turbo-folk culture. It was rebellious, it was about being individual, it was a liberating force.'

Dance culture wasn't new to the city. In 1989, when the illegal rave scene was taking over the deserted warehouses and open fields of rural Britain and, fired by a mixture of psychedelic drugs and electronic rhythms, sending reverberations of a generational culture shift right across Europe, B92 had begun to host a showcase for early house and techno tracks from Chicago, Detroit and New York. The slot was titled *Pimps, Pushers, DJs* after an album track by British acid house pioneers S-Express – because, explains Gordan Paunović, 'someone said that the only people who were working in this town were pimps, pushers and DJs. The rest were just having fun.' People who had spent time in London during the acid house uprising attempted to import that attitude to Yugoslavia with parties in abandoned state buildings, in the legendary Akademija, and later in the much-loved Soul Food club. But unsurprisingly, considering the economic conditions, the Belgrade club scene never managed to match the fervour of what was going on in Britain, Germany or Holland.

One party in the early nineties showed what might have been. A crew called Rhythm Zone brought over British DJ

Streets Ahead and a rapper for a party in what Paunović calls 'a kind of speakeasy for hardcore criminal types'. At first the atmosphere was awkward: no one could quite lock into the repetitive beats or comprehend the MC's rhyming. But when the gangsters' girlfriends started dancing, their men instantly jumped up to join them. 'They went crazy,' says Paunović. 'They realised something great was really happening in their club, they were drinking champagne and doing drugs, and they started to tip the MC, putting 100 Deutschmark notes in his pocket. When he got the first tip, he didn't understand what was happening and got really scared. But at the end of the night he had almost 2,000 Deutschmarks – more money than he was going to be paid in the first place.

'Those criminals thought it was the best party that ever happened in Belgrade!' Paunović laughs. 'But of course it never happened again because the promoters were shitting their pants and didn't dare to do it again because later someone got killed there.'

London techno DJ Mr C once described the clientele in the ideal dance club as a combination of 'the most ugly and the most beautiful people you have ever seen in your life, all in the same room; villains, thugs and on the other hand beautiful, well-groomed, nice, fashionable people': a mixture of underground culture and underworld sleaze.[23] Paunović believes that the failure to engineer a synthesis between clubbers and criminals was a missed opportunity to create the same kind of eclectic blend of outcasts and misfits which helped inspire the vital rave cultures of London, Manchester and other European cities. 'It was a crucial point when we missed the chance to get more criminals involved with the house scene. I think it would have really benefited the scene, because they had a monopoly on venues – in Belgrade, like everywhere else, criminals run clubs, not people like you and me.'

During the economic crisis of the early nineties, club culture slipped into catatonia, and it took an injection of inspiration from abroad to move things on again. Paunović, a perennially inquisitive former mechanical engineering student with an encyclopaedic knowledge of contemporary pop, had joined the *Rhythm of the Heart* show in the eighties and eventually become B92's head of music. He was, says one acquaintance, 'one of the few people in Belgrade who has this unique energy, who always has great ideas and wants to try something new'. In 1994, he travelled to London and experienced the euphoria of a full-on techno party for the first time. The club was called Lost; the DJs were seminal techno innovators Derrick May and Richie Hawtin, who liked their music hard, fast and almost unbearably intense. Paunović had never witnessed anything like it before.

'I was completely blown away, totally fascinated with the music and the atmosphere,' he recalls. 'I thought it was so great that I had to do something like it in Belgrade. When I got back I told as many people as possible about this club and how different it was.' He also learned how to mix using two turntables and, with fellow B92 DJs Boža Podunavac and Vladimir Janjić, launched a weekly techno party called Kozmik in a new venue, Industria, in the city centre.

Industria, sited in the basement of Plato's Pub, the bar of the Belgrade University Faculty of Philosophy, was little more than a black, humid cellar. Its decor was modelled on the stark, industrial design of Manchester's Haçienda club, the birthplace of Ecstasy culture in the north-west of England, and it would shape club trends in Belgrade for the next five years. 'When it opened, it looked so superior to everything else,' says Paunović. 'You had to walk downstairs, and it was like descending into hell with a thousand people all around you and this phenomenal lighting.'

Kozmik and rival DJ collective Integra both began to fly in DJs from the UK, Germany and America. In the absence of any other real contact with youth culture from 'outside' – the only decent bands who played in Belgrade in the mid-nineties were The Prodigy and Holland's Urban Dance Squad – the parties represented a lifeline to another kind of existence.

In the rest of Europe, the rave scene was an attempt to create free space to dream and play; in Belgrade, like rock'n'roll, it symbolised the refusal to accept isolation and xenophobia; an unspoken opposition to the dominant cultural order.

A new breed of rare nocturnal butterflies spread their wings and came out to play – many of whom were too young to know what came 'before'. Techno represented not only new-found freedoms but a spirit of tolerance and international communication – qualities which were in short supply in Belgrade that year. 'There was so much euphoria – it was a fresh spirit,' says clubber Ivana Vasić. 'Everybody knew each other and we all had this huge emotion of belonging. The parties were so special, so happy. It was a paradise.'

With techno came Ecstasy, although due to its high price it never became as popular as in the rest of Europe. Elsewhere, recreational drug use was the primary leisure pursuit for urban youth. In Belgrade, Ecstasy was a cult drug: a cherished secret. 'It was people who would travel to Amsterdam or London and bring back fifty tabs or something then save them for big parties. People weren't taking it on a regular weekly basis,' remembers Gordan Paunović. 'In 1996, the supply became much more widespread and there were the first cases of people arrested for Ecstasy possession and dealing. It stopped being exclusive.'

And, just as in the rest of the continent, the first casualties started to emerge as people began to burn out on their accelerating intake of pills. Some knew no limits, had nothing else to live for, and charged right over the edge, progressing rapidly from Ecstasy to heroin. 'As the years passed by, more and more people became ruined,' says B92 arts reporter and veteran clubber Maja Atanasijević. 'People here have a tendency to escape from reality and it's much easier to lose yourself in club culture in Belgrade. You can become a junkie in London or New York, yes, but if you become a junkie here where you don't have money, it's a different picture, if you are spending your parents' pay cheques to buy drugs.

'People were disappearing one by one. They either got bored and started families or got hooked and had to go to Moscow to get a shot from a doctor, some injection of chemicals which gives you unpleasant feelings if you take heroin, so you don't feel high any more. A lot of people went that way, which is very sad.

'It was amazing, it was decadent, it was crazy, but that escape from reality fucked the best crew in Belgrade.'

Heroin was the other, darker side of Belgrade's drug equation. This was a city where heavy opiates made perfect sense; what Fleka dubbed 'Zombie Town' was also a cradle of the walking dead, nodding out into the dream-sleep of oblivion. As in any European capital, smack had been around for many years. But the drugs trade had benefited from the Bosnian war, as narcotics traffickers expanded their business to deal in arms and oil, and sanctions-busters added heroin to their commercial repertoire as the long-established 'Balkan route' for heroin shipments from Turkey and the East into Western Europe flourished. The lawlessness of the militarised zone allowed shipments to travel unnoticed, and the warlords' 'special relationship' with the authorities granted them unprecedented freedom to operate.

'Drugs and arms are two branches of the same business,' stated an investigation into profiteering by *Vreme*. 'Many arms dealers were not averse to selling drugs since they were already risking their necks. The dealers' paradise was complete because there was no law to avoid.'[24]

According to a report from geopolitical monitoring group OGD, the Belgrade secret police and state security services were also deeply involved – just as US special forces were implicated in heroin transportation during the Vietnam war – as well as criminal kingpins like Arkan, with ordinary policemen grabbing their cut too. Simultaneously, in a sinister correlation, heroin addiction escalated in Serbia's capital, where one local doctor estimated that up to 30,000 people became hooked.[25]

By the time the Dayton Agreement finally ended the long war in Bosnia in November 1995, many veterans of the underground club scene of the late eighties who had remained in Belgrade were ravaged by addiction, enslaved by the fall-out from Milošević's military adventures.

# 4
# forward, forward!
# 1996–97

'It all began when, after I don't know how long, I got drunk out of happiness. I wasn't quite sure why I was so happy: the victory of the opposition in the local elections couldn't have been the only reason. It was a much bigger happiness, as if someone had given me back the last forty years, or at least made them better, more appropriate. It seemed that everything had been turned upside down, by some magic, and everything would now develop in the best possible way, that the misery of all the years gone by would vanish, and that everyone who had left would come back. Of course I knew that that was impossible, but I was happy to know that some of the good people here were still around, that some good new people had emerged and that the destruction was not complete.'

*Ivica Dolenc*, **Walking On The Spot** *(1997)*

The first thing to hit you was the noise. From a mile away it sounded like a thousand screeching tyres – a road race, like the Monte Carlo grand prix, cars circling round and round tight cobbled corners, or a distant football match, with angry fans screaming their displeasure at some poor refereeing decision. Then closer, and the shrill silver whinny, a piercing sheet of sound bursting from thousands of whistles, was under-pinned by the queasy low moan of cow horns lowing a mournful bass counterpoint in unison. And then the people: too many to count, a rolling surf of faces and bodies, each chanting, whistling, blowing hard until they had to catch their breath – and smiling, positive, innocent again with a sudden flush of wonder; a lost emotion inexplicably rediscovered.

A frail, headscarved old lady halted the marchers and passed out home-baked cakes. A ruddy-faced pensioner threw down cans of beer and packs of cigarettes from his fourth-floor balcony. A woman cradled her child in one arm, gazing down on the city's children, brushing away tears with her free hand. Tears welled up in the marchers' eyes as they saluted her with whistles and arms held aloft. From every towerblock, people were waving and cheering, showering the crowd with tiny strips of torn paper.

In the middle of it, a phalanx of funky drummers, woolly hats pulled low against the chill, stepped jauntily to a samba beat while fellow marchers banged along merrily on saucepans and cheese graters and tinny, tinkling cowbells; anything they could pull out hastily from a kitchen cupboard and carry along to make some noise, to shatter the silence, to synch to the beat which declared: we are here – now listen.

It was a carnival of resistance. Belgrade had woken up and opened its eyes. From nowhere, an intrepid spirit had sprung from the concrete boulevards; a hardy winter flower blossoming on barren ground. Everywhere you looked, someone was plotting and planning, trying to outdo the rest with the most outrageous and telling strike at the heart of the regime; the blackest joke, the most audacious allegory.

Across a frosty quadrangle and down the yellowing corridors of Belgrade University's Faculty of Philosophy, a bunch of students, clad in jeans and sportswear, were working on their daily news-sheet, the *Protest Tribune*, and arguing, laughing, joking, while upstairs their comrades huddled in sleeping bags – the night-shift, snoozing lightly for a few hours before it was their turn to resume command.

One of them stopped for a moment, rubbed his red eyes, lit another Marlboro, inhaled quickly, then explained, in the kind of hurry that indicated all talk was a waste of precious time that could be better spent on action: 'When we started we were full of enthusiasm. We thought if we carried on for ten days they would listen to us. Now it's cold, we're tired, we have exams coming up, we don't want to go on the streets. Milošević is ignoring us, hoping that we will get bored and break down. In 1991 and 1992 we failed, and each time we failed it got worse and worse. I don't know what will happen if we fail this time. We can't make any more compromises.'

This was Miroslav, an archaeology student, inflamed with lack of sleep and the urgency of a body clock running on double time. 'We learn about democracy, about justice, about human rights, but then we see the media blockade, manipulation all over the place, police on the streets,' he gabbled. 'They stole our votes. It's not like we were taught. Many people think nothing will change if the opposition come in. Maybe they're right, maybe they're wrong. But come on, let's see! We can't lose anything more.'

Thousands of police, he said, were parked up in the back streets, waiting to strike when the order came. He remembered 1991, when the tanks rolled in to the city squares and stood there, arrogant and threatening. 'We don't want any bloodshed, we don't want anyone to die, but if necessary I will be the first to lie in front of the tanks. They'll run me over: OK, no big deal – I don't want to live in a country where there is no freedom.'

Across town, in the dusty basement of the Faculty of Electrical Engineering underneath Bulevar Revolucije, another group of students, most of them no older than twenty, were sucking down bottles of Czech beer, huddled around glowing computer screens, their dishevelled clothes indicating that none of them had been getting much sleep. They were slightly nervous, worried that the police might discover the location of their guerrilla bunker, but simultaneously euphoric, urging each other onwards. Pasted on the wall was a chart listing the world's top 20 dictators, downloaded from the Internet. Slobodan Milošević was in at number 14 with a bullet. One of the students complained jokily: 'He should definitely be in the top ten!'

This claustrophobic room was the command centre for the young protesters' website. They wrote reports, took photographs, collated news, translated it into English, coded it and published direct to the world the same day. By Web design standards, theirs wasn't a slick, flashy site: it just did its job. 'The Internet is the only free media in this country, the only way to communicate with the international public,' said one, Igor. 'We are making connections with young people all over the world. We are saying: "Look at us, we are the same age, we think the same, we like the same music, we are also Europeans and we want to be part of Europe."'

He and his friends had been down in their strip-lit bolt-hole for weeks, toiling selflessly day and night. Their studies were on hold for the duration and they expected to have to spend another year at college to catch up. 'Most of our teachers and parents support us,' said Igor. 'They say it's better to lose one year of studying than to lose your whole life in the darkness.'

A year after the end of the war in Bosnia, Belgrade's citizens were back on the streets in some of the greatest demonstrations for change ever seen in the Balkans. From November 1996 to March 1997, they kept the pressure up for eighty-four long days and nights, through sub-zero frost, snow and cold rains.

The uprising seemed to come from nowhere. Never had Milošević seemed so secure and unassailable. The conclusion of the Bosnian war with the Dayton Agreement, which lifted the UN sanctions, had put the president in his strongest position for years. Although he hadn't succeeded in his aim of creating a 'Greater Serbia', although he had suffered serious losses both on the battlefield and as a result of mass emigration, and although the war had crippled Serbia's economy and impoverished its population, he still managed to claim a victory of sorts: the warmonger had become the peacemaker.

And while some nationalists accused him of betraying the Serbs' 'sacred territory' in Bosnia, the West accepted him as 'a man we can do business with' and bolstered his rule. One of his lackeys even proposed he should win the Nobel Peace Prize.

Milošević used his mandate from the West and his unchallenged mastery of state institutions to tighten his hold on the media. In 1994, after officials had accused the independent daily paper *Borba* of 'throwing mud' at its own country, *Borba* was told it had not been 'legally registered', therefore must come back into state hands. Now they grabbed back control of the independent TV station Studio B, declaring it had been 'incorrectly privatised', and culled its staff. It had been a rare outlet for opposition opinions. Western governments watched in silence, unwilling to upset their man by causing a fuss.

Milošević's wife declared that independent publishers and broadcasters were fifth columnists who, in league with the opposition parties, were conspiring to sell out Serbia to foreign powers – a now-familiar refrain after years of divisive wartime rhetoric. 'These mercenaries and informers, who with foreign currency organise "democratic" parties and "independent" media, naively think that the truth about their activity will not see the light of day,' she stated. 'And they naively hope that if trouble finds them, their financiers will protect them. But of course they will not.'[1] It was a thinly veiled threat to all those who dared to step out of line.

In Belgrade, the result was frustration and a grey fog of apathy. 'After Dayton it was clear that a long and painful struggle was ahead,' says Veran Matić. 'Milošević had the international community in his hand, and it was obvious that it would be very difficult to change things.'

But while he retained some grudging respect in the rural provinces, Milošević had underestimated the level of resentment which had been simmering in the urban centres. And for a rare moment, the bickering opposition leaders had set aside their career rivalries and huge policy differences, and united. Vuk Drašković's Serbian Renewal Movement, Zoran Djindjić's Democratic Party and Vesna Pešić's Civil Alliance of Serbia, in co-operation with other, smaller political groupings, had united to form Zajedno – 'Together' – to run as a collaborative bloc in the federal and local elections which were set for November 1996.

The federal elections progressed as normal. Milošević did no actual campaigning, relying on the compliant media to praise his virtues as a statesman and the sole architect of peace. His Socialists and his wife Mira Marković's United Yugoslav Left (JUL) party, a family coalition nicknamed the 'cosa nostra', won a firm majority, resoundingly beating Zajedno. But as the perennial gloom descended once more, the local council polls delivered a breathtaking surprise. Zajedno had taken all the major cities: Belgrade, Niš, Novi Sad, Kragujevac and many others.

Nobody could quite believe it; there was a feeling of joyful incredulity. 'Normally in Belgrade, people just walk along looking at the ground, nobody talks to each other, everyone's imprisoned in their own misery,' says one Belgrade resident. 'Then suddenly people on the streets were talking to each other, saying: "Did you hear? They won! The opposition won! We've got change!"'

Before the news had really sunk in, the regime acted decisively. Citing reports of 'irregularities', the election results were annulled. The opposition victories were declared invalid. This was shameless fraud on a nationwide scale; Milošević, who had stolen people's freedom, their livelihoods and their happiness, had now stolen their votes too. It was an unnecessary confirmation of a fact that had been obvious for years: although Serbia called itself a democracy, this was a flimsy façade which barely concealed the reality of what the country had become: a dictatorship.

Outraged, Belgrade's citizens poured out on to the streets to demand their stolen votes back. Within a week, their numbers had risen from tens of thousands to around 200,000, surprising even the opposition leaders themselves. The opposition coalition Zajedno's marches were mirrored by parallel demonstrations by Belgrade University students, who wanted the election results recognised and the university rector, a regime appointee, dismissed.

It was the students who provided the irreverent humour and creative imagination which would shift the demonstrations from political rallies into pavement fiestas. 'On the third or fourth day, I was standing in the centre of Republic Square and I remember thinking it was all getting a bit pathetic,' one B92 staffer recalls. 'There weren't so many people there and they were just standing around listening to the politicians and thinking, "OK, you've said that, now what's going to happen next?" It was becoming lacklustre.

'Then all of a sudden, out of nowhere, the students started to swarm into the square. It was completely cathartic, the whole atmosphere suddenly transformed, everyone turned round and realised this was something else, and that something bigger was going to happen.'

From their ad hoc control room in the dilapidated halls of the Faculty of Philosophy, the students' 'creative team' planned daily stunts and spectacles, weaving images from pop culture, film and rock'n'roll into a witty iconography of resistance. They employed the sophisticated visual language of advertising agencies to twist orthodox political protest into something smarter, hipper and infinitely more inspiring. Their essence was inherited from the student uprisings of the summer of 1968 (in which many of their parents had participated), but they were also influenced by the dramatic anti-war and pro-democracy actions of the mid-nineties – B92's presentation of babies to Milošević, the hundred-metres-long black cloth that was carried through the streets in 1993 in commemoration of the war dead. They drew yet more references from the surreal antics of *Monty Python* and the more unorthodox demonstrations during the overthrow of Communism in other Eastern European countries, like Lithuania's laugh-in protests, when citizens in the capital Vilnius directed synchronised cackles at occupying Soviet troops. Some even suggested this could turn out be a 'delayed echo' of the collapse of the rest of the Eastern Bloc.[2]

The students insisted that they were in thrall to no one, even politicians who preached democracy. They would lead their demonstrations, which continued to march separately from the party-led Zajedno walks right up to the end, with a banner reading 'Beograd je svet' – 'Belgrade is the world' – its slogan reaching out, like hands through the bars of a cell, to a global society that Milošević had shut out. There were placards decorated with cartoon characters, Smurfs and Bugs Bunny, pennants with the logos of CND, Jack Daniels and Ferrari, and quotations from Shakespeare, Kafka and Orwell. There were images of Bob Marley and lyrics from bands like The Prodigy and Rage Against The Machine. Some banners carried personal messages ('Ivana, I love you'); some were ridiculous ('I'll have a better slogan tomorrow, I promise') while others were obscene ('When the ruler is impotent, only the people arise'; or toilet rolls inscribed with the message: 'We've had enough shit'). Serbian flags were flown, but many carried the flags of other countries – Germany, Japan, France – intended as a symbolic break with the spell of isolation cast by Milošević (yet inevitably cited by regime loyalists as evidence of hostility to Serbian interests).

The best took the rhetoric of the regime, twisted it and fired it right back again. The slogan from Milošević's nationalist rallies in the late eighties had been 'Serbia's woken up'. Now a student's banner declared: 'Serbia's woken up. Someone make the coffee!' When Milošević's wife Mira visited India, a placard advised her: 'You'll be safe in India, they don't kill cows there.' And after Yugoslavia was beaten 2–0 by Spain in a football international, a satirist scrawled: 'Yugoslavia beats Spain 2–0. Signed, the Supreme Court of Serbia.'

Actors performed plays in front of the police barricades; the strangest being a post-midnight *Macbeth* which was intended as a parable for Serbia's descent into self-destruction. 'It was 1 a.m., it was below zero, we had two naked actors and we were pouring water on them,' says Borka Pavičević, director of the Centre for Cultural Decontamination arts foundation. 'One voice said "hell is dark" and thousands of voices responded: "Yes!"'

The actors felt that, for once in their stage careers, their drama could capture the collective consciousness. 'If any time the theatre really happened on the streets, this was it – this is what Brecht was talking about,' Pavičević continues. 'We wanted to say that you can't rehearse Molière during the morning then go on the demonstrations in the evening. We wanted to say that you should be on the streets all the time. There should be no separation between the theatre and the streets.

'I remember 1968 in Paris – I am from that generation – but I have never seen such literary and theatrical imagination on the streets. It was better than any theatre director could have invented.

'People wore their best shoes, their best suits; the women put on their best hats. It was amazing – the best of Belgrade came out. At the time we thought it was over for the regime, and that nobody could stop us.'

At Radio B92, the music spoke of hope and reached for victory, creating a feedback loop with the spirit of the streets: the lithe caress of St Etienne's *Nothing Can Stop Us Now*; the inspirational charge of Curtis Mayfield singing *Move On Up*; the insurrectionary techno of Underground Resistance, whose fearsome electronic rhythms called on the 'brothers and sisters of the underground' to 'wreak havoc on the programmers'.[3] B92's head of music Gordan Paunović captured the mood: 'Now people really feel that they can do it, they can finally change things. The time has come.'

The whistles and the drums, the uproarious racket which permeated the cityscape until long after dark, combined the

Dionysian abandon of Brazilian samba parties with the hedonist excess of rave culture which had recently erupted in Belgrade's clubs. 'The whistle is used as a mood amplifier,' suggested student protest organiser Lazar Džamić. 'A sonic doping, a satiny audio whip for the flagging muscles of the committed participants. Its very presence brings the resonance of a great party, a crowd with a common aim, totally positive, and an energy on the edge of control.'

While the demonstrations resembled open-air raves, the whistles represented both a voice for the voiceless and a symbolic reclaiming of official authority – suddenly the protesters, not the policemen, were directing the traffic. 'The seizing of that symbol, usurping the sonic tube and turning it on those who until then had been its exclusive users was in fact a symbolic scalping,' Džamić commented. 'Now we're going to whistle to them to stop! Now we're going to blow the whistle on their foul!'

The protest drum corps would mix up Cozy Powell's seventies percussion extravaganza *Dance With The Devil* (an appropriate title, they thought) with the traditional folk rhythms of Serbian rumba to create a kind of communal trance magic: 'They exorcised evil spirits,' wrote Džamić. 'They fought shame with noise.' The drummers inspired other protesters to form their own beat groups, rattling out amateurish grooves on battered saucepans with bits of cutlery. Belgrade, one observer suggested, 'looked like a tinkers' Olympiad'.[4]

The spectacular happenings inevitably generated intense international media interest. However, Gordan Paunović believes that this kind of creative invention was only a novelty for those who hadn't been following what had been going on in Belgrade in the nineties. It was, he says, a resurfacing of the local spirit which had almost been extinguished during the war years. 'These demonstrations were not a big surprise to people here, they were only a surprise to people who were raised on all the prejudices and media pictures built up of Serbs under Milošević – this role of us as bad guys.'

Two events since the Dayton Agreement had helped raise the spirits of Belgrade's youth and prepare them for action. Punkish techno crew The Prodigy had played in town; their album *Music For The Jilted Generation*, a raging cauldron of anti-establishment rant-and-rave ('Fuck them and their law!'), commanded massive resonance. The concert, ironically, was staged with the support of the local Socialist Party. 'They were proud of it,' laughs Dragan Ambrozić, who promoted the gig. 'But The Prodigy's message could only be understood by the kids, who knew that the songs were about rebellion. Those songs connect here; you could hear them everywhere on big sound systems during the protests. That's something politicians will never understand – politicians in the opposition parties as well as the government.'

The second was a Red Star Belgrade match against FC Barcelona. Red Star had lost, but played brilliantly nonetheless, and the event had provided the chant which would become the demonstrators' call sign: 'Ajmo, 'Ajde, svi u napad' – 'Forward, forward! Everyone attack!'

National leaders have often attempted to use football as a political tool. In neighbouring Croatia, premier Franjo Tudjman insisted that the country's finest club change its name from Dinamo Zagreb to Croatia Zagreb to boost his nationalist megalomania; it also emerged that the Croatian secret service kept files of football referees, and bribed them to rule in favour of Tudjman's favoured club.

But sport has also become the focus for political protest. A match in Tripoli in 1999 was the forum for the only public display of discontent with General Gadaffi's Libyan regime. After the team supported by the leader's sons was awarded a dubious goal, the crowd burst into anti-Gadaffi chanting, and many of the demonstrators were immediately shot on sight by police. And during the protests of 1996 in Belgrade, Red Star fans instigated anti-regime disturbances at an international basketball tournament, while supporters of the Yugoslav national team would ritually chant: 'Slobo, go! Slobo, go!'

At first, Radio Television Serbia all but ignored the demonstrations, damning them casually by remarking that only 'a handful of provocateurs and hoodlums' was on the streets. 'The first reaction of the official state media to the student protest was typical and almost boringly stereotypical: we do not report it, ergo it does not exist,' noted artist Jovan Čekić.[5] Instead there would be stories of 'progress' and 'co-operation', of visits by delegations of Russian businessmen, even reports of unrest elsewhere in Europe, but little about what was happening right below RTS's office windows. RTS portrayed a cosy, amiable country where the president had generously and wisely won peace and ensured prosperity, while the international community smiled benignly from afar. One protester responded with a banner declaring: 'I want to live in the land of RTS.'

'When state television interviewed people, ten out of ten were saying we were gangsters, hooligans, foreign agents,' says Borka Pavičević. 'If I was making propaganda, I would have eight against and two for the demonstrations, so at least it would be believable. But no, all ten were against, every time! So you think, good gracious, does anyone believe in such nonsense?'

Nevertheless, Veran Matić thought that privately Milošević was disturbed. 'He didn't even consider the possibility that he might lose,' Matić said at the time. 'The second thing he did not believe was that people would take to the streets.'[6] Others speculated that the noise people were making as they walked along was getting to Milošević psychologically. In private, the president raged that he could obliterate at a stroke the upstarts who dared to think they could run his city. This disquiet became public when a Socialist Party official went on the offensive, stating that the marchers were 'destroyers and violent individuals with all the characteristics of pro-fascist groups', and claiming they were 'manipulating children'. The students replied angrily: 'It is wonderful that you are so worried about us, but where were you when those of our own age, on the orders of the regime, went to their deaths around Vukovar and on other battlefields? While you shed our blood you did not worry at all about our tender years.' And one student marched with a placard declaring: 'I have an under-aged, retarded, impressionable, seduced, manipulated, pro-fascist temperament.'[7] Milošević's wife also attacked the protesters, suggesting they were trying to stir up a civil war. She couldn't quite work out if they were doing it on purpose or whether they just had 'sick minds'.

In those first days, there were signs that frustration might spill over into random violence. The Zajedno march would circle past the national parliament and the pro-regime daily paper *Politika*, then stop as people jeered and hurled abuse at the faceless bureaucrats inside. One day, as the snaking column reached RTS, someone pulled an egg from their pocket and hurled it at the building. Others joined in. Stones were lobbed and windows smashed. 'After someone threw an egg there were ten seconds of thinking, "Oh my God, what is going to happen? This could be the end. What the hell am I doing standing here?"' says one of the demonstrators. 'Then people started throwing eggs and it became clear that nobody was going to do anything more than that, and nobody would start shooting.'

The opposition leaders appealed for calm, but for days afterwards the eggs kept on flying, leaving a gloopy yellow slurry dribbling down the walls of the hated institutions and a crunchy mosaic of shells on the pavement outside. These eggs became a symbol of what was dubbed the 'yellow revolution'; a popular picture postcard of the time depicted an enormous cartoon egg smashed over *Politika's* HQ with the caption: 'Greetings from Belgrade.'

The police responded in kind. A life-sized dancing sponge puppet of Milošević, dressed in convict's garb, had been carried through the streets on the back of a lorry, operated by a 21-year-old student who jigged along merrily behind it. After the rally, he was arrested, beaten and tortured. The police told him they were only doing to him what he had done to Mr Milošević's effigy. He was then jailed for twenty-five days for 'obstructing the traffic'.

Radio B92 assumed even greater importance as the regime extended its media blackout. It was beginning to reach out beyond its fashionable urban liberal audience and become a source of information for all those opposed to Milošević. Aware of this, the state began to jam its signal. In some areas of Belgrade it was impossible to get clear reception, just a mess of fuzzy interference and static. A B92 video produced at the time shows one young man standing upright in his living room and putting his radio antenna in his mouth to enhance the signal, and a woman with her aerial wrapped round a vacuum cleaner pipe.

At 2 p.m. on 3 December, the fourteenth day of the protests, the signal cut out altogether: B92 was banned for the second time in its short history. Another youth station, Radio Index, was also shut down. In the B92 newsroom, amidst the customary fug of cigarette smoke and coffee fumes, a frenzy broke out as the reporters scrambled to find out what was going on. The station's bosses rang everyone they knew at the foreign embassies, pleading for support. The international press corps descended on the building and the story went global. 'It was a livewire atmosphere,' says Julia Glyn-Pickett, a British woman who launched B92's English-language news service. 'We didn't realise it at the time, of course, but history was being made at that moment. People were saying: "This is it, they've taken us off the air for good." '

The news editor managed to get Serbia's information minister, Aleksandar Tijanić, on the phone. He demanded: 'What the hell are you doing?' The minister responded: 'I'm acting under orders.' (Soon afterwards Tijanić would resign from his post and later became a born-again critic of Milošević.)

Bosnia was the first war to have Internet access. In 1993, a former Vietnam draft-dodger and a Greenpeace eco-warrior had got together to found ZaMir ('for peace'), a rudimentary e-mailing system which reached right across the frontlines of the former Yugoslavia. Before this, only the universities had been able to send e-mail, and only to other academic institutions, which suited the regime as it was easily censored. (Even this link was shut down during the protests of 1992.)

In November 1995, just before the Dayton Agreement, B92 established the first Internet service provider in Belgrade. Opennet, as it was called, was intended to offer access to the public and teach them about the online world, and to wire up the independent media, allowing them to reach out beyond the borders of Serbia. It became one of the routing points for Belgrade's emerging digital culture.

The concept of Opennet was inspired by B92's difficulties in contacting reporters in other Yugoslav cities during the war in Bosnia. It was headed by Dražen Pantić, a professor of mathematics at Belgrade University who had got involved with B92 because he liked its combination of 'libertarian spirit and urban sensibility – no other radio station in Serbia played Tom Waits, or Nick Cave'. He had long dreamed of bringing the Net to Serbia.

For months, the authorities had ignored B92's request for an Internet link, but through a university contact, Pantić secured a face-to-face meeting with a state telecoms official. The official told him: 'You, B92 people, are enemies of this state, but the state is not doing anything about introducing the Internet.' Against the odds, permission was granted.

Until then, the authorities had taken little notice of the Internet, but as soon as Opennet was launched, they started to pour money into local projects – although it was clear that the ruling clique itself hardly understood what the Net really was and what it could achieve. After Belgrade got wired, the only way to control the flow of information would have been to cut outside lines to the West. As the Net had such a small number of users in Serbia, this was pointless – it was a marginal medium preaching only to the converted, the regime appeared to think.

When B92 was shut down, it immediately began publishing its news bulletins over the Internet, short-cutting the censorship and appealing direct to the outside world. Its RealAudio sound files were picked up by the BBC and Voice of America and beamed back into Serbia. Ironically, its connection had only just been installed by the state phone company. As Dražen Pantić notes: 'The same Telecommunications Ministry that banned the radio station thus provided us with the means to evade the ban via the Internet.'

As soon as the Students' Protest Initiative Board was set up, the first move it made was to code a website to disseminate updates on the demonstrations and photos of its street stunts, and encourage its users to 'throw' files containing pictures of eggs at government e-mail addresses. Its site was 'mirrored' across the world to evade targeting. As one of the students declared: 'If they shut down the Belgrade server we can directly modem the information overseas. To stop that they will need to shut down every telephone in Serbia – which is impossible.'[8]

Although only around 10,000 people had Internet access in Serbia, the use of new technology gave the protests worldwide impact, opening new lines of communication. Virtually at least, Serbia was part of a global community again. This was, said the students, the first Internet revolution; the first test of whether global electronic interaction could undermine a dictatorship. (Three years later, Chinese activists would similarly claim that the volatile and evasive nature of the Net could open up closed societies: 'In 1989, I was in Tiananmen Square. We failed then. The Internet won't fail,' said one.)[9]

It was an irresistible story for a world fascinated by the digital boom. The stream of press articles generated by this hip, savvy bunch of wired dissidents triggered a barrage of international political pressure on the regime. They had turned to the Net because it was the only thing they had left, but it had more success than they could ever have imagined.

The exact reason for the shutdown of B92 remained unclear, says Veran Matić. Perhaps the government thought the station was swelling the protests with its reports. Perhaps it was worried that B92 had enhanced its position in the city by setting up an arts centre and a publishing house, printing books which exposed the hidden atrocities of the Bosnian war. Or perhaps it was just a personal vendetta dating back five years.

'It's often a grudge which results in pieces of repression here,' says Matić. 'B92 was banned in 1991 and afterwards our general manager gave an interview to a newspaper. The title of the story was "They're getting into a fight with someone stronger than them" – meaning RTS was getting into a fight with us, but we were stronger. The general manager of the technical department of RTS took that article very personally and never forgot it, so he could easily have been responsible for the second ban.

'This guy was general manager of RTS, he was also in the federal telecommunications ministry and on the Serbian commission for the allocation of frequencies. So if you wanted to get a frequency licence you had to apply to the commission – in other words, to him. That commission then told you that you had to get approval from the federal telecommunications ministry – also him, and from RTS – him again. So it was a vicious circle and it's pretty obvious it was created by Milošević to control things.'

B92 appealed to the streets for assistance. Its employees strung a banner from their window-ledge and installed speakers on the balcony to announce the news; their live audience reduced to whoever was in earshot. Srdjan Andjelić, the station's most popular and charismatic presenter ('because I incite revolution on the air,' he explains), cajoled the crowd. And the students, gazing upwards, began to chant the station's name, their breath steaming white in the crisp winter's afternoon. 'The people realised how much B92 meant to them, and B92 realised how important they had become,' says Borka Pavičević. 'It was the point when they became the focus of this civil rebellion.'

The news kept going out over the Net. The diplomats made their calls to their contacts in government. The students kept up their chants. A fax arrived stating the official reason for the ban: B92 was no longer transmitting due to 'water in a coaxial cable'. The newsroom fell about laughing – it was the weakest excuse they had ever heard.

Just over fifty hours later, through a combination of international pressure and people power, B92 was back on the air. It was a remarkable retreat. 'Forcing Milošević to back up and let B92 continue broadcasting was the first time he was defeated politically on his own ground, in Serbia,' says Dražen Pantić. 'And the Internet was the cause of that defeat.' The regime, so secure after Dayton, no longer looked so invincible.

B92's listenership shot upwards to three-quarters of a million, double what it had been a month beforehand. The protesters began to scent victory. 'It is like an earthquake shaking Milošević's castle. We will keep marching until the walls fall down,' said one student. 'I really don't see how we can lose now. It is just a question of time, and time is on our side.'[10]

However, a month into the daily rallies, Milošević remained cool. He merely sat back and waited for events to play themselves out, for people to become footsore and tire of their daily trudge across the cobbles. 'The state just retreated: the banks, the police, the government, they didn't care what was going on in the streets,' says Dragan Ambrozić. 'It was a huge display of cynicism. They were saying, "OK so we stole the elections – so what?"'

But as Christmas approached, it was Milošević who cracked first. On 24 December, the Socialist Party organised a counter-demonstration to prove to Belgrade that Milošević still could lay claim to the hearts of the people. His supporters came to town in requisitioned buses, driven up in convoy from his rural strongholds, waving red, white and blue Serbian flags and carrying framed portraits of their hero. Some wore plain peasant garb, others sported uniforms. Fed on a diet of RTS propaganda and fuelled by free food and drink, they raged at the opposition demonstrators: 'Shame on you! You traitors! You are betraying your own country!' The demonstrators shouted back: 'How much did they pay you?'

As brassy martial music signalled the start of the rally, scuffles broke out as anti-Milošević protesters threw water over the regime loyalists and tried to grab the flags out of their hands. The two factions began hitting each other with the stick handles of broken placards. Above the crowd hung an eerie sea of identical faces – a throng of disembodied Miloševićes, printed on placards, gazing implacably into the distance.

The two groups were cordoned apart by blue-helmeted riot police carrying perspex shields, their long black batons swinging low. Missiles and fists started flying and the police cordon collapsed; some people fell and were trampled on the asphalt. An old man wiped blood from his eyes. Another lay on his back on the paving stones, a red river flowing from his skull. The police looked on and did nothing. By the end of the day, one opposition supporter had been shot, and another beaten so badly that he died of his injuries two days afterwards.

Milošević's fans were outnumbered five to one by 300,000 Zajedno supporters. He was, one reporter observed, 'angered by the small size of the gathering', and he could hear the drums and whistles of the opposition nagging insistently, mocking him, as he addressed his people. The speech itself was a grotesque fantasy. It emphasised that he had brought peace to Serbia, made it rich and strong, and that now every-thing was just getting 'better and better'. The only force that could threaten this dream-come-true was the agitation of unnamed foreigners and their treacherous running-dogs in the opposition, he warned. It was a vision of the country that appeared in full colour each day on RTS, but no one had actually seen in real life: a virtual Serbia, a figment of the totalitarian imagination.

The crowd seemed to like it, though. One of them shouted to him emotionally: 'Slobo, we love you.' Milošević replied: 'I love you too.' His words were sampled for a B92 jingle, and from then on protesters would greet each other saying 'I love you' – and get the reply: 'I love you too.'

The next day the students 'cleaned up' the area where Milošević's loyalists had rallied using detergent and brooms. The temperature was well below zero.

In the final days of the Bosnian war, B92 had established itself as a focus for alternative thinking and independent action. When the Croatian army recaptured the Krajina region from the Bosnian Serbs in August 1995, tens of thousands of Serb refugees hastily gathered up their possessions and fled towards the border in lorries and on the backs of tractors. The Serbian government wanted nothing to do with them – they were an eyesore, an unwelcome reminder of failure and defeat. They were desperate and hungry; the wretched victims of Milošević's blunders who were bringing the war back home to the motherland. B92 appealed to the people of Belgrade to supply them with food and drink, and a convoy of cars and taxis made its way to the border where they had camped out.

'The message was: we don't want to see the refugees in our town,' says B92 managing director Saša Mirković. 'The TV was silent, no one was talking about the shame of this, how these people had been pushed into the war, given fake dreams and told that they would be protected, then betrayed when Milošević decided he didn't need them.'

The B92 relief operation compounded the embarrassment of a regime which wanted the refugees to simply disappear and be forgotten. The mayor of Belgrade twice summoned Mirković to city hall, telling him that he was a trouble-maker, that this must not continue. 'He threatened me, saying: "You are making a circus in the centre of town. Stop making this fuss." It was strange that the first support these people got was from us, who were blamed all these years for being "anti-patriotic".'

As the government took over Belgrade's cultural institutions, B92 also became a focal point for artists, writers, filmmakers and musicians. 'It was half-deliberate, half-spontaneous, because by that time there was practically no space to do anything other than what the government wanted. So we had to create this space for ourselves,' says Veran Matić, whose office became an impromptu art gallery. 'The whole alternative scene had disappeared, people had either moved out of the country or become reclusive in their apartments. There was no culture to report, so we had to organise something.'

As one local critic explains, the Belgrade art world had become dominated by the same turbo-folk ideology as the rest of Serbian popular culture: 'anti-modernism, anti-individualism, anti-intellectualism, wisps of national metaphysics and mythology, resistance to anything international, lack of irony and humour'.[11] Art was used as a political tool to promote the insular, backward-looking state mentality; the head of the Museum of Contemporary Art was purged; the staff of literary magazines were dismissed.

For artist Uroš Djurić, a veteran of the alternative scene of the eighties and a former member of punk band Urban Guerrilla, who painted phantasmagorical, iconic self-portraits with Fender guitars and comicbook superheroes, B92 was a last oasis of liberty and opportunity. 'It was a kind of soul ambulance; the only institution which was trying to keep alive this kind of alternative living model inside this ruined society,' he says. 'It attracted the cream of young authors and artists who did not want to get corrupted by the system.'

Being alternative had its pitfalls: B92 was accused of being wilfully obscure and unlistenable. Late one night, when Gordan Paunović was playing a set of minimalist techno, a woman rang in, a psychologist in her fifties, offering him professional help; the music he was playing obviously indicated some deep mental disturbance, she had concluded.

B92 also gathered around it the most innovative of the city's underground rock bands. It released the first CD from Darkwood Dub, and signed up an eclectic collective called Kanda Kodža I Nebojša, a group whose nonsense name belied their serious intent. Kanda Kodža created a new rebel fusion for the days of protest, a jubilant hybrid of American post-punk rock, Jamaican reggae and languid jazz-funk, its trenchant lyrics infused with Rastafarian imagery – the allegorical visions of an evil Babylon and the smoke-filled dreams of a mystical paradise in the next world. 'They had the kind of hope which comes from utter despair – but they were trying to get past this kind of alienation, to get people together,' says Dragan Ambrozić. 'They were not afraid of being a revolutionary band. Songs like *Their Time Will Pass* – everyone understood this.'

Singer Oliver Nektarijević had an almost shamanic presence on stage – he was variously described as 'a nineties Jim Morrison' and 'a kind of Serbian Ian Curtis'; he was swarthily handsome yet simultaneously angelic, and it was said that 'every other girl who likes rock music in Belgrade was in love with him'. Nektarijević was a mouthpiece for the pent-up frustrations of a generation which grew up during wartime, which was too young to participate in the alternative scene of the eighties, which had known nothing but 'the situation', which didn't know where to turn. A generation imprisoned by the consequences of someone else's grand plan. Nektarijević's best friends and his mother, who had been a well-known arts reporter on Studio B, had moved 'outside'; he was not even able to visit them.

'I cannot get regular documents so I can't work normally, and I have problems with my passport because I don't want to go into the army,' he says. 'I just refused. It's against my beliefs, I see that army as more my enemy than NATO – they are my personal enemy. I would do anything else rather than join up. If it was a normal army, if it wasn't this government's army, it wouldn't be such a problem – but in these circumstances, no way.

'I don't feel Serbian. I don't feel like I'm anything. I have more in common with an Albanian who is a good guy than a Serbian who lies, steals and cheats.'

He admitted, however, that the regime had helped him find his voice. 'For me as a musician, this situation is better. It gives you more creative energy, more inspiration because you have to struggle.'

The use of Rasta imagery was an attempt to frame the spirit of resistance in poetic form – just as Bob Marley and Peter Tosh had done in Jamaica in the seventies – so the lyrics didn't sound like banal social commentary. Nevertheless, hymns to the 'righteous ones' who would answer the 'final call' needed little interpretation. To outsiders, the bizarre Serbian-Jamaican inflection of Nektarijević's voice sounded not a little peculiar. 'I just use the language, I don't think I'm a Rasta,' he says. 'There are bands here who sing about Rastafari and Jah in Serbian and think they're Rastas; I'm not into that. I respect it but I don't think I'm part of it. You also have rap bands here who rap in Serbian and say things like "I'm a white nigger" – they're not a part of it but they imitate black people, they want to be something that they aren't.'

Signing up with B92 was a political statement in itself, he insists. Bands who worked with government-linked record companies to improve their PR opportunities and record sales were beneath contempt. 'We got offered a better deal from the publisher that is run by the government, but we said no,' says Nektarijević. 'We stayed with B92 because it is the only independent publisher here, and that's what counts.

'Many people who I didn't expect to went to the government's publishers with their music. I would never do that – even if they forced me with a gun. I would tell them to kill me. I have said many things in the press that I shouldn't have, and that has caused problems for me, but I don't care. If they want to stop me, they can – but they will have to do it by force.'

By the mid-nineties, B92 was operating like any other pro-fessional radio station, utilising trained and paid journalists, presenters and technicians. It had a staff of around forty-five people and a freelance pool of a further 150. However, its independent status would not have been sustainable without funding from liberal philanthropists and foreign media spon-sorship bodies. Advertising revenue was hard to raise in such an impoverished country, and marketing agencies which did choose to place commercials on the station often received 'visits' shortly afterwards from tax inspectors. 'Only a few companies have the courage to come to us,' says Saša Mirković. 'Private companies already have so many problems that they don't need any more by working with B92.'

The station's costs outweighed its income, so the courting of Western donors assumed increasing importance. B92 received funding from proponents of democratic media like IREX Pro Media, Press Now and the Open Society Institute, non-governmental human rights organisations like the Swedish Helsinki Committee, humanitarian solidarity groups such as the trades union-backed Norwegian People's Aid, European governmental alliances like the Council of Europe, plus various other international sources. It attempted to ensure that no single donor contributed over twenty per cent of the total funding 'as an internal safeguard against influence on editorial policy', as one B92 fundraiser puts it.

Socialist critics argue that many of the donors which support independent media in Eastern Europe promote a free-market capitalist worldview, either overtly or covertly. They believe that funding programmes in the Balkans still follow Cold War logic, and that their goal is to engineer US policy domination of the region. Some of the big American organis-ations operating in Eastern Europe undoubtedly have a definite strategic political agenda; one of the most prominent, the United States Agency for International Development (USAID), states that its goal is 'achieving both sustainable development and advancing US foreign policy objectives'.

Nevertheless, B92's staff insist that they never tailored their programming to suit the agendas of their benefactors. 'We never played anyone's game,' says Gordan Paunović. 'The projects we did, we did them because we believed in them. The projects we didn't believe in, we turned them down.' They refute any suggestion that they might have been manipulated or coerced by American anti-Communist or CIA front organisations which sought to promote US interests overseas. However, as one local analyst explains, whether they trusted their donors' motives or not, the Belgrade independent media had little choice – to refuse the cash would be tantamount to giving up: 'There are only two ways of doing things here. Either you get money from these foundations to do them, or you get no money and do nothing at all.'

But Nenad Čekić, B92's original executive editor, who was ousted in 1990 and remains bitter to this day, believes that, consciously or unconsciously, its programming was adapted to suit the agendas of its donors, and that B92 became a fashionable plaything for Western liberals who bought into the buzzwords of human-rights orthodoxy. 'It's difficult to explain what's going on to a foreigner, because here it's common to talk about one thing, do another, and think something completely different,' he says. 'In the community financing the whole thing, there is this kind of Newspeak, as in Orwell's *1984* – politically correct speech which disgusts me. "Multicultural", "multi-ethnic", "multi-lingual" – the rights of this and that, the rights of plants, the rights of cucumbers! They'll say whatever it takes to get the money. They speak like parrots. They see the catchphrase and repeat it.'

And even those who were labelled 'foreign mercenaries' for taking money from the West had few illusions about the motivations for their benefactors' generosity. 'When you are Tony Blair and you want to change something in Serbia, you can't go to Milošević and tell him to change it, because he won't,' states one B92 DJ. 'You must invest in something you know people will follow.'

The most notorious of the global philanthropists was the super-rich currency market speculator George Soros, who made over £1 billion on Black Wednesday in 1992, when he led the attack on the British pound. Soros, who had fled his native Hungary during the German occupation of the thirties, spent hundreds of millions of dollars, more than many Western governments, setting up branches of his Open Society Institute in Eastern European capitals to promote human rights, free speech and respect for minorities, and help realise his dream of an 'open society'.

Understandably, the leaders of those governments which wanted to retain control over their media were infuriated by his intervention. In Belgrade, Soros was accused of being an enemy of the Serbs, of calling for Western military campaigns against the country, and criticised for 'uncooperative behaviour' when he refused to distribute humanitarian aid through the state machinery, believing that much of it could end up on the black market. The state media insisted he was promoting 'Coca-Cola democracy' and that those who collaborated with him were blinded by 'a fistful of dollars'.[12] In 1995, his Open Society Institute was temporarily prohibited from operating in Belgrade.

The regime insulted Soros on the one hand for pushing an imperialist Western political agenda, while simultaneously attacking his beneficiaries for being tools of interfering foreign provocateurs. Milošević could have it both ways: while purging the state press and cracking down on independent broadcasters, he could also claim that free speech was alive in Serbia because of the continued existence of organisations like B92, however marginalised they were.

B92's journalists realise that the regime has used and misused them as an alibi in its dealings with the West. 'He was always playing this card,' says Gordan Paunović. 'He could say: "Look, you can publish whatever you want in Serbia, B92 can talk against me as much as they want, they are free." But although we were influential, our signal couldn't reach many people at that time. As long as Milošević thinks his personal power is not in danger he will let you do whatever you want – it's a kind of soft dictatorship. He lets unnecessary things fly around him like mosquitoes, without any effect, while he concentrates on centralising economic and military power and controlling media with serious influence on a national level.'

Some, like Nenad Čekić, accused B92 of being a cheap tart flaunting itself for the titillation of Western interests – a hollow cause célèbre of the international community, more interested in promoting itself than in building genuine alternative media in Serbia. Veran Matić, however, didn't delude himself that for many foreign reporters, the fascination with B92 was purely superficial, but was willing to play their game to get what he wanted: 'These global media like MTV and CNN wash their consciences by paying attention to cases like ours,' he says. 'It is exotic, it is something weird and paradoxical – a horrible dark dictatorship in which exists an institution which promotes world principles. You can either do what we do and consciously use these media and have some influence, or reduce yourself to a ghetto, unable to communicate. I think the battle for our principles is more important than the way it is all presented.'[13]

As the pro-democracy demonstrations continued to fill Belgrade's streets, after the clashes of 24 December and the humbling of his loyalist rally, Milošević began to take an increasingly tough line against the protesters. The 'obstruction of traffic' – a euphemism for the daily protest walks down Belgrade's spacious boulevards – was prohibited. Police set up cordons to prevent the marchers moving freely. But thousands continued to gather each day, and they invented increasingly imaginative schemes to bamboozle the officers who were attempting to rein them in. One such game was entitled

'Arrest the Traffic Lights': a crowd would wait until the green light showed on a zebra crossing, then rush into the road en masse, screaming 'it's green!' and bouncing up and down on the road like punks pogoing in a nightclub. Another encouraged citizens to drive their cars into the city centre and then mysteriously 'break down', causing chaos and gridlock while they lifted their bonnets and attempted to 'repair' their stricken engines. When asked by a reporter what had happened to his car, one man answered: 'Its soul has broken down. It has been broken for a long, long time.'[14]

At 7.30 p.m. each evening, all across the city and right out into the suburbs and estates of New Belgrade, people would gather on their balconies and batter their pots and pans in an attempt to 'drown out' the propaganda of the prime-time RTS news bulletin. While Milošević had attempted to create silence and acquiescence by pulling the plug on B92, now B92 started to broadcast the 7.30 p.m. noise live, attempting to amplify dissonance by retransmitting it. The noisefests proved so popular that a local saucepan company even used images of pot-bashers in its commercials.

Downtown, people paraded about in ridiculous fancy-dress costumes: one man wearing a tin helmet with red tulips 'growing' from its crown; an immaculately made-up woman in full Roman gladiator's gear; others in comic sunglasses, face masks and nurses' uniforms. Student girls would draw pink hearts on police riot shields, or gaily offer flowers to young constables, who accepted them shyly, unsure how to react. A jazz band blared out New Orleans trad classics in an attempt to 'blow away the cordon'. Sheep were paraded with placards around their necks reading: 'We support the Socialist Party.' After the students were banned from marching in certain areas – particularly the wealthy district of Dedinje, where Milošević, Arkan and other potentates dwelled – they produced and distributed a 'map of the Forbidden City'; another sad document of the narrowing options in Belgrade.

While the students' stunts were intended to keep spirits up

and retain the attention of the world media, the walks had also become a social occasion; a chance to catch up with old friends, to see who was still in town, to not be alone in your apartment. 'I never ever thought it was going to be a revolution – it wasn't focused in that way,' says one regular marcher. 'It was about feeling good about yourself, doing something that made you feel better, about speaking out. Only a small percentage of people were out there because they supported the opposition, most people were out for other reasons. It made you realise you weren't the only one who was miserable, there were other people and you could have a laugh with them about it.'

But some felt that the politicians, who viewed the protests as rallies in support of their own party programmes, were increasingly bleeding the fun out of the proceedings. 'The opposition leaders killed off the best action, insisting that the noisy local walks should end at the same old place, the Square, with the same boring speeches,' protester Ivica Dolenc said.[15]

Others worried that the limited agenda of the protests – *give us back our votes* – was burying deeper disagreements which would remain, festering, until some time in the future. 'The Kosovo problem and Serbia's responsibility for the recent war [in Bosnia] were not discussed at all during the protest,' wrote ethnologist Ivan Čolović. 'Even the occasional mention of Kosovo and the war showed how divided, or at least ambivalent, Serbs are on these questions, for all their spectacular protest and their championing of a new, modern, democratic and European Serbia. One student leaflet described the war as a national catastrophe which had ended in the loss of territory. On the other, there were slogans which dismissed Milošević as a war criminal.'[16]

For many, the peak of the protests came on New Year's Eve, when half a million people packed into Republic Square to celebrate. The drum corps hammered out a furious rhythm while demonstrators waved balloons and let off luminous red flares. The mass of jumping bodies resembled an open-air

rave; the showers of fireworks recalled the terraces at a particularly intense Italian soccer derby; the atmospheric clouds of
rising smoke, shot through with red and white light, were like
a scene from Francis Ford Coppola's Vietnam fantasy *Apocalypse Now.* And all the while, the snow kept on falling.

'The weather was terrible, but it was a state of spiritual
catharsis, a massive explosion of frustrated energy, of souls that
had finally opened up: this was a real experience,' says artist
Uroš Djurić. 'In all the demonstrations before 1996, we didn't
have a real idea of what were we fighting for, why and how.
Somehow they were pathetic – not many people will tell you
that, but that was what I felt. The protests of 1996 weren't
pathetic any more. Fuck Serbian archetypes! Fuck Serbian
romanticism! Fuck nationalism! We were fighting for our lives,
for our dignity.'

The demonstrations continued throughout January, each
side refusing to back down. The Serbian Orthodox Church
condemned the regime as 'godless and satanic' for annulling
the election results. In early February, police in body armour
charged the marchers again, running amok with truncheons,
coshing anyone in range and smashing their bones as they fell,
then beating their bellies and skulls as they were handcuffed
and dragged away. As the protesters attempted to fight back
with bottles and stones, water-cannon opened fire and plainclothes officers drew batons and assaulted anyone who had
strayed from the main body of the march. Scores of people
ended up in emergency clinics with fractured limbs and broken
teeth. Television cameramen from international news agencies
were attacked and their equipment smashed.

A couple of days afterwards, Milošević wrote to his prime
minister asking him to frame a piece of legislation to recognise
Zajedno's election wins. It was victory – of a kind. Because
while this 'lex specialis' gave Zajedno its prize, its unusual
nature also signified that power would remain within the remit
of one man alone; his act of grace showed he was above any
parliament and any law. Nevertheless, on 21 February, 150,000

people celebrated Belgrade's new opposition party rule in the city centre. Zoran Djindjić, head of the Democratic Party, became the new mayor. A few weeks afterwards, the rector of Belgrade University resigned, and the students too concluded their protests.

However, while most students were overjoyed, some felt unfulfilled, even betrayed, by their leaders. At the outset they had insisted that their protests would be non-partisan and have nothing to do with party politics. But some of their leaders had joined Djindjić's Democratic Party, leaving them open to allegations of bias. It was seen as a sell-out. 'They said they were different, then they just got co-opted,' one angry student says. There was speculation that party bosses had acquired favours and influence from some of the student organisers in return for financial resources.

The Zajedno coalition would not last long either. Vuk Drašković's Serbian Renewal Movement announced it would found a committee to reinstate the monarchy in Serbia, a suggestion which riled Drašković's more liberal Zajedno colleagues, who wanted no truck with royalism. Zoran Djindjić was also displeased that Drašković assumed he would be the Zajedno candidate in the forthcoming presidential election; Djindjić would have preferred to put up a 'Serbian Vaclav Havel' for the job. By June 1997, so soon after its victory, the Zajedno alliance had collapsed entirely.

Many had never trusted the opposition politicians, and this confirmed their worst fears: these people were egocentric careerists who played to the crowd but cared nothing for them. 'One mistake that everyone made was to give the opposition the benefit of the doubt,' says B92's Julia Glyn-Pickett. 'Someone said to me that we at B92 were never critical enough of them so we didn't prepare the public for the shock and disillusionment of their falling apart, which was totally inevitable if you knew anything about them. Everyone had known it would happen but hoped maybe they would realise and put the interests of ordinary people before their own egos. But they didn't.'

Perhaps the politicians had never really comprehended the deeper social significance of the protests, muses Glyn-Pickett: 'Through their own arrogance and vanity, they thought that people were there because of them. They didn't understand that people were there because they wanted to live a normal life and control their destinies.' Indeed, a Belgrade University poll of marchers revealed that only around four per cent of them had joined the protests to back the party hacks, while nearly sixty per cent were spurred by non-partisan desires for freedom and justice.

And perhaps simply forcing Milošević to accept the local election results wasn't enough – there had to be a strategy for what would happen afterwards. 'The politicians led people to believe they could make everything right by just walking through the streets, that they could change the remains of Communism which lasted for fifty years by walking for eighty days – but of course the regime is stronger than that,' says student protester Milja Jovanović. 'The whole world was watching us and seeing there was a seed of democracy here – not just democracy as in a parliamentary system, but the way people walked, the way people said things, the way people acted.'

The politicians hadn't grasped that people wanted a break from the cynicism and corruption of the past – that the liberation movement had made a quantum leap into a new way of thinking. They were still locked into the mind-set of the past – the bear-pit politics of power-plays and ego battles, of which Milošević was the past master. 'They were just pleased with the attention that they got and never tried to go beyond that,' says Jovanović. 'Of course it was a great show of strength and will and stubbornness, but it was not enough and nobody told those people that it was not enough.' (Some, however, make the counter-accusation that the independent media did not support the opposition's new local governments in their attempts to make change and condemned them as failures too quickly.)

A deep and weighty hopelessness set in; a depression of overwhelming finality — a feeling that people had tried to change things, that they had battled as hard as they could for as long as they could, but they had failed, and that now nothing would ever change. 'We just lost it,' says singer Oliver Nektarijević. 'We gave our best for a while but didn't get anything in return. We felt used and desperate, and most of us don't feel we can trust anybody now.'

# 5

# collateral damage
# 1998–99

'When reality doesn't work any more, we move to the virtual world. But the pain is real and it stays with us.'

**B92 'Net Aid' manifesto (1999)**

In July 1997, a few short months after the fiercest and most sustained uprising Serbia had experienced in decades, Slobodan Milŏsević was elevated to the presidency of Yugoslavia – a new title which confirmed that not only had he survived the winter of discontent, but had come out of it stronger than ever. In his inaugural speech, he promised his people 'peace, progress and prosperity'. He would deliver exactly the opposite.

The opposition, meanwhile, pressed the self-destruct button. To the annoyance of the other parties and the disgust of those who hated the regime. Vuk Drašković met Milŏsević for talks and then gave an interview to the state TV channel RTS, which had been one of the prime targets of the protests of 1996. And worse, he made light of the betrayal: 'This time I have come without eggs,' he joked, referring to the egg attacks on the 'Bastille' the year before.[1]

His party, backed by the Socialists and the ultra-right nationalists of the Serbian Radical Party, moved to eject Democratic Party leader Zoran Djindjić from his position as mayor of Belgrade and capture control of the local TV station Studio B. Drašković said Djindjić had 'betrayed' him, so he had to have him 'eliminated' in an act of personal revenge. It highlighted how fractured the opposition had become in less than a year. Djindjić's supporters came out on to the streets to protest at his ousting and were immediately attacked by riot police. As political analyst Robert Thomas noted: 'For Drašković to be implicated, even indirectly, in an episode where force was used by the police against demonstrators was particularly damaging for someone whose political image had on previous occasions been centred on the idea of his being the victim of state-directed violence.'[2]

Drašković then decided to join the Socialists in a 'government of national unity', his desire for influence over-riding his previous hostility to Milošević, further tainting his image as a man of the people. Nevertheless, this unholy union was short-lived – Drašković's party fell from favour and was unceremoniously abandoned after it had served its purpose. (Less than two years later, Drašković would dally with Milošević once more, this time joining his government for a brief period as deputy prime minister.)

After compromising Drašković's image as a democratic icon, Milošević established a new alliance, this time with the Radicals, led by the neo-fascist firebrand Vojislav Šešelj, who became the new deputy prime minister. The Radicals had benefited from the opposition's disarray as Šešelj capitalised on the loss of faith in the Zajedno coalition and captured the votes of those who were dissatisfied with Milošević and wanted change in any form, whatever its political colour.

Šešelj had regularly participated in a kind of unofficial coalition with the regime, despite the fact that his Radicals were a far-right party while Milošević and his wife's organisations were Communist. This bizarre fascist/Communist alliance shared in common both violent xenophobia and hatred for the West. During the eighties, Šešelj served time in jail for 'endangering the social order' with his nationalist views. He was once a close associate and friend of Vuk Drašković and had helped him form the Serbian Renewal

Movement, although he quickly left to set up his own party. His Chetnik paramilitaries were implicated in ethnic cleansing in Croatia.

The ascendance of Šešelj bred fear and insecurity; he was nasty, brutish and unpredictable, and now he had a licence to cause trouble. As Robert Thomas wrote: 'With the apparent blessing of the Serbian government Šešelj was able to act as if he was above the law.'[3] While he was mayor of the Belgrade suburb of Zemun, he gave one of his cronies a flat belonging to a Croat family while they were on holiday; after a TV debate his bodyguard beat up a respected human rights lawyer who was a fellow guest. Vitriol was never far from his lips.

A feeling of lawlessness and sudden, random violence affected everyone in Belgrade. Even those at the highest levels of society, where business, war and crime were interchangeable concepts, were deeply disturbed. In February 1997, Vladan Kovačević was killed. He was a Milošević family friend who once sponsored their peroxide-haired, sports-car-driving son Marko's attempts to become a racing driver and later was alleged to have collaborated with him in the cigarette-smuggling trade. Two months later, police minister Radovan Stojičić, who was responsible for the Miloševićes' personal security and represented the link between the paramilitary ethnic cleansers and the government during the Bosnian war, was shot dead by a masked assassin. Milošević attended his funeral along with the gang overlord Arkan and his wife, the singer Ceca. In October, businessman Zoran Todorović, a personal friend of Milošević's wife and general secretary of her political party, was also murdered. None of the killers was identified or apprehended.

In February 1998, in the southern province of Kosovo, an armed attack on Serbian police by the ethnic Albanian guerrilla fighters of the Kosovo Liberation Army was met with a massive offensive by the state security forces (allegedly led by the same anti-terrorist unit which had been active in beating up protesters on the streets of Belgrade in the winter of 1996). Milošević then launched an all-out assault against the guerrillas of the Kosovo Liberation Army and Kosovo's ethnic Albanian population, which was fighting for independence from Serbia. The war in Kosovo had begun.

The outbreak of hostilities coincided with an escalation of the regime's crusade against the independent media in the rest of the country as Milošević stepped up his efforts to dominate the entire public landscape. His wife Mira Marković railed against 'evil forces' and 'collaborators' who she said were plotting to destroy the country from within. Non-conformist radio and TV stations in the provinces were shut down under the pretext that they had flouted technical regulations; newspapers were harassed by the tax police.

In Belgrade, Veran Matić warned that the regime was 'preparing the public for a mass physical showdown with independent journalists', involving bans, closures, censorship and possible violence. Milošević was taking his toughest line ever because, Matić argued, in the absence of any political alternatives, the independent media had become the only genuine opposition movement in Serbia.

Its reports also encouraged resistance to Milošević's nationalist adventures in Kosovo. However, it was becoming increasingly clear from the information which, despite censorship, was filtering through to Belgrade, that this was a renewed campaign of ethnic cleansing which an emasculated opposition could do little to prevent. 'We could all see what was going to happen but it didn't matter what we said,' says B92's Julia Glyn-Pickett. 'It was like watching this horror movie unfold in slow motion and realising how powerless you are to influence events.'

In the autumn of 1998, the NATO military alliance advised Milošević that unless he reined back his operations against the Kosovo Albanians, Serbia would be bombed. Belgrade's alternative media, which maintained close links with Albanian-language newspapers and radio stations in Kosovo, opposed any NATO military intervention, although not simply for reasons of self-preservation. They believed that such action would only strengthen the dictator's position. Veran Matić warned that air raids would 'put a powerful weapon into the hands of all conservative and nationalist forces and cause desperation to all those who have for years now stood up to the policy of hatred and violence'. Milošević would use NATO to 'prove' that there was an international conspiracy against Serbia and unite the population around him.

'Military action will not bring to an end the crisis in the Balkans,' Matić insisted. 'It is more likely to bolster Milošević's totalitarian regime and pile more misery on the people of Yugoslavia by guaranteeing more years of international isolation.' Ironically, Matić himself had been accused on a state news agency bulletin of asking NATO to bomb Serbia; he was labelled a 'fifth columnist' and the report claimed he possessed a 'disloyal gene'.

The storm clouds were gathering once more; the horizon had darkened. People were nervous and edgy, fearing the worst. NATO attacks seemed imminent; events in Kosovo were deteriorating. 'The situation is very dramatic,' wrote Gordan Paunović at the time. 'All the bad things are 100 per cent virtual – Milošević, scenes from Kosovo, sessions of the Yugoslav parliament with pathetic patriotic rhetoric – all that you can only see on TV, while everything else seems to be normal. But seriously, everyone is scared to death, especially the older people.'

B92 tried to organise a benefit party for Kosovan refugees in Montenegro, but cancelled after the city authorities who ran the venue insisted the money went to the cause of their choice. Three Belgrade independent dailies were banned under a government decree on special measures in response to the NATO attack threat; one was told it had 'spread fear and panic' due to its reprinting of articles by Kosovo Albanians. The signal of local independent news broadcaster Radio Index was jammed, then the station was shut down. People grew increasingly scared that the regime, under threat of destruction from the West, was preparing for one last stand: an all-out war on dissidents and the establishment of a dictatorship. The threats were becoming harsher, the insults more terrifying. Journalists were accused of inviting foreign aggression and betraying their country. 'Media that continue spying and anti-state activities will be closed down, their equipment confiscated and the editors responsible arrested in the event of wartime,' Vojislav Šešelj declared.[4]

The minister of information ordered all TV and radio stations to cease retransmitting programmes made by overseas networks like the BBC, Voice of America, Deutsche Welle and Radio Free Europe, stating that they constituted 'a conscious involvement in espionage activities'. Interviewed on B92, Šešelj accused the station of broadcasting 'foreign psychological propaganda'.

The sustained hate campaign against 'enemies within', interfering Western politicians who were seeking to impose their own 'new world order' and the Albanian 'terrorists' of the Kosovo Liberation Army was plainly recognisable to those who had lived through the build-up to the wars in Croatia and Bosnia. This was a concerted attempt to brainwash Serbs into a hysterical, paranoid mind-set, a feeling that they were surrounded on all sides and must fight to protect their identity. It was the insidious propaganda of mobilisation.

For those who sought to close their ears to the martial fanfares of RTS, the only alternative was the fluorescent escapism of the television entertainment channels, offering round-the-clock Serbian pop, Hollywood films, soap operas, football matches and hours devoted to horoscopes and clairvoyants. TV Pink, the foremost of these, was run by a man once dubbed 'Europe's most unlikely Marxist', Željko Mitrović, a former rock star who had hooked up with Mira Marković's JUL party. Another MTV-style pop-video channel, TV Košava, was run by Milošević's daughter Marija. These turbo channels offered their viewers all the virtual fun they could consume, plus the added attraction of scantily-clad bottle blondes with surgically-enhanced figures. In the world of TV Pink, life was a glossy concoction of make-up and merry-making, all vapid smiles and dancing girls.

The assaults on the independent media climaxed later that October with the passing of a new Public Information Law. This Draconian piece of legislation enabled huge fines to be levied on editors and publishers and the seizure of property and equipment for unpaid penalties. The Serbian prime minister warned: 'If you write like you're supposed to you won't have to worry.'[5]

Newspapers which gave space to opponents of the regime or Kosovan Albanians were hit hard. Some were driven out of business altogether. The editor-in-chief of the *Dnevni Telegraf* (*Daily Telegraph*), Slavko Ćuruvija, was fined over four million dinars and sentenced to five months' jail after refusing to pay. Papers which tried to get around the censorship by publishing in neighbouring Montenegro were seized at the border. The overall result, wrote columnist Petar Luković, was that 'the Serbian public was much better informed about the wars in Croatia and Bosnia than it is about Kosovo today'.[6] The information blackout enabled Milošević to launch his new ethnic cleansing offensives almost unnoticed.

Just after the Public Information Law was passed, B92 was presented with the Free Your Mind free-speech prize at the 1998 MTV Awards. The entire ceremony was broadcast live on TV Košava. As Veran Matić received the prize from members of the American rock band REM and began to make his acceptance speech, the TV Košava announcer translating the proceedings into Serbian – who at first didn't seem to realise exactly who the award was going to – began to stumble over her words, and then the picture cut out completely.

There was also a renewed campaign of censorship in the universities – a calculated response to the outbreak of student militancy the year before. The students, like the independent media, were now one of the last remaining sources of potential opposition, and as such they had to be crushed. Vlada Tedosić, a government-appointed official at Belgrade University's computing centre, ordered that users of the Yugoslav academic Internet system be prevented from accessing Opennet, B92's website. It was reported that he acted after Opennet carried a political cartoon picturing him in a Nazi uniform, with another university administrator caricatured as a monkey. Tedosić had been central to the implementation of a new University Law earlier that year, which required all professors to sign what amounted to an oath of loyalty to the government – another attempt to ensure that the mass protests of 1996–97 never happened again. Those who refused to comply were sacked.

The victory of the opposition in the local elections of 1996 had liberated many regional radio and television stations from the control of the ruling Socialist Party. In June 1997, using this new-found freedom, B92 had instigated the creation of the Association of Independent Electronic Media (ANEM), a country-wide network of over thirty broadcasters. ANEM members initially retransmitted news programmes from B92 and the Serbian section of the BBC World Service. Each day, four hours of programming was sent via the Internet to Amsterdam and then on to London. The BBC then uplinked the broadcasts to its satellite, from which ANEM local radio stations would download and then rebroadcast them across the Yugoslav airwaves. It was an audacious attempt to go right up against the national dominance of RTS.

Some of these local ANEM stations, isolated from the relatively liberal heartland of the capital, experienced even greater traumas than B92. Radio Boom 93 in the deeply conservative town of Požarevac, birthplace of Milošević and home to his son Marko, was shut down for nine months in 1996 and many times afterwards. Harassed by local authorities who were in thrall to the whims of the dictator's playboy offspring, who seemed to run the town like his own personal fiefdom, Boom 93 found it impossible to obtain a licence and was forced to operate, guerrilla-fashion, as a pirate, broadcasting only when conditions were favourable. It wasn't exactly safe to criticise the president in his own back yard.

B92's attempts to win a wider, more mainstream audience would have a critical impact on the station's programming. When it topped the Belgrade ratings chart during the protests of 1996–7, many listeners who tuned in for news of the demonstrations found it hard to comprehend the uncompromising, often provocative music the DJs were playing. 'Each day we would get about 500 phone calls of support,' says head of music Gordan Paunović, 'and ten per cent were saying, "Can you please play anything but this – anything at all!"'

Initially Veran Matić stuck by the system which gave each DJ autonomy of selection, feeling that the policy of musical independence was as vital as political independence, and that both were integral parts of B92's mission to establish a genuine social alternative. As he once told a listener: 'Yes, they might be complaining about the music, but if I changed the music they wouldn't believe the news any more.' However, after ANEM was established and a listenership survey was conducted, he decided that a playlist had to be imposed to smooth out the ragged edges and accommodate an older listenership which found it impossible to digest the nuances of drum'n'bass or indie rock, but wanted to keep tuning in for the reports they couldn't hear elsewhere. A British radio consultant recommended by the BBC, Graeme Moreland, was flown to Belgrade to advise the music department on how to organise the programming to make it more accessible.

According to Gordan Paunović, Moreland arrived with the kind of formatting guidelines which would be recognisable to listeners of any commercial radio station anywhere in the world: a playlist system arranging output into stylistic streams: classics, current hits, breaking singles and so on. His plan was to accommodate the casual listener by establishing logic and order. Some staff, particularly those who preferred an element of creative disorder, were afraid that their shows would lose their individuality, and sarcastically compared Moreland to Harvey Keitel's character in the Quentin Tarantino film *Pulp Fiction* – the 'cleaner' who washes up the bloody mess after a murder and disposes of the dead body.

Paunović admits that a few slots were a mess, some presenters were incompetent and that a number of DJs 'couldn't control themselves and they were just playing to make themselves happy'. But although he felt that the music department could have sorted out the daytime programming themselves, he decided to work with Moreland 'to stop him making too much shit'. Instead of using the typical categories of golden oldies, eighties hits and contemporary pop, the music department created their own strands, and the evening shows were unaffected.

'We bought the formula but we filled the categories with the music that was our trademark,' says Paunović. 'Mr Cleaner left us a book containing all the Top 40 hits in the history of music and said "this is the Bible of a successful radio station". Of course I never opened it. We will not play Mariah Carey or Phil Collins as he would have liked, but we'll play Massive Attack and Pulp and Paul Weller on rotation. We got rid of the extremes and got something that's like a quality mainstream.

'I think what we did isn't bad, although this repetitive formula of rotation is killing the excitement about the station in a way. It's a formula meant for people who listen for ten minutes at a time. There's no way you can wake up at 9 a.m. and hear Sonic Youth, although you can still hear bands like that because we created a category called "off" – which means "off limits".'

Some felt that B92 had lost its nerve and chosen the soft option. 'The easiest thing you can do is use a formula to make your radio station successful in a commercial way,' says Paunović, 'but if you want to play a more subtle game, not to make compromises and still keep your listenership, it's fucking difficult.'

Matić believes that the changes 'brought some balance into the overall programming and made the station more easy to listen to'. He also says the transition took place 'without too many earthquakes within the station itself'. Although some disagree and remain resentful, many indeed felt that compromises were necessary. 'We were scared at first but it turned out to be good for us; we lost that unpredictability but we managed to stay almost the same,' says DJ Vladimir Janjić. 'Nothing changed much and we got more listeners. We retained our real underground side but we made a compromise with the daytime programming because of the older listeners.'

There had long been disagreements between the news team, which wanted a more commercial policy, and the music department, which felt that B92's alternative ethos should be reflected throughout the entirety of its output. 'There is no point trying to stay independent from the regime and the opposition parties in your news programmes and then having something that is not independent in the rest of your programming,' says Janjić. 'We were fighting for years with the guys from the news department. We are friends but they would prefer a station with more local music and more pop – but that would make us just like every other radio station in Belgrade.'

After the changes, B92's popularity continued to rise, although some of its veteran fans felt betrayed, believing that it had sold out its uniqueness, turned mainstream and discarded its original mission for the sake of audience figures. One suggests the new policy was introduced to mollify international donors who were only interested in B92 as a news broadcaster with a wide outreach, not as a cultural force. Another says simply: 'Music itself was part of the message – a playlist was definitely not part of that message. We lost it.'

Nonetheless, both B92 and ANEM thrived. The foundation of a broadcast network covering seventy per cent of the country was an audacious move which, as its first listen-ership figures indicated, inspired hopes that a coalition of independent broadcasters could seriously rival the previously unchallenged supremacy of the state media.

Veran Matić travelled to London and Washington to lobby British foreign secretary Robin Cook and US secretary of state Madeleine Albright for political and financial support for the network, and to warn them that the situation in Belgrade was rapidly turning critical. Inevitably, this was seen by Milo-šević as a direct appeal to the enemy. During the nineties, B92's journalists had become used to being denounced as a fifth column in league with outside forces to destabilise Serbia, and had learned to laugh it off as the wild ranting of dema-gogues. But with war looming again, the insults now felt much more sinister. They began to fear for their safety. 'In an autocratic system, everyone who thinks differently is a traitor or a spy,' says B92 reporter Zoran Mamula. 'During peacetime, it's no problem, but in wartime it's a licence to kill.'

At around 8.15 p.m. on 24 March 1999, air-raid sirens sounded in Belgrade city centre. Negotiations between Milŏ-šević and NATO had broken down after the president had defied the latest in a five-month series of 'final warnings' to quit his savage campaign in Kosovo, and the West launched missile attacks on military installations all over Serbia. Oper-ation Allied Force was Europe's largest military action since 1945, the start of a 'moral war' aimed at forcing Milošević to back down, quit his Kosovo offensives and avert the kind of humanitarian catastrophe which he had helped cause in Bosnia. 'There are times when you have to stand up and fight for peace,' stated British prime minister Tony Blair.[7]

Belgrade's citizens couldn't quite believe that it was finally happening – only weeks before, a poll had shown that seventy-eight per cent thought NATO would never bomb. One reporter noticed old couples walking through the streets, taking the air, and a woman roller-blading down the road despite the orange flashes over the skyline and the sound of explosions from an airbase under twenty miles away. Many didn't seem to know where their nearest bomb shelter was. 'Although we all had a few months to "prepare", as it were, none of us really ever experienced anything remotely like this, so the first siren did sound, to say the least, unfamiliar,' said Jelena Subotić afterwards.

By 1 a.m., Belgrade was eerily silent. 'Belgrade is *totally* in darkness. And I mean it! There is no street light, no blinking neon banners, no light in houses and apartments. Darkness everywhere . . . No clouds, no lights, only a half-moon is shining over the city,' wrote young computer programmer Slobodan Marković in a diary he circulated over the Internet. 'Totally amazing, scary and claustrophobic decoration . . . Too bad you need to have a bloody war situation to experience such a view . . .'[8]

As the onslaught began, B92's reporters started ringing the authorities responsible for ensuring civilian safety. They were given short shrift. 'The regime had done nothing to prepare the population for the war, starting from the basic things like where to go to shelter to the psychological preparations,' says Veran Matić. 'We contacted all the institutions who were in charge of organising things in wartime, and all of them didn't really want to talk. We were expecting that, we knew our reporting was irritating the government, but what was strange was even the people in charge of protecting people didn't want to talk to us.'

Just before 3 a.m., after Matić had gone home, a group of policemen entered B92's fifth-floor newsroom. 'Good evening, ladies and gentlemen,' one said. 'Madam, take your hands off the keyboard. Everyone else, stay away from phones and mobile phones. If anyone touches a mobile phone, it will be confiscated.'

The policemen, accompanied by two telecommunications inspectors, stated that the station had overstepped its permitted transmission power, and that they must confiscate B92's 'exciter' – a crucial part of its transmitter. 'They were quite polite, just like ordinary cops on duty, as if they were thinking: "OK, I was just catching a criminal, now I have to shut down a radio station, then I must go and arrest some hookers",' says programme director Milivoje Čalija. 'They just said: "We have come to shut down this radio." There was no violence. No one shouted.'

Over the airwaves, the final announcement came: 'You have been listening to Radio B92. You will not be listening to it any more because of technical problems.'

Veran Matić realised that B92's signal had disappeared and phoned the office. Nobody answered, so he put his clothes on and left for the studio. Outside his apartment he noticed two plainclothes policemen, who followed him all the way to the B92 building. When he entered the studio, he was asked for identification, then told that he had to accompany the policemen to the station.

'In the police car I was with a very young policeman who didn't seem to approve of what was going on. He said he realised it was very disturbing being arrested and thought that I wouldn't be kept in custody very long and perhaps police would soon be able to come to the radio for a cup of coffee and everything would be OK,' he recalls.

Matić asked to call his wife to tell her he had been arrested. The policemen refused, saying they had been told to conduct the operation with the utmost discretion. The police station was almost deserted.

'They took my personal belongings, my belt and my shoe-laces – the usual procedure. I was put in a cell with another guy who was dressed up perfectly in a suit like he was going to some ceremony. He was lying on the bench, sleeping like a baby. When he woke up, we started chatting and it turned out he had been in the cell for two days. He used to be the general manager of a security company for [Milošević's wife's party] JUL and he was there under investigation for attempted murder. He couldn't believe I was a journalist; he insisted I must be a policeman who had been put in there to get a confession out of him. So even in a cell, the lunacy continued.'

Matić spent eight hours behind bars, after which he was released without charge and with no explanation given. The next day, a regime official stated that the clampdown was justified because during the air strikes the station would act as the 'main radio locator guiding NATO aircraft to targets in Yugoslavia'. This time there was no point appealing to Western diplomats for a reprieve; their countries were already bombarding Serbia. As Saša Mirković puts it: 'Any kind of reaction from Madeleine Albright or Robin Cook, who could before have had an impact, would have been counterproductive. And what could the international community have said to Milošević – "reopen B92 or we will bomb you"?'

As well as shutting down B92, the government imposed immediate limitations on the rest of the media. They were ordered to act solely in the 'service of the state's current interests', and those who did not comply were threatened with closure and detention. Reports on Yugoslav army casualties were prohibited; police and army manoeuvres were to be described only as 'defence activities' or 'the struggle to defend the country'. Enemy losses were to be reported using the terms 'neutralised', 'incapacitated', 'paralysed' and 'liquidated'. No information which would 'spread defeatism and panic' was to be published. As well as the censoring of their reports, journalists' vocabulary was strictly regulated: the Kosovo Liberation Army was to be referred to as 'a gang', 'terrorists' or 'criminals', while NATO had to be called 'the aggressor'.

B92 switched its news programming to its website, as it had during the shutdown of 1996, and tried to report the war as best it could under the blanket restrictions imposed by the regime, while attempting to get its reporter, an Albanian from Priština, out of Kosovo before reprisals began. 'There was certainly a body of opinion that said we should have refused to go on air because we couldn't report freely,' says Julia Glyn-

Pickett. 'We argued that our loyalty is to our audience in Belgrade – no, we couldn't tell them everything, but what we had to make sure was that we didn't lose those listeners because if we did lose them, when all this was over, what were we going to do if we had absolutely nothing left to rebuild a future with? They needed information about what was happening and where the shelters were, because there was so much misinformation about basic things like that coming out from the government. We never put out the government propaganda – we basically put out community service information.' Nevertheless, B92's website was soon attracting over a million hits per day.

The radio silence was an indication that all opposition to Milošević was now impossible, that there was nothing left to do but keep quiet, suffer, and wait for it all to end. 'Part of our strategy in the first few days was: wake up and listen to B92,' says an adviser to one of the opposition parties. 'If you hear there is no B92, don't come to work that day, sit down, phone each other and work out what to do. It was a sign: no more bullshit, you can't say a thing, we are entering a different reality. No freedom of speech, no freedom of expression, no possibilities of any sort of action, and great repercussions for anyone who dares to do something. B92 was the test: when they shut them down, that's it, now it's really started.'

Veran Matić felt let down by his friends in the West and painfully disappointed that his predictions that bombing would mean the annihilation of all independent thought had gone unheeded. He knew that the radio stations of his Albanian comrades in Kosovo were also being muzzled by the authorities, and that the staff of *Koha Ditore*, the independent Priština newspaper, had gone into hiding. The first collateral damage was to democracy.

'Perhaps someone out there would prefer to see us removed completely – as the final proof that Serbia is home only to nationalism, war-mongering and sheer brutality,' he speculated angrily. 'The more I think about that, the more I realise that this has become a direct consequence of the US policy in the Balkans. To destroy and silence all alternative democratic voices and peace initiatives in order to make Yugoslavia a European Iraq and a pariah state for the next ten years.'[9] It seemed clear that the same British and American politicians who had once hymned B92 with fine words and bolstered it with cash were also more than willing to cut it loose when it suited them. The people at B92 felt betrayed by those whose culture they so admired – and felt the West had betrayed the values of free speech and human rights which it had once so enthusiastically propagated.

Matić wondered at the naivety of some Western commentators who expected not only B92 and the Belgrade opposition to support the NATO offensive as a strike against Milošević, but to come out on to the streets to demonstrate and welcome the fighter planes with open arms. People did come out on to the streets, not to oppose the regime, but to protest against the bombing of Serbia, which they saw as an attack on them, not simply on their president. NATO's bombs may have been smart, but they weren't discriminating. As Matić said, 'the sins of the government have been visited on the people'.[10]

He noted that the West had directly supported Milošević on a host of previous occasions: selling him equipment for the Serbian police and special forces, colluding in the $1 billion sell-off of the state telecommunications network, which helped fund one of his election victories, not delivering promised funds to independent trades unions and media, and tolerating the transfer of Serbian investments overseas.

Each day there were anti-NATO concerts in Republic Square, where bands would play and thousands of people would defiantly display humorous banners damning Clinton and Blair, and hold up target signs as if to say: 'You know where I am – come and get me.' Others would gather at night on the bridge over the River Sava, which they believed would inevitably be bombed.

Some saw the protests as a continuation of the spirit of the student uprising of 1996–97: 'Shiny, smiling faces, people wearing paper targets on their clothes or foreheads. Slogans, both in English and Serbian, are witty, ironic and striking like haiku poetry – "Monica, clench your teeth" (people mock Clinton mostly for his fatal fondness for fellatio, and Monica Lewinsky becomes a funny symbol of opposition to Clinton's policy). Shop windows are full of slogans and cartoons. In the word NATO, the letter "T" is sometimes replaced by a swastika, since this NATO aggression is equalled to fascistic aggression in 1941,' one participant explained.[11]

But others found the concerts and bridge gatherings repulsive, an outpouring of cheesy, patriotic turbo-fervour orchestrated by Milošević loyalists for the benefit of the regime. 'If they were just concerts against the bombing, that would have been cool. But how could I be against Albanians all of a sudden?' asks one. Many felt it was distasteful to party while others were dying.

The sun shone, but now even the sunshine could be menacing. 'Yes, the weather, it is beautiful, we all enjoy and fear it: the better the weather, the heavier the bombings. I wish I only knew, do we need good or bad weather to stay alive?' wrote Belgrade resident Jasmina Tesanović in a war diary she published on the Internet.

She feared NATO's attacks, but was also reluctant to spend all her time in the bomb shelters. 'I think it is part of the local propaganda to keep people underground, not to worry about their moves and more than elementary needs,' she explained. 'When the sirens come on I deliberately go out on the street, says a friend of mine. The situation is the opposite of demonstrations in '97 when everybody was outside. Maybe we should set up an underground state with its new democratic laws: maybe a state run by women and children, according to their needs and morals.' When asked why she braved the danger outside, she replied: 'Yes, I am afraid, but

I am even more afraid to stay for the next twenty years obediently underground, whatever happens outside.'[12]

Radio Television Serbia's propaganda machine went into overdrive, pumping out paranoia and hysteria day and night. For RTS viewers, the NATO attack had come from nowhere, unprovoked and unjustified – they knew little of the realities of Milošević's campaign in Kosovo. NATO was repeatedly compared to Hitler's Germany in films linking the air attacks to the Nazi bombings of World War Two. Tony Blair, Robin Cook, Bill Clinton and Madeleine Albright were lampooned in cartoons and photo-montages – Cook as a silly, squealing appendage to Blair's sinister puppetmaster, Albright as a mad housewife and Clinton as a lascivious, green-eyed monster. Like the revellers in the squares and on the bridges, RTS taunted NATO, daring it to do its worst. 'Our address is 10 Takovska Street,' said one presenter. 'Work out the co-ordinates for yourself.' Most other TV stations ceased making their own programmes and simply retransmitted RTS's output.

'We were thrown into an information black hole,' says Borka Pavičević of the Centre for Cultural Decontamination. 'You could only see on official TV what was bombed and where, and usually just on a map. Can you imagine the madness – you hear something then you have to look at CNN or Sky News to see what is happening practically 500 metres from you in Belgrade! Many people were getting calls from friends abroad telling them what was about to happen here. It showed how those who are ruling us are actually against their own people – why, if you want to protect people, are you taking away their information?'

Civilian casualties were an essential propaganda tool for Milošević. When RTS was ultimately attacked on 23 April all its senior management were out of the building, aware that bombing was imminent, but they left a number of technical staff on site. Sixteen of them were killed when the missiles hit. The next day RTS was back on air triumphantly, demonstrating that although it had contingency plans to continue broadcasting, these did not include the evacuation of its workers. 'They were sacrificed,' said the mother of one of the dead, suggesting that the regime cynically benefited from the casualties.[13]

Some Belgraders could hear the Serbian-language programmes of the BBC, Voice of America and Deutsche Welle coming from a powerful transmitter located at a UN base just outside the country, and people with satellite dishes could watch CNN and Sky News. But for those with a keenly-honed antenna for spin, Western TV, with its agenda rigorously shaped by NATO's media HQ in Brussels, and by briefings at the Pentagon and the White House in Washington and the Ministry of Defence in London, seemed like just another form of propaganda, if less virulent. Their suspicions would prove justified: as Philip Knightley's book on the history of the war correspondent, *The First Casualty*, outlined later, the majority of Western journalists either believed in the moral imperatives behind the 'intervention' – which was never referred to as a war by their leaders – or swallowed NATO's line wholesale. A year after the bombing, evidence that NATO misled the press over its attacks on civilian targets, the numbers of ethnic Albanians killed by the Serbs and the extent of the air strikes' destructive impact on the Serbian army was still emerging.

In Belgrade, the atmosphere was one of complete unreality, compounded by the disembodied wails of air-raid sirens and the parallel misinformation of RTS. 'Some people strive to retain an air of normality,' Petar Luković wrote in the first week of the war. 'They go to work regardless of the fact that schools, the university, post offices and banks are closed. Most of the shops have switched to shorter working hours, most private stores are locked, and in the evenings on the ghostly deserted streets, there are no cars nor taxis.

'There is no news on the Kosovo drama. Nothing about what is actually happening in the famous province Serbia supposedly cares so much about. There is no concrete information on what the NATO bombs hit and destroyed. All that is broadcast is bare, hardcore propaganda celebrating "the firm, dignified politics of Slobodan Milošević". And the most vicious language against the "fascist aggressors" of the West. The US president now has a range of new titles: "Killer Clinton", "Satanic Clinton", "Scumbag Clinton", "Worm Clinton", "Mental case and sexual deviant Clinton", and best of all, "Adolf Clinton, the biggest criminal in the history of the world".

'With nothing but patriotic songs, old war films, meaningless news and the incredible war-mongering language, it's a real Catch-22 with the media here: you'd have to be a crazy person if watching it doesn't make you go mad.'[14]

During the first ten days of the war, B92 was visited repeatedly by secret service agents, asking questions and demanding lists of employees' names and addresses. Some were served with call-ups to the army; others received threats over the phone.

At 8 a.m. on 2 April, a deputation of stern-faced men arrived at the studio: court officials, uniformed policemen, the head of the Youth Council of Belgrade and about ten beefy, crew-cut minders wearing black leather jackets, the unofficial uniform of the Eastern European thug. They entered the office of managing director Saša Mirković and told him that he had been dismissed and was to be replaced by a new director, Aleksandar Nikačević, who immediately sat down in Mirković's chair. The Internet broadcasts were instantly halted and the journalists ordered to leave the building.

Nikačević, a government loyalist who some claim had been involved in attempts to undermine the protests of 1991 as part of a state-backed students' union, stated that the Youth Council of Belgrade was the legal controller of B92, and therefore had the right to appoint its own director and editor-in-chief. B92's lawyers responded that the company was socially owned and thus managed by its employees, and that the

Youth Council was acting illegally. The regime was exploiting
the complex legal situation caused by the break-up of former
Yugoslav institutions to put its cronies in charge of B92 and
neutralise the independent media under cover of the darkness
of war. The station's Rex cultural centre and equipment
owned by ANEM – an entirely separate legal entity from B92
– was also seized.

Locked out of his office and sitting dejectedly in the coffee
bar on the ground floor of the House of Youth, Matić told
reporters: 'It's over. The NATO bombing has destroyed us.
The hatred is now spinning a spider's web that is out of
control. There is no opposition any more. We are all losers.
Only the extremists can win and the only beneficiary is
Milošević.'

B92's staff were told to report to work on Monday under
the new management. Nobody knew what would happen;
some feared that all the men would immediately be shipped
out to the frontline. In the event, they were addressed by
Nikačević, who told them that he hadn't taken over the
station, but saved it. The news programming, he declared,
must 'work in defence of the state'. One reporter asked what
this meant. She was told: 'It is a national interest to love
President Milošević.' The DJs were ordered not to play any
more English-language rock'n'roll or Western techno, only
Yugoslav music or records from 'friendly' nations like Russia
or Greece. Next to Nikačević's computer was placed a snap-
shot of the new director with Slobodan Milošević – except
that it appeared to be a photo-montage, assembled digitally
to give the impression he was close to the president.

Some of the staff kept on coming in to the studio for the
next few days, pretending to work but actually smuggling out
CDs and personal effects in their bags and under their coats,
or tying them to ropes and lowering them to safety from the
fifth-floor window. They were searched on the way in, but
not on the way out. One security man told a journalist whose
handbag they were going through: 'We're worried about what

we might find. You wouldn't believe some of the things we've found. We found a [digitally-altered] picture of Mira Marković *with tits!*' She responded: 'What, Mira Marković has no tits, then?' Another told one of the DJs that they had discovered 'satanic' records in the studio.

Veran Matić says that Nikačević and his colleagues knew little about the logistics of radio; they were simply Party members with a job to do. The only one with any kind of experience was a former horse racing correspondent. 'What we did was start a kind of game with them. It involved negotiations – however fake they were – to try and prevent persecution and blackmail,' Matić explains. 'Our guys were so persuasive and their acting was so good that the new management naively believed they could take over the team. Our tea lady remained there undercover at the office and managed to get quite a lot of our personal belongings out.' No one realised that the black plastic rubbish bags that she was constantly 'throwing away' were actually full of records and other essential documents. 'That shows the loyalty to the project from the top to the bottom,' says Matić.

However, some listeners argue that it was Matić and his staff who had been naive; after Matić's arrest, they should have evacuated their equipment immediately rather than staying on, easy targets for takeover. 'How quickly they allowed it to be destroyed,' one sighs. 'There was no clear strategy, they were unprepared for it. Too unprepared. They should have taken it more seriously, moved some equipment.'

Nenad Čekić, B92's first editor-in-chief, who had set up his own local independent station, Radio Index, says the loss of the studio was a result of sheer arrogance, and that B92 unwittingly became a major donor of technical equipment to the Milošević regime. 'Look at the building, which had two floors totally equipped and an expensive transmitter on the top, which were just given over to the government. They could have avoided such a grand takeover. They could have done it differently, like us, we tricked the government people who came to take us over – we gave them a bar-code reader and said it was a transmitter. It only cost $100 and it looked very much like a transmitter to those who are not familiar with such things. But it doesn't actually do anything, it just blinks.

'They thought the government didn't have the guts to strike at them, they were so full of themselves and thought they were so significant that no one would dare. B92 and ANEM are the biggest disasters which could have happened to Serbian independent media. They have wasted a lot of money without really doing anything.'

Veran Matić admits that they had become a little complacent and the belief existed that with the establishment of ANEM, 'B92 had become so powerful that the regime could never again seriously jeopardise it'. But it was the very strength of ANEM, he realised later, that helped galvanise Milošević into action.[15]

Saša Mirković insists that no more could have been done to protect the equipment and the transmitter. 'No. All that speculation is wrong,' he says. 'It was impossible because it was a state of war. The law was so restrictive that I couldn't ask anyone to bring equipment out because they might be arrested, sentenced to jail or even killed. We saved some of the equipment, but what is most important is that we saved the people – that we all stayed together.

'This is a rare example of people sticking together in our country. They didn't split up like a lot of people expected, because that's the nature of Serbs, you know, to divide themselves. We have a saying: "Two Serbs, three political parties." You see what the opposition is like here.'

B92's decision to work quietly to protect what was left of its network was perceived by some as defeatism. 'Some people expected us to be prepared for war – to have built an infrastructure for local radio stations including a network of correspondents and to become mobile, dangerous and elusive for the regime,' Matić said afterwards. 'We didn't do anything like that because we thought we wouldn't stand a chance in any case.'[16]

The pretence of collaboration with the new management continued until it felt too risky to go on. On 11 April, Slavko Ćuruvija, publisher of the *Dnevni Telegraf*, was shot dead in a mafia-style execution by black-clad hitmen outside his home.

Ćuruvija had once been a confidant of the Milošević family, but had fallen out with them and begun to criticise the government. In an open letter he co-wrote the previous October, he accused Milošević of leading the country towards lawlessness, terror and dictatorship, and creating a feudal state run by patronage where the president's friends were rewarded with the rich pickings of nationalised industries while the old were forced to root through dumpsters looking for food because their pensions went unpaid. The letter won him an enormous fine under the Public Information Law. He refused to pay and was sentenced to jail.

A few days before he was murdered, a state daily newspaper had referred to him as a 'national traitor' who supported NATO aggression, and said his treason would not be forgotten. The headline read: 'Ćuruvija has finally got his bombs.' (Ćuruvija, like the rest of the independent media, was opposed to the bombing.) He had been warned to leave town because his life was in danger, but didn't want to emigrate, telling his friends: 'A man cannot run from his fate.' His partner Branka Prpa believes the newspaper's report amounted to an unequivocal call for a public lynching, and that the murderers were so blasé about not being caught that they made no attempt to act surreptitiously. 'It was carried out ritually, in the centre of Belgrade, at half past four in the afternoon with a whole crowd of potential witnesses, and the killers weren't concerned at all about how many witnesses would be present during the murder,' she said. 'They chose the house, not some deserted quay on the Sava or the Danube, to execute Slavko right before my eyes.'[17]

Branka Prpa looked on as Ćuruvija was finished off with

several bullets to the head: 'It suddenly seemed to me that some terrible wind had begun blowing because a lot of dust flew up. I thought that Slavko, who was holding my hand, had stumbled and begun to fall, I had absolutely no idea what was happening. I tried to turn, but was then struck on the head and fell beside him. Then somebody dressed in black came up to him and shot him in the head in front of me, as he lay there,' she said afterwards.[18]

The state media did not report Ćuruvija's murder, and the independent press simply noted it without much comment. Even some of his colleagues dared not attend his funeral for fear of reprisals. The killers were not detained. The message was clear: criticism of the regime will not be tolerated. These are the consequences. So now you know.

'After Ćuruvija was assassinated, the prevailing feeling was that we could suffer the same fate,' says Veran Matić. Indeed, a local journalist heard a rumour that Matić was to be next. A month after Ćuruvija's death, men in military uniform came looking for Matić at his old address. He left Belgrade for Montenegro soon afterwards, became involved in making a programme for Kosovan refugees, and did not return until the war had ended. 'Later on I found out there was a plan to draft me into the army and send me to the Albanian border,' he says.

Ultimately, none of B92's staff journalists or freelances remained to work for the new management. Like hundreds of thousands of others across Serbia who had lost their jobs when the bombing started, they were now unemployed and penniless. But there was no attempt to set up a pirate studio or publish any kind of samizdat literature. After Ćuruvija, it seemed too dangerous. As one observer says: 'They behaved, and that saved their lives.'

They met in cafés, trying to keep the last vestiges of the station's spirit alive amidst the climate of intimidation. 'You could feel this red spot on your head,' remembers programme director Milivoje Čalija. 'I don't mean that some sniper was on the rooftop, but that everyone became more paranoid. We just tried not to be paranoid. We tried to stay in touch.'

The days were long and dull, the nights terrifying. A magazine columnist, writing anonymously, described the scene: 'Terrible tectonic explosions shake buildings and windows, thick black smoke billows from various parts of the city, fires and reflections light the horizon. The advance clips for George Lucas's latest *Star Wars* film seem like nothing compared with the battles raging in the sky over Belgrade every evening: anti-aircraft tracers streak overhead, the sound of missiles rips through the night, and deafening explosions shatter any temporary, unreal night peace. Indeed, when it comes, many hours after midnight and enveloped in total darkness, silence itself seems ominous.'[19]

People began to lose hope, to become trapped in torpor, traumatised by battle stress. 'We don't care about our personal lives anymore: most of us don't go to shelter, don't think of leaving the country,' wrote Jasmina Tesanović. 'We are just being here, who cares for how long, we have no decent way out, we are hostages of our own life without power.'[20]

Unwilling to participate in the anti-NATO concerts, B92 organised a small, low-key gig in town with free beer and a few bands, and a couple of club events which were broadcast on the Internet to keep the station's name alive. 'We had no intentions apart from bringing people together,' says DJ Vladimir Janjić. Ten days into the war, the Industria club opened up and DJs would play records quietly each afternoon for people who had little else to do with their time. 'I read an article in a British newspaper saying there was a party scene going on during the war, but it wasn't true – it was just to let like-minded people gather together and not have to be with the people who support this government. Nothing special, it wasn't a party at all,' Janjić explains.

'You had nothing to do during the day. We had been kicked out of our jobs, other people had lost their jobs, you couldn't sleep well at night, you'd wake up in the morning, hang

around, come home and just wait for another round of
bombing. Go on the Net and watch TV if there was electricity,
smoke and drink a lot, and that's it: nothing for two and a
half months.

'So many people were so scared. Before they had no connection with all the shit that had been happening for nine
years and this was the moment when they woke up and
realised how serious our problem is. It's a terrible thing for
someone to find out what's really going on in his life after
such a long period.'

There was fear of bombing, and renewed fear of conscrip-
tion. As Petar Luković reported: 'The mobilisation has not
yet reached its maximum level, but a great number of young
people are in hiding, spending nights away from home, trying
to avoid a knock on the door to fulfil their "military obli-
gations". Yet the state media constantly provides updates on
the "huge number of volunteers" joining the army to
"defend the homeland." '[21]

The media repression continued. An editor at a TV station
in Sokobanja, eastern Serbia, was found guilty of 'disseminating false information' after displaying a poster bearing the
words 'Free Press Made in Serbia!' with an image of someone
languishing behind bars made of newspaper and a B92 logo.
The court stated he had 'provoked unrest among citizens and
caused them to mistrust the decisions of state agencies'. He
was sentenced to one year in prison.

The bunker mentality was infectious. People became
obsessed with catching the spies which RTS said were everywhere, or capturing the pilots of downed NATO planes.
There were bets on which building or bridge would be hit
next. After dark, during the bombing hours, local TV stations
showed non-stop pirated crime thrillers from America and
endless hours of South American soap operas like the enor-
mously popular *Cassandra*. TV Košava even rebroadcast the
signal of a Chinese news and entertainment station – a bizarre
manifestation of solidarity with one of Serbia's last remaining

international allies. Democratic Party leader Zoran Djindjić was regularly accused of being a NATO supporter on the evidence that US and German flags had been waved during the protests of 1996–97. The relentless propaganda rammed home the message that Kosovo was worth sacrificing everything for: your job, your city, your life.

But as the second month of air raids passed, there was some slight evidence of disquiet. The power cuts were unsettling; soldiers were deserting from the front; mothers were demonstrating for the return of their conscript sons. After Milošević's residence was bombed, graffiti appeared on walls around Belgrade, complaining: 'Slobo, when we needed you most, you were not at home.'

Kosovo was the first time armed conflict was reflected by simultaneous battles in the new realm of cyberspace. The American, British and Serbian governments and the Kosovo Liberation Army all ran combative sorties over the digital landscape, while the inclusive nature of the Net allowed individuals to stage their own low-level propaganda fire-fights and 'flame wars' via e-mail. Only the voices of ordinary Kosovo Albanians, expelled from their homes and without access to computers, went largely unheard.

During the Bosnian war, the ZaMir network had hooked up Belgrade with Sarajevo, Zagreb with Ljubljana using a low-tech chain of modems and packet radio. But since the Dayton Agreement the number of Internet users in the former Yugoslavia had expanded to make the Net a mass medium which allowed unfettered communication across the borders. Its potential as a tool for evading censorship was first demonstrated during the student protests of 1996–97, but nevertheless, until the NATO bombing started, the Milošević regime had not really taken the Net seriously as a propaganda weapon (indeed, pro-regime newspaper *Politika* had even published an article claiming that the 'www' code for the worldwide web represented the numbers 666, insinuating that the Net was some kind of diabolical conspiracy).

The Net's most significant impact was at the purely personal level – one-to-one communication across the closed borders of the warring countries. Hundreds of chat rooms, e-mailing lists and Web discussion forums transformed themselves into hectic, fractious hubbubs of conversation and violent argument, enabling ordinary people who were suffering the impact of the conflict to talk directly, without mediation, to those whose governments were carrying out the ethnic cleansing on the one side or sending the stealth bombers airborne on the other.

Some were literally typing as buildings burned outside their windows. As the first air strikes hit Serbia, Vladislava Gordić, a university professor from Novi Sad who used the online pseudonym Insomnia, wrote: 'I was sitting at my computer when my building started shaking with detonations. The sky was lit with yellow and orange flame from the explosion nearby. The attacks were unexpected and sudden, many atomic shelters in apartment buildings and cellars in private houses were locked, damp, dilapidated and unprepared, since no one expected this to happen.'[22]

There were also the voices of those who feared NATO had extinguished any hope for change in their country. 'Although logically it should be feasible to oppose both the NATO action and the Serbian regime at the same time, in reality this is no longer an option,' wrote one, anonymously. 'The air strikes have effectively destroyed what opposition existed, even more efficiently than the repression of the past decade. And, with the dissidents silenced, Milošević has truly emerged as Serbia's supreme and unchallenged ruler.'[23]

And then there were the screams of purest rage, hastily typed with little thought for punctuation or grammar and blasted straight down the wires, like this e-mail from a Serb calling himself 'Baža': 'Good fucking morning to you too. fucking fucking fucking! early morning, 4.50, all fucking

windows were shaking fucking strong, fucking close if anything happen to my son, i will fucking do something nasty,
really nasty i am fucking scared, i am fucking angry, i must
be fucking dangerous and do not anyone EVER dare to
fucking brainwash me about fucking military targets NEVER
FUCKING AGAIN'[24]

Online theorists argued that the Net was 'bringing the war
back home' to the West – into people's living rooms, on to
their desk-tops, and that ignorance of its human cost was no
longer possible. Just as photography, television and CNN-style
24-hour rolling news broadcasts had brought the reality of
battle progressively closer, virtual communication made war
more, not less, real. As one Serb noted as buildings around
him were blasted into rubble: 'This time it's personal.'

At times the arguments reached the level of information
overload, the sheer volume of messages, claims and counter-
claims almost defying comprehension. Initiatives like the
Kosovo Privacy Project attempted to provide forums for ethnic
Albanians, publishing personal letters from refugees on the
run, often unbearably tragic notes to missing loved ones, and
used encryption programs to ensure anonymity and freedom
from surveillance. On the other side of the lines, the much-
celebrated 'cyber monk', Father Sava Janjić, e-mailed eye-
witness reports of the refugee exodus and pleas for peace from
his monastery in Kosovo.

Computer hackers also began to turn the Net into a virtual
battlefield. A Russian pro-Milošević group called CHC broke
into American, British and Chinese websites and replaced
their pages with messages attacking NATO's 'hyper fascism';
another, named KpZ, invaded a NASA site, leaving a picture
of cartoon characters Beavis and Butt-head and the slogan:
'NATO stop killing.' An American cell, The Arbitrary
Command, fought back, breaking into a Serbian university
site and declaring it would be 'held hostage' until three US
airmen captured by Milošević's forces were released, while
another group of US hackers obliterated a Japanese website

with a barely literate manifesto ranting that Serbs 'deserve to be bombed' and demanding that NATO 'burn Milošević's ass'. One hacker simply posted the words: 'Fuck democracy – kill 'em all!'

When a NATO server was bombarded by e-mails, causing it to collapse for twenty-four hours, the Milošević regime claimed it as the 'first Yugoslav victory' of the war. But soon afterwards, the Serbian information minister was forced to admit that his own site had itself been hacked too. American and European government servers were pounded with 'spam' – junk e-mails – by Milošević loyalists. Electronically-altered pornographic pictures of Bill Clinton and Madeleine Albright were circulated.

As the war progressed, the number of Internet users in Serbia grew from 25,000 to around 55,000. Many used it to access the latest developments from the CNN and Sky sites, gathering in the apartments of friends who were online and sharing terminals. For them, it was the only source of alternative information. But some thought the mythologisation of the Internet war masked its lack of genuine impact; propaganda aside, it could do little to protect the refugees in Kosovo or preserve the independent media in Belgrade. 'This new medium has proven particularly vulnerable,' wrote Geert Lovinck of Dutch digital organisation Nettime. 'Not yet war proof. Not much "routing around". A clear lack of satellite telephones, crypto software, laptops and digicams.'[25]

One European Internet activist suggested that techno-journalists could have instigated guerrilla media resistance in the streets of Belgrade, using digital cameras linked to sat-phones to upload images and sound direct to the Net. However, Gordan Paunović of B92 says this simply demonstrates the reality gap between the wired utopians and what was actually happening on the ground in Serbia: 'It was ridiculous. They would have either been arrested and had their equipment stolen – or just killed.' For Paunović, who had left B92's music department and was now the head of new media at the station, the war highlighted the vulnerability rather than the strength of the Net.

Reading from afar, many others simply felt that the heart-rending e-mails confirmed their utter powerlessness to do anything worthwhile. 'Could it be that a real war, with real pain and suffering, reveals just how incapable the Internet and, in particular, online conversations are of enacting real strategies for helping others?' worried technology commentator and author of *Cyberia* Douglas Rushkoff. 'All I see is people who'd like to do something and don't understand why their keyboards can't help them.'[26]

Evicted from their studio, the B92 team tried to campaign for international support with a series of 'Net Aid' webcasts, 24-hour sessions featuring DJs and bands from around the world, transmitted from Amsterdam, Vienna and Belgrade. But B92's Julia Glyn-Pickett has few illusions about what the online concerts achieved. 'It kept us out there. If we hadn't been on the Internet we would have disappeared. In the situation where every minute decides your future, your survival, you have to be there. You have to be doing something. Not only that but on a really basic level it kept people sane. It kept the team together, knowing they were doing something useful.

'In terms of news impact, no, I don't think we were the most important during the NATO air strikes. We weren't in the position to be. Other news sites had a greater impact than us because they were doing live coverage of the air strikes. It wasn't our role to do that.'

The most important achievement, she says, was to 'keep alive a flicker of the other Serbia': once again, just as during the Bosnian conflict, the whole country had become identified with the Milošević ideology. 'We were in a situation where Serbia *was* Milošević and his henchmen, so we were always saying: "No, it's not that simple, there are other people too." It was very difficult doing that because of the propaganda machine that was working on both sides. Challenging the

NATO version of events which one day was "this is against Milošević, not the Serbian people", and the next day "well they're all genocidal lunatics so they get what they deserve". So we carried on and did what we could.'

The Internet did provide a perfect platform for satire. One circular which was passed around the global e-mailing lists offered tourists a unique travel opportunity: 'Experience the explosions and detonations by Tomahawk cruise missiles, cluster bombs and many other radioactive bombs with all known and unknown NATO arsenal on the spot, LIVE! You will experience demolishing of factories, hospitals, schools, buildings, apartments, so as killing innocent civilians and children in a direct vicinity! For our guests with a skin-deep pocket, we offer private accommodation among many mouldy shelters around and below buildings, which will be generously shared with Yugoslav old people and children!'

It also promised a special 'safari tour' ('travel with the refugees across the country, enjoying a unique trip on the red tractors!') and sporting activities ('three miles running and exercise, breathing freshly depleted uranium'). The tour operators named themselves 'JEopardized BIzarre Tourist Entertainment of SErbia', or JEBITESE – Serbian for 'go fuck yourself'. Another prank e-mail offered battle 'souvenirs' for sale, including parts of shot-down US war planes ('F-117A Nighthawk wing structure, 3.3 kg, damaged, $150. Price excludes delivery costs').

The American and Serbian governments became locked in a propaganda duel. The US Information Agency created a Kosovo site and supplied material to sites all over the world in Russian, Albanian and Serbian as well as English – a latter-day re-creation of its now-redundant Cold War role. Special operatives were assigned to monitor online discussions and 'make information available to participants on the spot'.[27] The Serbian government established a similar team of rapid-response e-mailers.

Milošević was a more recent convert to the Internet. His

own Socialist Party site was dull and uninformative, although that of his wife Mira Marković featured page after page of text and pictures and a photo of the JUL leader with a flower in her hair and the message: 'The new world is coming. More rich, more just and more universal.' Son Marko's website, a promotional project for his nightclub Madona, the largest disco in Serbia, was full of the latest browser gimmicks and multimedia applications. He later launched his own Internet service provider, Madona Net. On the official state media sites, photos of bombed buildings were interspersed with rhetoric condemning NATO 'barbarians' and images of children protesting against the air strikes, holding up banners bearing slogans in broken English: 'Chelsea, what is the feeling to be a daughter of children mass killer?'

Although intelligence operatives on both sides took a close interest in the flow of e-mails, neither took the step of directly attacking the Internet's infrastructure. Belgrade TV reports suggested that Milošević envisaged the Net as another weapon in his media armoury to weaken Western resolve, while NATO believed that the free flow of information could undermine his regime by diluting Serbian morale. However, military planners at the Pentagon in Washington did prepare a document on the potential of launching cyber assaults on Serbian computer networks to disrupt the operations of Milošević's forces, raid bank accounts, shut down electricity plants and terminate phone connections. These were rejected because the Defence Department's lawyers believed they could lay the US open to war crimes charges – although it was confirmed that America had begun to assemble a 'cyber arsenal' for use in future wars, including 'computer viruses or "logic bombs" to disrupt enemy networks, the feeding of false information to sow confusion and the morphing of video images on to foreign television stations to deceive'.[28]

As other outlets fell silent, the war inspired the creation of a new independent media initiative in Belgrade. Galvanised by the information ministry's censorship and what they perceived as the bias of Western satellite channels, a group of student activists and computer programmers, many of whom had been involved in organising street protests throughout the nineties, got together a few days after the NATO air strikes were launched to found a new Web magazine called, optimistically, *Free Serbia*.

'We wanted to break the media blockade which was imposed from both sides. Our slogan was "anti-NATO, anti-Milošević",' says programmer Janja Bobić. 'It was very amusing because we were receiving e-mails from abroad saying we were Milošević's servants, just another Serbian propaganda site, and e-mails from Serbia telling us we were traitors and mercenaries. So we knew we were doing the right thing because *everyone* hated us.'

*Free Serbia* attempted to document civilian casualties and discover what was happening to Albanian refugees in Kosovo, collating information via e-mail, bulletin boards, ham radio and reports from human rights organisations in Priština. It also tried to counter state disinformation about the level of bombing damage in Belgrade. After the death of Slavko Ćuruvija, some of its staff received warnings that they were being watched, but there was no attempt to censor the site.

'I don't think we make some kind of revolutionary impact,' admits Bobić. 'It just makes us feel better because there is not much you can do in this country. I spent the whole of my 20s out on the streets protesting and nothing changed, but with this website, I feel I'm making some kind of difference. That's what holds us together.'

Just as the war itself was virtual, fought by air crews and thousands of technicians at computer consoles rather than soldiers and tanks, and real death and suffering remained relatively abstract concepts as far as NATO countries were concerned, the only interesting things happening in Belgrade during its bombardment were completely virtual too. The Cyber Café site, an urban pop webzine, covered clubs, bars, sex and fashion – all the glittering trinkets of lifestyle consumerism which didn't actually exist in the real world at that time. Unlike life itself, Cyber Café was bright, shiny and optimistic. 'It was a kind of therapy. We were doing it and pretending there was nothing going on outside,' says programmer Slobodan Marković, who also ran the Internodium e-mailing list, a discussion forum for open-source software enthusiasts and do-it-yourself MP3 music freaks. The only drawback was the intermittent power cuts: 'At times we were praying to [Supreme Allied Commander] Wesley Clark not to disconnect our electric grid. Every time we heard a siren we would say: "Oh Wesley, not now, please!" But most of the time he wouldn't listen.'

Marković spent the war circulating reports on the psychological condition of the city over the Internet, and discovered that many foreigners assumed everyone in Belgrade supported Milošević's Kosovo operation. 'The hate mails I received usually sounded like they weren't addressing me, but Slobodan Milošević himself – they were saying: "Why are *you* killing Albanians in Kosovo?" One guy from France even asked me whether I was one of Milošević's ministers.'

On 9 June, after seventy-eight days of bombing, the war ended as NATO troops entered Kosovo. Milošević was charged with war crimes, but remained militarily undefeated. State television announced that the president's peace policy had triumphed, and Serbia was the victor. It was time to celebrate.

'North or south, all is destroyed,' wrote one Belgrade journalist anonymously. 'Bridges no longer exist, the motorway is history, the energy system is trashed and the electricity out. The entire country is ruin: bricks, cement, shards of glass. We have been bombed into the past.

'There is no economy. Optimists say that more than three million are unemployed, while pessimists project the figure at four million. The post office does not function, newspapers look like fascist party bulletins, the state of war remains in place. Yet what is this compared to the fact that the policy of our president has won?

'Intoxicated by peace, touting placards of our president and reports that Kosovo has defended itself, we, the zombies of Yugoslavia, know that we are the Best, the Strongest, the Brightest, the Heavenly. It will just take a few centuries for the rest of the world to acknowledge it.

'See you in the next war.'[29]

# 6

# surreal life
# 1999 – 2000

'Now is the worst time in Serbia this decade. This repression,
people being killed, people disappearing. We have gone from
Germany in the thirties to South America in the eighties . . .
what a trip!' *Srdjan Andjelić, B92 presenter (1999)*

The conclusion of the NATO bombing left Belgrade in its
worst ever psychological state. Disillusioned, angry, impoverished and downtrodden, its social life, like many of its public
buildings, in ruins, its independent media crushed, its political
opposition cowed and impotent.

The economy was devastated; an estimated fifty per cent
of the adult population was unemployed and seventy per
cent were living on the edge of the poverty line. Pensions
went unpaid for months. Teachers and civil servants did not
receive their salaries. Doctors demanded tips due to lack of
wages. Disability and child benefits were months in arrears.
Tens of thousands of citizens relied on food hand-outs to eat.
Electric power and oil were in short supply, with restrictions
expected for the coming winter. According to official statistics,
the average monthly income had dropped to around eighty
Deutschmarks, and the gross national product was down by a
fifth. A new wave of emigration began to swell.

'Reconstruction and economic recovery are proceeding
successfully,' stated deputy prime minister Dragan Tomić.

Each day, state TV service RTS had wonderful news for its

flock. Its publicity campaign, entitled 'The Reconstruction Of The Country From The Consequences Of NATO Aggression', regularly featured pictures of cheery officials and jolly workers opening up bridges, roads and factories which had been damaged during the bombing. Milošević spoke of bountiful harvests, plentiful oil for heating and the imminent revival of industry. As the acutely pessimistic Petar Luković noted: 'We have triumphantly defeated NATO, defended Kosovo, and managed to return the United Nations to its rightful place. Now we have embarked on the glorious Reconstruction.'[1]

Unfortunately, some of these fantastic feats of renewal were not actually taking place in the real world, only in the fantasy Serbia of RTS. Daily newspaper *Blic* reported that a film crew turned up to document the rebuilding of a bombed-out house and organised a crowd of curious bystanders for the occasion. Once they had finishing shooting, the crowd and crew both left, and no more work was done on the house.

Entertainment channels like TV Pink and TV Palma also delivered a relentlessly upbeat message, their gaudily-dressed presenters grinning inanely over the tinkling backbeat of Balkan techno-pop. 'Just watch Pink TV and you'll see what their idea of Serbia is: we are fun, we are clubbing, we are dancing, we are saying stupid things about love, we are rich – it's beautiful!' sneers Luković. 'Forget about the war, forget about everything, enjoy yourself!'

There were now two countries called Serbia, the real world of poverty and depression, and the surreal world where life was getting better each day and the citizens basked in the warmth of the love of their president.

'If I was him, our dictator, I'd no longer be afraid of anything,' wrote young playwright Biljana Srbljanović. 'I wouldn't worry about electricity cuts, as I have a generator. I wouldn't worry about water shortages, as I have my own supplies. I wouldn't worry about any future military inter- vention, as my bunker is indestructible. My subjects would receive the punishment for me, and I would interpret that as loyalty to the regime. If I were a dictator in this world I'd promptly send a thank-you note to [NATO headquarters in] Brussels.'[2]

Those who couldn't cope with reality turned to the paranormal for comfort. Magazines with names like *The Twilight Zone*, *The Third Eye* and *Phenomena* proliferated. One of them explained how NATO's global domination drive was actually the masterplan of evil aliens who had possessed the brains of Bill Clinton, Tony Blair and other Western leaders. 'If one were to switch off the impulses radiated at the US president by the extra-terrestrials, only a sax player would remain,' it insisted.[3]

Another suggested that an 'Order of the Fourth Reich' was intent on establishing a new world order as decreed by their master, the devil. The only ones who could stand up to it were the Serbs, who it was explained had set up a special para-psychological task force to combat the US army's nefarious voodoo and save the world from eternal subjugation. The magazines often mirrored the familiar nationalist ideology of Serbs as victims, but cloaked it in the extraterrestrial hoodoo of the *X-Files*.

The aliens who came from slightly closer to home – the Serb refugees who had fled Kosovo – were accommodated in camps whose existence was denied by the government and their locations concealed to avoid embarrassing evidence of defeat which contradicted the exultant official line.

Even schoolchildren were given a lesson in propaganda. Education supremo Jovan Todorović ordered that a message be read out at the start of term telling the kids how they had suffered in a war between 'hypocrisy and truth, high technology and classical weapons, cold-blooded mass murderers and dignified defenders of the homeland, formalised manipulative religion and the true faith'. He signed it, rather touchingly: 'Yours, Uncle Education Minister.'

Meanwhile Bill Clinton – along with Madeleine Albright,

Tony Blair and sundry other American, British and French dignitaries – was called to stand trial in the district court of the small town of Valjevo, eighty miles from Belgrade, to answer charges of war crimes against Yugoslav civilians. It is not known whether Clinton actually received the summons, but he did not make an appearance in court on the appointed date.

War heroes were feted for their role in the victorious campaign. Mira Marković's JUL party proposed that the president, although indicted as a war criminal by the United Nations, should be decorated as a 'national hero', hymning him as 'a symbol of our freedom, our existence and survival, our faith and hope, our present and future'. Milošević strived to portray himself as a world leader who retained the respect of the international powers that mattered, the ones he referred to as the last remaining 'free states': China, North Korea, Libya and Iraq. The state newspapers were constantly full of news from China, which had provided Serbia with $300 million in aid.

It was suggested that the Chinese and Serbia's other 'true friends' might combine in a new post-Soviet bloc to wage what the information minister referred to as the 'struggle against American imperialism and hegemony'. For those who still dreamed of democracy and an end to isolation, the suggestion of an international alliance of oppressors was terrifying. 'You can laugh at this – I'm laughing – but at the same time the effects of this idea are here and very serious,' says Petar Luković. 'We are living in the past and every minute we are going further and further back into history.'

However, the president's 'glorious victory' was not universally popular. Directly after the ceasefire, in a spontaneous outburst of rage, crowds of people poured out on to the streets shouting abuse about Milošević's loss of Kosovo or demanding the names of those killed and missing in the war. They were joined by reservist soldiers who had discovered they would not be paid for fighting in Kosovo, and demonstrators calling for the president's resignation. A TV producer in the town of

Leskovac was jailed for thirty days after airing a video inciting people to protest against Milošević in a break during a televised basketball game; tens of thousands came out in support.

In September, a group of opposition parties which had united under the banner Alliance for Change began daily demonstrations all over the country. The regime's response was vicious. When 30,000 people tried to march on Milošević's Belgrade home, they were met by riot police with armoured cars, batons and water cannon; more than sixty were injured in the beatings. One activist who was so badly clubbed he became disabled was charged with causing injuries to the policemen who attacked him. The printing firm which produced the Alliance's leaflets was hit with fifty-two charges of 'publishing an unlicensed paper'. The first brace of convictions resulted in a total of 1.65 million dinars in fines.

The Alliance leaders were, predictably, demonised as foreign spies and Clinton's puppets. Mira Marković's party even played on traditional Serbian homophobia by accusing them of 'having a weakness towards the same sex' and being mentally unstable delinquents. After the Alliance's representatives met a US special envoy in Hungary, Vojislav Šešelj's Radical Party announced that they were receiving new orders for conquering Serbia on behalf of NATO.

However, the Alliance for Change protests never accumulated the momentum of the 1996–97 uprising. They couldn't summon up the same vivid imagination, creativity and wit. The familiar shrill of whistles – far fewer this time – sounded more desperate than defiant, and Vuk Drašković, still a charismatic and inspirational presence on Belgrade's boulevards despite his spell in the government, refused to join the coalition, depriving it of his hardcore of street toughs. The columns of protesters were pitifully ragged. By December 1999, exhausted and unhappy, the daily walks around Belgrade had dwindled to mere hundreds, and were eventually cancelled.

But the new student movement which was gathering force

in the capital was less easily intimidated. Otpor (Resistance) had been founded by fifteen friends at Belgrade University in October 1998 in response to the repressive University and Public Information decrees. Sick of the endless compromises, defeats and endemic apathy, Otpor demanded the repeal of both pieces of legislation, the democratic overthrow of Milošević and a stronger role for students – those who had not been tainted by collaboration with successive Yugoslav despots – in shaping the Serbia of tomorrow.

In a purposeful break with the student movements of the past, Otpor became a kind of urban vigilante sect which operated on a non-hierarchical, cellular structure, with no leaders, no hierarchy, no voting procedures and no set ideology other than the replacement of the president. Similar to Western environmental protest factions like Earth First! and Reclaim the Streets, Otpor was an ad hoc, often anarchic collective whose members were encouraged to organise and take responsibility for their own actions. They were galvanised by the failure of the 1996–97 demonstrations, in which many had participated, and were determined to learn from their mistakes, particularly the co-option of certain student leaders by opposition politicians and the way that, once the student demands appeared to have been met, the impetus simply fizzled out into inertia.

Otpor had made an immediate and explosive impact. In November 1998, four students were arrested after spray-painting the organisation's clenched-fist symbol on walls in central Belgrade and jailed for ten days. Then Slavko Ćuruvija published their quasi-poetic manifesto in his *Dnevni Telegraf* newspaper: 'Don't wait until someone you love gets killed, don't wait until the last source is poisoned, don't wait until it's too late for everything – resist.'

The Otpor fist began to appear everywhere. People were confused: this was a traditional socialist image; what could it mean? Was it some new government propaganda? Vandals, perhaps? Or something more sinister?

'Those first two or three months were incredible,' says Milja Jovanović, an intense young indie rock aficionado who was converted from her initial distrust of any political activity by Otpor's emphasis on individualism. 'You would hear people on the bus talking about the fist, who is behind it, is it just another regime scam, is it just some party trying to create a different image. The police were very nervous about the fist so it was risky to wear an Otpor badge or a T-shirt, they could harass you, ask you for ID, make you pay some fine for whatever reason.'

During the NATO bombing, Otpor had suspended its activities: the climate was too unstable. 'We went to see Slavko Ćuruvija about three weeks before he was killed and he said: "You will be in great danger because you are very important to the regime." So we didn't do anything for those three months, just stayed in touch,' says Jovanović. 'We knew if we did any actions during the war, it would be used against us. We all stayed undercover, some of us in our homes here, some of us elsewhere in Serbia. Some were drafted to the army and it was terrible because somebody could have killed them and just said a bomb fell on them because a lot of the bodies of young soldiers never came back home. A lot of parents don't know where their sons are buried.

'We knew there was repression of Albanians in Kosovo, and of course they fought back. We were against NATO but we had the sense that NATO wasn't our business; there was something nearer that was our responsibility – the regime which let NATO bomb Serbia. It's very hard to talk about that because patriotism is very strong in Otpor – healthy nationalism, you could call it, because we all have a mutual enemy, the system which made strangers like the West, Croats and neighbouring countries our enemies.'

In July 1999, the protests resumed, as they parodied and poked fun at the establishment, playing games with its words and turning them against it. The government placed collection boxes in Belgrade streets to raise funds for farmers. The boxes carried the slogan: 'A dinar for sowing.' Otpor responded with its own collection, entitled 'A dinar for resignation',

To celebrate the year 2000, Otpor staged a concert in Republic Square. While the crowd of 10,000 was waiting for the fun to start, a four-minute film of Serbia's horrific recent history was shown on a huge screen. Then they announced: 'Serbia doesn't have any reason to celebrate anything, not even the new millennium. It was 1999, it's now 2000, but nothing has really changed. In fact it's all getting worse. And you must go home now without your celebration, because you have no reason to celebrate.' The crowd dispersed without protest.

They also staged a demonstration outside the military court where thousands of cases were ongoing against young people who refused to be drafted into the army. The demonstrators were Otpor members who decided not to evade the call-up and had actually joined the army – the people the regime hymned as 'patriots' were standing up for those who were demonised as 'traitors'.

Jovanović – another activist claiming influence from *Monty Python* – describes the movement's actions as a kind of allegorical, absurdist performance art. But if they were fun, they were also perilous; Otpor's first year saw 150 arrests and a host of police beatings. The students carried on regardless – after a decade of setbacks, they felt they had nothing to lose.

From its outset, Otpor chose not to act in the traditional slapdash, ill-planned, careless manner of Serbia's political opposition. Theirs was a sophisticated marketing campaign, co-ordinated from a bustling first-floor flat in downtown Belgrade, employing the same tactics as advertising agencies use to promote their product. Their posters, badges and T-shirts were meticulously designed, each one using identical corporate typefaces and black-and-white colour schemes. Stencils were distributed for graffiti campaigns; Otpor matchboxes handed out in bars; a series of gigs was staged all across the country with bands like Darkwood Dub and Kanda Kodža I Nebojša. The idea was to make the imagery of organised dissent – the fist – ubiquitous. To let people know they weren't alone. It was an infectious, self-replicating virus that began to break out all over Serbia; many of its supporters, wearing clenched-fist badges and scrawling slogans on walls, weren't even eighteen years old. The appearance of anti-Otpor posters in Belgrade depicting them as slaves to the Yankee dollar and sweethearts of Madeleine Albright because of their acceptance of funding from Western benefactors only served to confirm their growing influence.

Although some Otpor activists were members of political parties, and the opposition tried its best to drag the movement into its orbit, the students retained a healthy distaste for the realpolitik of collaboration. Otpor would amount to nothing if it didn't stay clean. 'The opposition parties made such fools of themselves because they all worked with the regime at some level,' says Jovanović. 'We never did and this makes the regime very nervous when they see the fist.'

Hers was the last generation, says Jovanović, with genuine memories of old Communism and the Tito years: 'A lot of older people still remember how they cried when Tito died – I remember how there were no cartoons on TV.' Otpor, she believes, was becoming a training camp for the leaders of the future and an education in independent thought for ordinary Serbs. 'The long-term aim of our movement is creating a second political generation in Serbia – not just politicians who think differently, but public opinion which will be careful about who it supports,' she says.

'We can blame Milošević for everything, but that's not right. We can acknowledge that he is responsible for the state of Serbia, that he fought wars that brought a lot of pain to a lot of people, a lot of people were killed and expelled from their countries – but he is not the only one to blame. If I didn't have enough strength, enough time, enough will to resist, I, like every other person in Serbia, must bear a small part of the responsibility for everything that has happened.'

With the opposition impotent, Otpor rapidly established

itself as public enemy number one. After senior Socialist Party politician Boško Perošević was shot in May 2000, the government accused Otpor of being complicit in his killing, and announced an imminent crackdown, threatening to arrest anyone who acted against it. Otpor members were called hooligans, terrorists and paramilitaries, and compared to the Hitler Youth. Milošević himself warned that fascism, in the form of the opposition, was rising again to menace Serbia. In the weeks that followed, scores of Otpor activists were seized in a wave of arbitrary detentions. Nevertheless, they vowed not to give up.

'I'm not afraid of what will happen to me personally,' says Milja Jovanović. 'If I get tired, if I give up, if I'm arrested and put in jail, if I'm shot – I don't know what may happen – there are a lot of other people to continue this. We are trying to build a system that is completely different from the one we grew up in. Maybe it will take twenty years – OK, we are prepared for that. The regime can be changed with one election, but the system will take much longer.'

'This is Radio B2–92. Serbia calling. This is Serbia calling. Radio B2–92.'

Announcer: 'B2–92 programme. 99.1 FM. From morning to dusk.'

Sampled voice of Veran Matić: 'Free B92.'

Announcer: 'The third channel of Studio B.'

Sounds of a flushing toilet and a gong banging, then the sampled voice of Slobodan Milošević: 'This is a great achievement. I congratulate you on it. I wish you a lot of success.'

Gong bangs again, followed by the sampled voice of Vuk Drašković: 'You'll not sleep, you'll not rest. Let us clean the ears of the deaf.'

Gong followed by sampled voice: 'Almost all our men here can speak in rhymes.'

Gong followed by sampled voice: 'How much milk do you get per cow?'

Gong followed by sampled voice: 'Everyone has as much information as he wants.'

Announcer: 'Radio B2–92, morning news bulletin.'

On 2 August, 1999, this impudent collage announced that Radio B92 was back on the air again. Except it was no longer called B92 – that name was still being used by the state-imposed loyalist management which had taken over the station back in April. This was B2–92. And it was no longer based in the House of Youth in the heart of the city centre, but on the seventeenth floor of Beogradjanka, the tallest office block in Belgrade, a creaking carbuncle whose design was a capsule tribute to the bad taste of the seventies; a rhapsody in brown from its carpet to its fittings. B2–92 was using a spare channel owned by Studio B, the radio and TV station run by Belgrade city council, which was now under the control of Vuk Draško-vić's Serbian Renewal Movement. It relocated to Studio B's office complex. A borrowed frequency, borrowed premises and, perhaps, borrowed time.

The news and music policies remained the same, but streamlined and computerised to suit the new slimmed-down, potentially temporary circumstances. Broadcasting hours were reduced to twelve per day. Many wondered whether Draš-ković, whose Studio B television news displayed a hefty bias towards his own party's activities, would insist that B2–92 cut him some favours. While the RTS building was known as the 'Bastille', Beogradjanka was called the 'little Bastille', an indication of how Belgraders rated Studio B's integrity. Studio B television was nicknamed 'Vukovision'. Drašković had recently joined in the attacks on the independent press. Others thought he was using the dissident broadcasters to rehabilitate himself in the eyes of voters who had not forgiven him for the time he spent cosying up to Milošević earlier that year, or that he had succumbed to American pressure to give B2–92 a frequency.

'It was a big test for us when we started again because

everybody was thinking, will it still be the old B92?' says managing director Saša Mirković. 'We said of course it will, but told them they had to listen for a few days to be sure.'

Veran Matić insists that he would never have accepted the frequency without a guarantee of total independence. 'Vuk Drašković and the Serbian Renewal Movement are a significant political factor. Without Drašković it is difficult to imagine the current regime being replaced. That's a fact, whether you like him or not,' he states. 'That it was Studio B which enabled us to broadcast is also a fact. But that doesn't mean that anybody, especially Vuk Drašković, is interfering in our programmes. We would never accept anyone interfering in our work.'

He promised that if Drašković ever decided to make another deal with the regime, the agreement would be off. But there was also the further worry that if the Socialists took back the leadership of the city council, and with it Studio B, B2–92 would be kicked out without notice. One DJ noted laconically: 'The frequency is, from a legal point of view, safe from government attack. But that doesn't mean anything, as we know.'

The station's declared independence meant that it hadn't maintained a cosy relationship with the opposition parties over the years. Many of their leaders believed that anyone opposed to Milošević should automatically give them unequivocally positive coverage and never criticise their failings or expose their fallings-out. In a media environment which had been tightly controlled by the political elite since World War Two, with no traditions of public-service or commercial broadcasting, most politicians found the concept of editorial autonomy hard to fully comprehend.

'For many people, independence automatically means opposition, which is not true,' says Saša Mirković. 'You have opposition media which directly support opposition parties, then you have independent media like us. We used to say: "When you are independent, everyone hates you". Governments are attacking you because you criticise them; the opposition hates you because you are criticising them too, because they have no ideas and they're not smart enough.'

'We have good relationships with the opposition parties but sometimes they get angry because they think we should portray them as angels,' adds news reporter Zoran Mamula. 'But sometimes they are wrong, so we criticise them and they ring up and shout at us. But we don't give a damn.'

In the past, the station hadn't spared any politician's feelings. 'Opposition parties have their own agenda,' continues Saša Mirković. 'The majority of them, during the wars here, have been nationalistic, and when war started nobody wanted to defend us. Now everybody is fighting for their position for the future. A lot of opposition parties think B2–92 could be a possible political rival or partner – they're afraid that we have political ambitions.'

He believes that certain politicians would have been happy to buy off B2–92 journalists with offers of apartments, cars or money, or to blackmail them for taking bribes from other parties – 'but of course they can't do it because we haven't received anything'. These pressures didn't always come from within Serbia – despite the regime propaganda portraying the station as a NATO quisling, it also caught flak from its American donors when it refused to support US foreign policy and condone the NATO air attacks.

Within a few months – and despite a degree of criticism for having become too formatted and unadventurous – B2–92 had risen to third place in the ratings chart for Belgrade. The impostors who had usurped their premises had fallen to twentieth. Matić was overjoyed: 'It's important for us to have our revenge on the regime and come back even stronger than we went down,' he smiled. And the ANEM network's out-reach was edging nearer and nearer to that of state radio. 'In 1997, we had 1.5 million radio listeners, and they had 2 million,' says ANEM co-chairman Milorad Tadić. 'In 1999, we did more research and we had 1.3 million listeners – some local stations had been taken over by the regime – and they had 1.5 million. So we are very close. We are becoming a serious problem for them.'

The court cases instigated to regain control of the old B92 offices and equipment were progressing slowly, although the outcome looked unpromising without political change at the top. Many of Veran Matić's staff were still furious about losing their studio, but some had become blasé, saying that eviction was just another mantrap in the dangerous terrain they chose to inhabit. 'Maybe one day they will all be removed from there so we can all go back, but now I really don't care,' says DJ Vladimir Janjić. 'At first I was down, but then I realised the only thing they really took was our name. They will get what they deserve one day – I'm not going to take part in it, you know, but one day they will pay for what they did to us.'

Wooden and unimaginative, the puppet B92 more than deserved its lowly showing in the radio ratings chart. Its bulletins were taken direct from the state news agency or ruling party press releases (sample headlines: 'Price Rises Are Slowing Down'; 'President Milošević Receives A Delegation From The Communist Party Of China'). It played a constant procession of mainstream pop hits, with evening shows dedicated to chirpy seventies disco or the recordings of superannuated rockers like Jethro Tull.

The new head of music, Branislav Boksić, an electrical engineering student with a ponytail and thinning hair, claimed to despise politics and simply wanted to entertain, unlike the DJs he replaced, whose music he found amateurish and unpleasant: 'We don't play things that are too ugly or too cheap. Before you couldn't hear the Rolling Stones, you couldn't hear Boney M, you couldn't hear Diana Ross. You only heard bands that people didn't even know the names of. It was just alternative, alternative, alternative,' he complains. 'I don't think an alternative musician is a real musician – he is alternative because he can't sing or play well.'

The entrance to the studio was guarded by crop-haired

young bruisers in shell-suits. In the management office, middle-aged men in suits and ties sat around smoking cigarettes and chatting idly while bottle blondes in short skirts plastered on layers of make-up. Compared to the frenetic pace of the B2–92 offices, the almost total lack of activity was striking. The phones rarely rang. Little work was done. No one seemed to care much. Posters for films produced by the old B92 team remained on the walls; the new management had kept their archives, their videos, books and CDs. One of B92's CD releases, a superb drum'n'bass and techno compilation album entitled *Millennium Funk*, had been completed only days before the takeover. It was a big hit in Belgrade in the summer of 1999, and the new bosses sold off the entire edition for a tidy profit.

The puppet B92 staff were told that their predecessors were no longer working there because they had been involved in illicit currency dealings and had libelled politicians. But loyalist boss Nikačević and his cronies had problems too; many of their workers departed hurriedly within the first few months. Even music editor Boksić thought that his bosses weren't exactly consummate professionals: 'It's hard. Some of the management don't know too much about radio,' he says. 'I've got two dogs at home, I think sometimes they understand more than people who are working here with me.'

Boksić's programming policy also included plenty of vintage Yugoslav rock from the eighties – a time increasingly viewed with wistful nostalgia. Peaceful, prosperous and safe in its post-Tito stagnation, Yugoslavia was still one great, paternalistic country which took care of its citizens, cocooned by the watchful benevolence of the Communist Party. B2–92 DJ Tomislav Grujić describes the cult of eighties rock as 'music for oblivion'. 'It's an anaesthetic for the masses. It's like someone is saying to you, look what a great life you had and *they* ruined it – the Croatians, the Bosnians, the Slovenians, the West, the whole world. It's not that this music is bad, but the connotations are bad. It means something else, it means these times were really great, these times should not have changed, no one should have allowed different political parties, this was the cause of all this shit that has happened. Let's stay in the past and sleep on.'

The impostor station's mediocrity – a daily fare of nostalgia, insularity and thoughtless entertainment designed not to stimulate or provoke – demonstrated how intertwined culture and politics had become in the Milošević era. Music reinforced the political message: ask no questions.

Belgrade's entire cultural scene had been devastated by the conflict. The city, says journalist Duška Anastasijević, had been turned into a village. 'It's so claustrophobic and suffocating here now. You can't meet new people, it's a closed circle, you know everybody and you know everything about everybody.

'Your circles shrink: first you judged your friends according to their views on the wars in Croatia and Bosnia, and you fell out with some of them, then you judged them on Kosovo, which was a test for many people who opposed the war in Bosnia but then thought Albanians should be killed. Then you judged them on the NATO bombing – OK, I didn't approve of it but I could not say, "oh, the West is crazy", because I could understand the rationale behind it. Everything has become so political. I could never imagine dating someone whose political ideas were different from mine. It's sad but it's a fact.'

Bars and clubs in the Old Town were open again – many had worked on through the bombing – but few people could afford to spend much money on leisure. Gigs were even more rare than before. 'We don't have any culture left now,' suggests Petar Luković. 'All we have is history, nationalism, politics and craziness, and there is no way to escape it. All the events that are going on here – a few records, a few books, a few gigs, a few films – are just a virtual reality. They are just one per cent of what we had before. This is not real life, this is not real culture.

'The most important question is how to survive, and if you

are faced with this question, all other things seem abstract, reserved for the privileged. Nobody is interested in the things we are talking about now. They are just for a few bizarre people like me. Go into the street and look how people are going through dumpsters every day: for them, the question of culture has become irrelevant. I'm sorry I sound pessimistic, but there is not one single fucking reason for me to be optimistic.'

Club culture had also lost its sparkle as poverty emasculated the hedonistic impulse. 'You can't talk about clubbing in Belgrade now. It stinks,' says clubber Ivana Vasić. 'You want to go out, but it's all fake, it just looks like a simulation of life. It's not real. I can't relax, I can't be happy like I used to, because of what happens to you during the day you can't just switch to another kind of emotion when you go out at night.

'You can't afford to drink as much as you want. You have to wear old clothes, never anything new. You just can't *afford* to be happy.

'Sometimes when I go out I try to pretend that I'm somewhere else and to see it through different eyes – as if it was all colourful and cheerful. But it doesn't work. I don't know whether it's better for someone to have been somewhere and seen something better and to remember what they saw, or not to have seen anything at all and not to know that there is anything better.

'It's exhausting. You don't think in terms of what you are *able* to do, but what you are *allowed* to. I know it's a cliché, but I don't want to stay here any more – if I stay I'm afraid I'm going to turn into a bitter and unsatisfied and angry person like all our parents are.

'This is just a ghost town now.'

The near-fatal condition of Belgrade pop culture could be seen each week on the first floor of the Student Cultural Centre, where bootleg traders would assemble to sell racks of pirated CDs and computer games at around three Deutschmarks a throw. The albums, complete with amateurishly laser-

copied sleeves, ranged from the latest Western pop releases to
Balkan rock bands, obscure jazz, Chicago house mixes and
the entire back catalogues of stars like David Bowie and the
Rolling Stones. The bootleggers would even assemble their
own unique compilations of their favourite artists. The room
would always be packed with audiophiles browsing furiously
and vendors counting wads of notes. The bootlegs, it was said,
were manufactured in Bulgaria – and as one rock journalist
says ironically: 'We used to laugh at the Bulgarian music scene,
but now we rely on it.'

While the global corporations which dominate the music
business could easily afford to lose a tiny sliver of their profits
– not that they released CDs in Serbia anyway – the indigenous
music scene was hit hardest. A legitimate copy of a local band's
CD would cost far more than a pirate version of a Western
release, therefore sales were decimated and it became increasingly difficult to survive as a musician in Belgrade and afford
to make decent-quality studio recordings.

The pirate vendors operated without interference from the
police, which some found suspicious. 'The regime just doesn't
care about piracy – or else maybe some of them or their
children are involved in that business,' says Vladimir Janjić,
who co-ordinated the production for B2–92's CD label.
'There is an official copyright agency here, I go there every
time we have a release to get a licence to produce the CDs,
and they are also completely scared because they cannot do
anything either.'

The legitimate CD market was dominated by businessmen
with links to the regime. City Records – an offshoot of TV
Pink, whose owner was close to the JUL party of Mira Marković – was the most hated. The label managed to sign bands
with opposition sympathies who had, some believed, traded
their principles to further their careers. 'They are giving an
alibi to somebody who is corrupt – it's selling out of the worst
kind,' says Milja Jovanović of the student movement Otpor.
'It's not like being on an independent label in Britain and

then signing to a major label – not that kind of subcultural "selling out" – it is giving an alibi to a regime that represses you.'

Nor was Hollywood exempt from the pirates' touch. State television regularly showed illicit copies of blockbuster movies before their official release dates. On the day of an opposition demonstration in April 2000, a trio of hit films – *American Beauty, The World Is Not Enough* and *Eyes Wide Shut* – was screened in an attempt to keep people at home in front of their televisions. The state might have despised the West and all its cultural artefacts, but it was not averse to making use of them when it was needed.

Piracy and bootlegging weren't confined to pop culture; they were evident everywhere in Belgrade and had infected the entire economic life of the country. The boulevards were lined with men in scruffy trainers and dirty shell-suits with hand-written signs scrawled on ripped pieces of cardboard selling petrol and diesel from plastic fizzy-drink bottles. Old women hawked boxes of Lucky Strikes, while returning exiles brought bottles of spirits and expensive disposable nappies across the border to their impoverished relatives. This ad hoc economy even had its own smell: the reek of gasoline as drivers siphoned bootleg petrol into their cars and the acrid smell of low-grade benzene burning.

In every neighbourhood, money-changers with ill-barbered moustaches and battered brown leather jackets lolled on the corner, offering to swap Deutschmarks for dinars: an instant gauge of how the economy was faring. These were Serbia's dealing floors, and the slightest upward fluctuation of the exchange rate revived fears of a return to the hyperinflation of 1993, as people worried that Milošević might be printing money to cover the costs of rebuilding the country and risking financial meltdown. 'As this is a closed economy, even one newly printed dinar's impact can be felt,' said one black-market dealer.

This was survivalist capitalism at work; brutal and unforgiving. Serbia was run on a mixture of patronage, bribery, illegal import–export, nepotism and physical force. Despite the professed socialism of the ruling party, the state had retreated, taking the spoils with it, and left the people to fight amongst themselves over the scraps.

The long years of sanctions meant that corruption and smuggling had become inextricably bound up with the economic survival of the country. Criminality was institutionalised, as companies close to the regime made deals with gangsters to circumvent the international boycott. By 1999, according to the anti-corruption agency Transparency International, Yugoslavia could boast the most corrupt officials in Europe. Judges could be bought, as could university professors. A degree could be purchased for 6,000 Deutschmarks, it was estimated. Humanitarian aid for refugees was siphoned off and resold. Corruption was omnipresent; bribery almost an everyday necessity.

All businesses existed, at least in part, in a grey area on the very edge of the law. Legally, they were compelled to exchange foreign currency for dinars at the official rate – which was much lower than that offered by the black-market money-changers. Everyone used companies – often those who advertised themselves as 'marketing' firms – to change cash for them. Although this was the only way most businesses could ensure their survival, it laid them open to the constant threat of legal action from the financial authorities. This, naturally, suited the regime as it could then close down any operation whose activities did not meet its approval.

'I would be the happiest person in the world if I could change money at a normal rate, not losing a third of the amount,' says one young executive. 'But the problem is this system has been created in such a way that the government is pushing you to work on the edge of legality, and using that for political purposes so they can attack you if they want.'

The state-sponsored degradation of the judiciary and the

police force meant that Serbia had become a kind of lawless zone. 'Anything goes here. You can do whatever you want, because nobody cares,' says Julia Glyn-Pickett of B2–92. 'Someone I know was carrying a camera over the border at the airport and got asked: "What's that for?" He thought, OK, I can't say it's for training people in news production. So he said: "It's for pornography." And the Customs officer smiled and said: "OK, no problem, away you go." Picture the reverse coming into an EU airport: training and news production would be no problem, but pornography? No way!'

A local club promoter summed up the situation simply: 'In Belgrade, everything is possible and nothing is possible. Everything is permitted and nothing is permitted.'

This pervasive feeling of lawlessness spread despite the exponential growth of the police force. Milošević, who treated the police as his personal paramilitary guard, had increased its numbers and its power. Police checkpoints were everywhere, on insignificant street corners as well as the major highways and boulevards. Drivers expected to be stopped regularly and asked for their papers. Policemen would check tyres and lamps and exact the occasional on-the-spot 'fine'. They were augmented by the patrols of interior ministry officers in combat fatigues carrying automatic rifles.

Belgrade citizens were encouraged to spy on their neighbours, checking for indications of potential Albanian 'terrorism'. Police announced plans to call on every home in the capital to check documents were in order, and men of fighting age were asked to visit interior ministry offices to have their home addresses confirmed.

Serbia was visibly being transformed into a police state, dressed up and armed for repression. The perpetual sense of impending violence was heightened when a series of key political players was attacked in the space of a few months. In October 1999, Vuk Drašković narrowly escaped death in a head-on collision with a truck which killed four of his friends and colleagues. It was, Drašković alleged, unquestionably an assassination attempt: 'At one point, out of the blue, and with no reason, without anyone overtaking anyone, five metres before passing by, the truck swerved into our lane. It was then clear to me that he wanted to kill me.'[4] Members of a group calling itself the Serbian Liberation Army were later arrested, although many believed the hand of the regime was at work. Three media organisations were fined huge sums under the Public Information Law for reporting a statement which suggested government involvement. (In June 2000, another attempt would be made on Drašković's life, when he was shot and wounded by a gunman in Montenegro.)

Zoran Djindjić, head of the Democratic Party, also claimed that he was under constant surveillance and feared assassination by the authorities. But it was one of their own – the paramilitary leader, football club owner and smuggling magnate Željko Ražnatović, alias Arkan – who would be the next to die. His violent demise, in January 2000, aroused suspicions that the regime was striving to erase evidence linking it to war crimes in Bosnia, or that a gangland war was about to erupt. In the previous year, three other major figures with links to gambling rackets and the underworld had also been executed, like Arkan, with shots to the head. The police had at least 500 unsolved murders on their books. There was speculation about the existence of an organised squad of bully boys – known as the 'men in black' – who could be summoned at any time or tipped off by a network of informers to defend the regime's interests. People began to ask: 'Who's next?'

A month later, defence minister Pavle Bulatović was fatally wounded as he sat eating in a Belgrade restaurant. No one, it seemed, even the most powerful, was safe now. As Gordan Paunović said: 'They are getting closer, step by step.'

The regime had manufactured lawlessness and economic uncertainty to create a sense of overwhelming fear and render the population insecure and unable to act. It had undermined its own legal institutions, fostered corruption, enforced universal poverty and summoned the spectre of fear of threat of attack from both outside and inside the country. Serbia had become a nation of twitching paranoiacs, afraid for the future and hardly able to cope with the present.

In the early months of 2000, attacks on the independent media were stepped up. Three independent newspapers and more than ten radio stations were shut down, and millions of dinars in fines exacted. The regime swelled its coffers as it crushed its opponents. Journalists in regional towns saw their cars burned and houses blown up. B2–92 received daily visits from tax investigators, searching for evidence of irregular transactions involving foreign currency. When they found nothing, ordinary policemen began to visit the studios. They would sit around, drink coffee, chat and attempt to be friendly, then occasionally ask pointed questions such as: 'So who is this Veran Matić then? What does he do?'

'They said to us: "Oh, we know who you're in contact with, we are listening to your mobile telephone," ' says Saša Mirković. 'That's the government strategy – to make us afraid. We have to waste time and energy going around town to secret places to make plans, we have to switch off the telephone because they are listening. This is not paranoia – you do have to hide some of your activities from them. I am always asking myself: "Why are we doing all this? Is it hopeless?" From time to time you want to give up. But then you think you've come so far, it's stupid to give up now.'

After the killing of defence minister Pavle Bulatović in February 2000, deputy prime minister Vojislav Šešelj gave an interview to B2–92, accusing it and other journalists of being part of a conspiracy to murder organised by the West. 'You kill off statesmen like rabbits here, thinking you're safe. You're making a big mistake. You're working against your own country; you're paid American money to destroy your country. You're traitors, you're the worst kind! There's nothing worse than you! You're worse than any kind of criminals!' he ranted. 'You journalists think you're some kind of sacred cows. Some of you are cows, all right, but not sacred.

'The gloves are off,' he threatened. 'You should know by now that I am afraid of nothing. Absolutely nothing! Why would I be afraid? It's you who should be afraid . . .'[5]

Šešelj's wild rhetoric, as anyone who could read the runes understood, was inevitably the prelude to a physical crack-down. On 6 March, five men in camouflage uniforms beat up a security guard and a technician and disabled Studio B television and Radio B2–92's transmission equipment, then drove away carrying bits of the broadcasting gear in a police jeep. It was the second burglary at the site in two months. As Gordan Paunović said afterwards: 'The opposition is very sterile and inefficient, they cannot even issue a proper press statement. Most of them are happy not to be personally endangered so why should they care about anyone else in this country? We are practically cut off from the rest of the world, no interference or monitoring is possible. We are somehow aware that no international help or solidarity will be possible, after so many disillusionments and disappointments. Now this really looks like Chile or Argentina in the seventies.' The next raid, he speculated, would come, undoubtedly, 'sooner or later'.

A few days later, Studio B was fined almost half a million Deutschmarks for 'temporary frequency use', and the telecom-munications minister warned that over 200 other broadcasters also owed him large amounts of money. Both Studio B and B2–92 continued transmitting using improvised set-ups, and fretted that worse was to come.

The talk now was of impending war. Milošević appeared to be gearing up for his endgame: a final showdown between the 'patriots' and the 'traitors'. In Belgrade, people began to speak about it as if it was inevitable: 'War is coming – civil war. I don't know how it will happen, but it's coming,' whis-pered one local record producer. 'Secret police are everywhere. They are listening to our conversations on the phone, watching us on closed-circuit TV. They can do anything they want. Horror is all around us.'

Some worried that, after skirmishes between Serbs, UN troops and Albanians in Kosovo, NATO might instigate a second air-raid campaign. Others feared that a new internal conflict was imminent after the breakdown of relations between Milošević and the government of Montenegro, the only other remaining part of the Yugoslav federation, which had started to move towards reconciliation with the West. In the provinces, postmen began to deliver call-up papers to all men of drafting age, although the military denied it was mobilising for battle. Portents of impending disaster were everywhere, and for many these signs were the same as those which preceded the wars in Croatia, Bosnia and Kosovo.

'This regime has a pathological affinity to provoking conflicts so it can just stay in power,' warned the Belgrade peace group Women in Black. 'There have been so many incidents in a short time that it is difficult to absorb them all. The unsolved murder of a high government official; arrests and beating up of students from Otpor; the continuous financial penalising of the "disobedient" daily newspapers and TV stations; the satanisation of the opposition; the constant talk of the imminent return of the "Serbian rule over Kosovo" . . .'[6]

Milošević, an international pariah, the first sitting head of state to be indicted for war crimes, no longer had anything to lose. Borka Pavičević of the Centre for Cultural Decontamination blamed the regime for invoking the apocalypse of civil unrest for its own ends: to frighten people and ensure their submission: 'If you say something critical, they say you are calling for civil war. They are constantly repeating that they are doing everything they can to stop it − in the very same way as at the beginning of the war in Bosnia when they were constantly accusing the other side of what they were actually doing. But how will we start a civil war? We don't know how to shoot. It's logical: the only people who can do it are those who are armed.'

She hoped that the electoral process might, against all odds, be their salvation: 'I will vote for anybody who will not kill: this is enough. Whatever I might think of what the opposition leaders have done in the past, I don't care. Just stop digging graves all around us. They can say: "We will be hungry, we will have nothing, I don't know how tomorrow will be, but there will be no more killing, nobody will attack you and you will not be forced to attack anyone." And that would be enough to start the future, without fear of the next war or that something will be forbidden or somebody will be killed. That would be enough.'

To a more cynical eye, the likelihood of electoral transform-ation was remote. 'High hopes are pinned on free, fair and especially democratic elections. Only an idiot could believe Milošević will allow any elections, never mind "fair" elec-tions,' wrote Petar Luković. The opposition remained paralysed, split into a score of competing factions and strategies. 'While Milošević controls all with precision and proficiency, the opposition is totally lost, running around like headless chickens,' Luković continued. 'The majority of Serbian opposition leaders can find only one major fault with Milošević – he lost the wars. Had he led the country to victory, then there would be no problems!'[7]

Some raged against the prevailing pessimism, but even they admitted they were in a minority. 'People should stop being pussies and do something,' says B2–92 arts reporter Maja Atanasijević. 'Be a fighter! I know it's a cliché, but if you want it enough and try hard enough, you can do something to make your life better. A lot of people are pissed off because they know how it *has* been and how it *could* be. And everyone is expecting that someone else will do it for them, that's the problem.' Few now looked to the West for salvation.

Veran Matić believed that only by facing up to its past could Serbia begin to construct its own future. 'The realisation of the truth about what has really happened, especially in Kosovo, as well as the establishment of responsibility, are part of the necessary changes,' he suggested. 'People in Serbia say, with self-irony, "Our past is awful, our present terrible: it's lucky that we don't have a future."

'The recent wars have completely submerged the truths and responsibilities for the tragic events which have been consequences of Communism's ideological showdown with its opponents from 1941 to the present day. This internal civil war has never really finished.'

Matić lay his hopes in a Serbian 'truth and reconciliation committee', based on the one set up to investigate the legacy of apartheid in South Africa. This would explore the aftermath of the fall of Communism and deal with guilt and responsibility for everything from the Srebrenica massacre to the siege of Sarajevo and the Kosovo conflict. B2–92 began a weekly programme, *Catharsis*, exploring the war crimes of the past decade, and began organising meetings which brought together representatives of all sides to set the process in motion.

'Everywhere on the territory of the former Yugoslavia where there was war there are sound reasons for unsealing the truths and for those societies to face their pasts, both recent and distant,' Matić said. 'Only then may we say that the process of treatment and healing has begun.'[8]

On the surface, to an outsider's eye, little looked amiss. Smart young people dressed in Nike and Adidas, smoked Marlboros, drove new VWs, ate Big Macs and drank Coca-Cola; packed bars throbbed to the latest tracks from the Chemical Brothers and Fatboy Slim; the only beggars on the streets were little gypsy ragamuffins. Food was plentiful and cheap, bread heavily subsidised. But all this surface normality was just a façade, a superficial image masking the deep-rooted disturbances beneath. In the surreal landscape of Belgrade in 2000, the only thing which remained certain was uncertainty. People spoke often, sometimes with horror but occasionally with admiration, of the bloody overthrow of Romania's Ceauçescu dynasty. A series of surveys by the Centre for the Investigation of Alternatives and the Belgrade Institute for Social Sciences found that while half of those polled still believed in peaceful change, thirty-five per cent would willingly use force to eject the Milošević clan. It seemed, at last, that the decade-long drama was moving into its final act, although its conclusion was still unclear.

Few imagined that, after losing all the wars he had started and destroying his own country in the process, the president would quit power peacefully. Mira Marković had once spoken dreamily of herself with her beloved Slobodan, happy in retirement, holidaying in Switzerland, eating ice cream with a flower in her hair. Now the possibility seemed more remote than ever. Petar Luković predicted: 'This regime will not exit the political scene of its own free will. It will not resign. It will not retreat to the castles, villas and factories it appropriated. Is it possible to imagine Slobodan Milošević as a pensioner? Or Mirjana Marković walking in the city without ten bodyguards? Is it possible to envisage a democratic handover of power, in which no blood is shed? It isn't.'[9]

Even if Milošević was deposed democratically, the vested interests of Party apparatchiks and the noxious tentacles of the criminal nouveau riche − what one commentator labelled the 'Kalashnikov generation' − were so deeply entrenched that the entire infrastructure of the country would have to be painstakingly torn down and rebuilt from the ground up. Xenophobia and violent nationalism would not simply disappear overnight with the president's clique. 'Even when Milošević is gone, I do not think it will be possible to say that war is over,' says Veran Matić.

And even those who had grown up in the nineties, who had stuck it out through the hard times while their friends and colleagues emigrated, wondered now whether it was still worth the interminable heartache; whether they would ever inhabit the kind of world about which they fantasised and whether their parallel reality would ever exist in real time − or whether they were simply extras in a bad movie, chasing a vision which would never materialise. Were they condemned to be a lost generation?

'This is a science fiction country, and we are the extra-terrestrials. Belgrade is our city, but we do not belong here, we do not fit in with the kind of Serbia which exists now. We are aliens here,' says Maja Atanasijević. 'I don't want people to feel sorry for us, I don't want people to say "Oh, you poor Serbs". We don't need pity. It is our problem and we have to solve it.

'We all know the end is coming – sooner or later. But when? How long must it take?'

# 7

# he's finished
# 2000

'I still can't deal with it at all. I'm in some kind of traumatic shock. So many things have happened in such a short space of time.' *Milivoje Čalija, B2–92 programme director (2000)*

As 2000 progressed, the sequence of events began to accelerate. With each new development, a colossal, irrevocable change seemed to be edging closer – but it would arrive sooner than anyone realised.

At 2 a.m. on 17 May, armed police entered the Beograd-janka building in central Belgrade and occupied the premises of Studio B, Radio B2–92, Radio Index and the popular tabloid newspaper *Blic*. The government announced that it had seized ownership of Studio B from the Serbian Renewal Movement-run Belgrade Council because the station had called for a violent overthrow of the system. Its offence was screening pictures of a rally addressed by Vuk Drašković at which he insisted he would resist Milošević's regime 'by all means possible'. When some of his supporters responded by firing guns in the air, Drašković said: 'Save your ammunition – you'll need it.'

Regime officials labelled Drašković a violent subversive, and said that Studio B was part of 'NATO's war machine'. They called for new anti-terrorist legislation to deal with the Serbian Renewal Movement and Otpor, which was growing in strength by the day.

Studio B's management was dismissed and replaced by loyalists. It remained on air, broadcasting pro-government programmes, while on the captured frequency of B2–92 – which Veran Matić referred to as 'collateral damage' in the takeover – there was only music. Staff were prevented from entering the premises. 'It's like history repeating itself. Everything is gone again,' said one B2–92 staffer, surveying the aftermath of a fourth shutdown in a decade.

Opposition leaders said that Milošević had finally declared civil war on his own people, and that Serbia was now under unofficial martial law. That night, tens of thousands joined a rally in downtown Belgrade. It progressed peacefully until police attempted to turn back thousands of FC Red Star supporters, whose team had just won the league and cup double and who were streaming into the city centre after a late-season match at which they had flown Otpor flags and chanted the name of Studio B. The football fans serenaded riot police with their latest terrace anthem – 'Save Serbia and be a man, kill yourself, Slobodan' – then fighting broke out as the demonstrators attempted to break through the police cordon and join them. Bystanders were beaten and tear-gassed, while the Red Star fans set dumpsters alight and threw bottles and rocks.

Some hoped that the unexpected intensity of the clash signalled a new phase in the resistance – the end of apathy. 'Thank God Red Star were playing. Thanks to the football fans, something finally happened,' said one observer. 'At least there was some rage and energy. A spirit has returned.' But the demonstrations that followed drew dwindling numbers, and within days optimism began to fade.

B2–92 moved to new premises, which it had been equipping in case of such an outcome, using satellite transmissions and Internet broadcasting, producing programmes for the nationwide ANEM radio and television network, and preparing to launch its own TV station. It was now effectively operating underground; 'on the brink of illegality', as Veran

Matić described it at the time. 'I often change locations where I work, trying not to be easy prey,' he said. 'We make sure that internal communication is encrypted, so our intentions are not revealed.

'From the legal point of view, we have the right to do our job: we are officially registered. But the regime's policy treats us as an illegal organisation. At press conferences of government officials, whenever any of our reporters introduces himself or herself before asking questions, the regime's representative immediately asks: "Aren't you banned?" or "Do you still exist? We must see what to do with you" – always followed by insults and accusations of us being spies.'

He predicted that before too long the regime would strike at the station again, silence it and confiscate its equipment. Ultimately, he worried, this could mean it would have to resort to 'deep underground work and emigration, and activity from the outside'.

The mood was one of complete uncertainty. 'These months were probably the worst of our professional lives because the psychological pressure and general repression was peaking. It was like being in some high-budget American thriller – life was like a rollercoaster,' says B2–92 programme director Milivoje Čalija. 'We were working in this kind of bunker situation. Most people in Belgrade didn't know we were here – although that doesn't mean the police didn't know the address.

'We were trying to convince people that we could still be heard even though they couldn't actually hear us – to show that we were still alive and kicking. It was a psychological thing. But in reality, unfortunately, we were only able to be heard in the provinces.

'We had a feeling that the end was close, but we didn't know how close. Our biggest aim was to stay calm and stay alive.'

B2–92 cut deals with radio stations in Bosnia and Romania, close to the Yugoslav borders, to relay its material back into the country. The broadcasts, which managed to reach as far as the suburbs of Belgrade, were jammed by the regime with transmissions of white noise on the same frequency, but each time it was gagged, B2–92 moved on again. 'Whenever they set up a new jamming device, we immediately showed up on another frequency with a different kind of news feed. We put them in the position that they could silence us only if we were physically eliminated,' says Veran Matić. Nevertheless, the result was that, through the ANEM network, provincial citizens were better informed than those living in the capital – which would prove hugely influential in the coming months.

'The government thought it was very important to control Belgrade,' says Čalija. 'Two million people live here and they thought it was a potential critical mass, and that the provinces were not so important. They thought if they controlled the capital, they could control the whole of Serbia. But the process backfired – in the end, the opposition movement erupted in the provinces and then moved to Belgrade.'

During the summer, something remarkable had happened. New federal, municipal and presidential elections were scheduled for September – and for the first time since 1996, the opposition parties, after months of wrangling over strategy, set aside their many personal and political differences and announced that they would field a joint list of candidates. They would also select a collective figurehead to run against Milošević for president. The coalition named itself the Democratic Opposition of Serbia (DOS); a united front comprising everyone apart from Vojislav Šešelj's Radicals and the increasingly eccentric Vuk Drašković's Serbian Renewal Movement. Vojislav Koštunica, head of one of the numerous smaller parties, the Democratic Party of Serbia (not to be confused with Zoran Djindjić's Democratic Party, of which Koštunica was once, briefly, a member), was then confirmed as DOS's presidential candidate.

A lawyer by training, Koštunica had been ousted from his position at Belgrade University in the seventies for criticising

Tito, and had subsequently collaborated on a daring legal study of the advantages of democratic systems over Communist one-party rule. He was considered modest and unassuming, and seemingly uncorrupted by his years in politics; his plain suits and old Yugo car regularly cited as evidence that he hadn't been bought off (although some worried that his image wasn't media-friendly enough). Unlike others, he had never cut deals with Milošević.

He also had strong nationalist credentials – he had damned Milošević for signing the agreements which ended the wars in Bosnia and Kosovo – and the state media found it hard to smear him as a traitor to Serbian interests. All *Politika* could fabricate was the stunning revelation that he owned 17 cats (he didn't) and as such, like a cat, was selfish and egocentric – and that he had no children, therefore was not a 'family man'. Koštunica was nicknamed 'Šešelj in a tuxedo', referring to his image as a slicker, more palatable version of the right-wing ranter. However, his nationalism was less extreme and more pragmatic than this nickname suggests. He had opposed the NATO bombing, and now spoke out against the war crimes court at The Hague and its attempts to bring Milošević to trial. But – despite his party's failure to join the Zajedno coalition which won the municipal elections of 1996 – he had also been a long-time opponent of the president. One of his slogans ran: 'No to the White House, no to the White Castle [Milošević's residence, once home to the king of Yugoslavia].'

'Koštunica was a clever choice,' says journalist Duška Anastasijević. 'Of course I myself resented that I would have to vote for him, but sometimes you have to do unpleasant things. He is a nationalist – never condemning anything that happened in Bosnia, not questioning the bombardment of Sarajevo – but he really behaves like a decent man. This is very important, to bring back decency to political life, because the political scene was very contaminated, dominated by bullies.

'He was not vulnerable in the same way as other politicians. They could not attack him for being a swindler or being engaged in any dodgy business, or say that he was pro-Western and had kissed Madeleine Albright's hand.'

The prognosis for Koštunica's chances was promising, with opinion polls showing DOS running way ahead of the Socialist Party's candidates. DOS promised to inspire sweeping democratic changes, end sanctions and renew ties with the rest of Europe. It was hoped that Koštunica could appeal to those voters, both liberal and nationalist, who were sick of the misery of the Milošević years but also tired of the in-fighting and factionalism practised by Djindjić and Drašković. He could unite disaffected citizens of all political persuasions and win over elements of Milošević's support in the more conservative provinces.

Unlike Djindjić, who had agreed to take a backstage role as Koštunica's campaign manager, Vuk Drašković – to the dismay of the rest of the opposition – announced that he would field his own presidential candidate, the mayor of Belgrade, Vojislav Mihailović, and that his Serbian Renewal Movement would not participate in the DOS coalition. It would prove to be a colossal error on the part of the turbulent individualist, and one which he would later regret publicly.

When Milošević named the date for the election, he had felt certain of victory. 'From his point of view, he did his homework thoroughly,' says Duška Anastasijević. 'He had the anti-terrorist law, which was really scary; it was a phantom law that was not enacted but was used as a threat. Everybody who saw the draft of the law could recognise himself or herself as a terrorist. It really induced fear in Belgrade.

'The opposition was showing no sign of any unity or solidarity and Milošević was doing well, people had got used to the status quo. The discontent was present but never really articulated.'

As the elections drew closer, however, the fortunes of the ruling clan looked increasingly shaky. Fuel shortages and scarcities of basic goods had undermined the public's residual passivity. Internal squabbles between members of Milošević's Socialist Party of Serbia and his wife Mira Marković's Yugoslav United Left were hindering their election preparations. In their hometown of Požarevac, where Marko Milošević presided over his business empire, a boycott launched by opposition forces after the president's son's bodyguards were involved in a fist-fight with Otpor activists was hitting Milošević junior in the wallet. The Otpor members had been arrested and charged with the attempted murder of Marko's goons, but the incident backfired as local clubbers stayed away from his expensively refurbished Madona nightclub, forcing it to close. His showpiece Bambipark leisure complex, which cost an estimated one million Deutschmarks to build, was virtually devoid of paying customers, and subscribers were deserting his Internet company.

Nevertheless, Milošević senior still exerted wide-reaching influence over the media, using it to push home his electoral message: freedom, independence, reconstruction and affluence for all. He told a rally at the Zastava car plant that 'everybody in this country will have higher salaries, more free time, a better standard of living and better conditions for health care and education'.[1]

He sought once again to present himself as the guarantor of security, playing on the fears of those who had suffered war and impoverishment yet still feared that worse could be around the corner. He invoked the familiar 'war between patriots and traitors', portraying the opposition as agents of a sinister, anti-Yugoslav New World Order, the fellow-travellers of terrorism and anarchy.

Milošević was convinced that the opposition – whom he labelled 'rabbits, rats and hyenas, a group of dissatisfied, unsuccessful, blackmailed and bribed persons' – could never unite behind a single leader, and that his self-proclaimed post-war reconstruction had impressed public opinion.[2]

What remained of the independent media also came under

further pressure. Reporter Miroslav Filipović was tried for espionage in a military court and jailed for seven years after reporting on Serb atrocities in Kosovo – another warning to any journalist considering stepping out of line. Anti-establishment playwrights and film directors were ridiculed on state television. As writer Filip David observed: 'The Milošević system needs enemies like a man needs air. Manufacturing enemies is a highly developed industry in Serbia.'[3] Judges who supported a dissident colleague who was dismissed for his membership of Otpor were also sacked.

Two British policemen and two Canadians working for the Organisation for Security and Co-operation in Europe were arrested in Montenegro and accused of plotting military sabotage. They were paraded on television as proof that an international conspiracy against the Serbs was gathering pace. The state news agency Tanjug reported that the American government was flying in experts in psychological warfare to its embassies in bordering countries to help destabilise Yugoslavia. A second show trial of NATO leaders and senior US and European politicians was staged in the Belgrade courts. Again, Bill Clinton, Tony Blair and 14 others failed to appear in the dock, but were convicted in their absence for crimes against the civilian population of Yugoslavia and sentenced to 20 years in jail. The court said it would issue warrants for their arrests.

On 25 August, Ivan Stambolić, the Communist boss who had been ruthlessly usurped by Milošević when he seized the Serbian presidency in 1987, disappeared while jogging in a Belgrade park. Eyewitnesses told his family they had seen him being dragged into a white van. It was uncertain whether he had been kidnapped or killed, and rumours intensified as the pro-regime media remained silent over the incident. (Documents leaked after the elections indicated that state security had played a role in his abduction.) Stambolić had recently become close to Otpor, and had stated that Milošević had transformed Serbia into 'a prison'. Some speculated that he had intended to return to politics – possibly to stand against Milošević – and was eliminated to avert the potential risk to the president's position. Former information minister Aleksandar Tijanić said he believed more arrests and abductions were inevitable in the coming days.

As the elections approached, those with connections to dissident activists or human-rights campaigners began to feel increasingly uneasy about their own safety. 'I was wondering whether people passing my flat were working for state security; was I being followed or not?' says Duška Anastasijević. 'Not because I was so important but because I liaised with people who were in trouble – my brother had problems with state security and had to leave the country; I was working with the Humanitarian Law Centre and the army threatened its director, Nataša Kandić, that they would file criminal charges against her – she had uncovered war crimes committed by Serb policemen in Kosovo, she knew lots of names. I had been reading those files; I was her adviser. I just didn't know what they had on me. You never knew when someone might call you to the police station for a "conversation". I don't know . . . you started thinking about these things.'

Many Western commentators have claimed that the NATO bombing hastened public disillusionment with Milošević; destruction, defeat and the effective loss of Kosovo causing Serbs to rouse themselves from apathy and break with their perennial loser of a leader, giving the West's Kosovo intervention a final justification. Some in Belgrade agree with this analysis: 'It started with the war; people wanted change and Milošević didn't have any answers any more,' says one. Others disagree, saying that the war actually delayed the emergence of a united political opposition by rallying the public around Milošević and the national cause, and insist that the combination of economic misery and visible repression was the real catalyst. 'Bombing made people more frustrated – in that sense only, it was successful – but it was completely the wrong strategy,' one suggests. They also point out that after propping up Milošević in the post-Dayton years and then demolishing the country's infrastructure, the West could hardly call its interventions in Yugoslavia positive.

As in 1996, it was the public, not the politicians or foreign governments, who became the instigators of change – above all, the increasingly influential Otpor movement. Otpor had grown exponentially in the post-war period, and it now commanded a national network of some 20,000 enthusiastic activists, organised into 'action teams' in 120 towns throughout Serbia. No longer exclusively made up of students, it had renamed itself People's Movement Otpor, and launched its own campaign to undermine the president.

Otpor's battle cry was 'Gotov je' – 'He's finished' – which activists pasted over every Socialist election poster they could find. The symbolic resistance of the Otpor fist logo was ubiquitous, on T-shirts, badges and graffiti. Otpor had become a political youth cult, and its advance was unstoppable, as increasing numbers of young people were won over by its audacious exploits. In short, identifying with Otpor was cool. 'Otpor made it fashionable to be against Milošević,' says B2–92's Dragan Ambrozić. 'They made things that looked impossible happen.'

The second front of Otpor's mobilisation was a nationwide rock tour under the banner 'Vreme je' ('It's time') in collaboration with B2–92, ANEM and other non-governmental organisations. Its aim was to persuade apathetic youth to use their votes, and it took the best Yugoslav bands on a gruelling cross-country caravan which covered a distance of over 2,000 miles, staging gigs in 25 cities and ultimately attracting more than 150,000 people.

'This was the biggest tour in the history of Serbian rock music, as far as I know,' says Ambrozić, who worked on the project. 'We wanted to try to establish a different social context in which change was possible – to promote the idea of social responsibility which started with going to vote on the 24th of September. We knew Milošević would try to steal votes, so the only way to stop it was to have a mass of people out voting. We wanted to make a miracle possible.

'It was a combination of artistic and social activism – it was not based on political propaganda, but on seduction. Bands like Kanda Kodža I Nebojša and Darkwood Dub were already transmitting the messages we wanted. Those bands grew up with this generation and had its experiences in their lyrics. All we had to do was put them together and the message was already there. They didn't even have to say "go and vote".' The election results would ultimately show a remarkably high youth turn-out.

The growth of Otpor inspired an immediate physical response. As it transformed itself from an underground cell into a mainstream movement, arrests and attacks on its members increased. In May 2000, it had applied for official registration, but had been rejected by the courts on the grounds that it participated in 'illegal activities' and called for 'people to rebel and violently overthrow the constitutional order'.[4] On 4 September, its Belgrade headquarters were raided, and computers, disks, posters and stickers seized. In the previous four months, more than 1,200 Otpor sympathisers had been detained all over Serbia – some for no more than wearing a T-shirt decorated with the fist logo.

This only strengthened the movement's resolve – it knew now that it was being taken very seriously indeed. 'When Milošević started all this repression against us, when he started pushing us hard, we knew he was already losing,' says Otpor activist Marija Baralić. 'Because why should he bother with us? We were just funny little students doing funny little things.'

It also proved to be a grave mistake. By targeting ordinary young people, the regime revealed itself to the voters as cruel and intolerant. 'It made people see Milošević as a real enemy,' says Duška Anastasijević. 'This repression brought him into everybody's home.'

While Otpor activists in the relatively liberal capital might have been spurred by romantic idealism as much as political conviction, their comrades in the provinces had to endure the harsh, physical backlash of an angry state. In September, five Otpor sympathisers in the town of Vladičin Han were detained, hung by their feet from the ceiling, and severely beaten around the genitalia, kidneys and heads by drunken officers.

'I spoke to their parents, they were not particularly in favour of Milošević but they might have voted for him to preserve the status quo and their state jobs, they didn't really like him but they thought it was too costly to confront him,' says Anastasijević. 'But then they saw their kid taken to a police station and tortured Gestapo-style just for wearing an Otpor T-shirt, and it became more personal. Lots of people were affected by that.'

B2–92's editor-in-chief Veran Matić agrees that Milošević, in his paranoia about 'enemies within', went very visibly over the top, and this ultimately benefited the opposition: 'This may sound perverse, but in a way, we were glad about the repression. We knew that each arrested student and each beaten demonstrator showed weakness and increased the rage of the people. As for me personally, I was closely followed by government. I did not bother too much, although I knew I was at the top of the possible execution list.'

Otpor had come a long way since a young woman spray-painted the first fist stencil on a Belgrade wall in 1998. Its members were regularly interrogated by state security agents, wanting to know who were its leaders, where its money came from, how its activists exchanged information, and whether they had weapons. Many were offered bribes to become informants. There was also evidence that the police were insinuating undercover officers into the organisation, posing as ordinary members. 'Police infiltration was taken very seriously; we were constantly afraid of it,' says Marija Baralić. 'Of course they had people in Otpor, it's normal practice. Some of them were discovered.

'A lot of people were taken to state security and threatened with violence, or had their family threatened with violence, and they got scared. So when they came back they told the rest of us not to tell them anything important: "Don't share anything with me because I am a danger to you now." So we knew what was asked in these "informative talks", and we knew not to share information with people who could be pushed into talking.'

Otpor, believes Veran Matić, 'became an obsession for Mira Marković and her allies in the secret police. They saw future guerrillas in it – urban guerrillas. It also contributed to major hesitations and indecision within the regime. It was a brand-new formula of resistance and struggle.'

In the months leading up to the election, the European Union pumped more than £350,000 into Serbian independent media, stretching EU rules on aid to counter Milošević's TV and radio propaganda and enable opposition newspapers to purchase paper for publishing. 'It was a really effective operation,' stated EU External Affairs Commissioner Chris Patten.[5] Veran Matić says that the actual amount of cash delivered was considerably less, although he does admit that 'at the moment when strong determination that something definitely must be done emerged inside the country, serious determination to help it from outside also emerged. However,' he qualifies, 'no money would have been able to help us had it not been for our faith and conviction to fight and endure.'

Otpor was also the beneficiary of foreign funding. Off the record, some activists admit that the influx of Western money was a significant factor in the organisation's development. But its spokespeople insisted that influence could not be bought. 'The most important thing is that the West must co-operate with us, and not try to co-opt us into their own scheme of things,' said activist Vladimir Radunović. 'It's obvious that Otpor is aiming to create a democratic and free state in Serbia. So these rumours are circulating, mainly that we are paid by NATO, and are going to collaborate with NATO in the bombing of Serbia, but they are too ridiculous to even deny.'[6]

Otpor's relentless motivating swelled a rolling wave of optimism. This time, people began to believe, victory was within
reach. Yet nobody imagined that, even if defeated, Milošević
would forsake his position easily. Although most expected
Koštunica to win, with all opinion polls placing him ahead of
the sitting president, a survey by the Institute of Social Sciences
showed that 46 per cent thought Milošević would nonetheless
remain in power. As political commentator Petar Luković
wrote: 'The whole psychological make-up of the Milošević
regime precludes defeat. How can a "National Hero" lose?'
The escalating repression, Luković surmised, was a clear
message to an electorate on the verge of making the momen-
tous decision to break with the past: 'Don't mess with us,
we're armed, we have tanks, special forces, cut-throats with
pedigree. Don't think a vote is going to save you.'[7]

There were worries that Milošević could send the army
into Kosovo, reigniting the war in the southern province, or
engineer a showdown with the Montenegrin police force.
Reports emerged that Milošević's army was gearing up for
battle in Montenegro, which was showing signs of wanting to
break away from Yugoslavia. Montenegrin journalists believed
that the Belgrade leadership was drawing up plans to take over
essential services and telecommunications links. Soldiers could
be seen patrolling the roads and aircraft flew low over the
Montenegrin capital Podgorica. NATO and the EU drew up
contingency plans and shipped in reinforcement troops to the
region in case of unrest. Montenegro's deputy prime minister
Dragisa Burzan said that he feared a 'staged fifth Balkan war'.[8]

Most simply believed that Milošević would rig the election,
perhaps by stuffing ballot boxes with phantom votes, as he
had done at previous polls, and declare victory for himself,
whatever the real result. After all, he had only been defeated
twice since 1989 – in the Serbian municipal elections of
1996 where attempted fraud sparked mass protests, and the
Montenegrin elections of 1998, where the pro-Western Milo
Djukanović had triumphed.

'I knew that something would be different after the elections, but I didn't know what,' says Duška Anastasijević. 'I was a pessimist. I thought they would clamp down, that he would declare victory quickly and launch large-scale intimidation.' Nevertheless, like many others, she didn't believe Milošević could hold out for ever. 'I thought there would be serious urban guerrilla action and counter-offensives. Even if Milošević won and introduced a more classic form of dictatorship, his days were numbered. I didn't think he would last more than a year.'

Meanwhile, B2–92 was making plans to go further underground if events went against the opposition or a state of emergency was declared. 'We would have tried to work illegally, and we would probably have moved part of our team to some provincial town in Serbia, to one of our affiliates,' says Veran Matić. 'We planned to pick a station that was most convenient to be defended if necessary.

'As the final option, we planned moving part of our team to Bosnia or Romania to do broadcasts of programming that would have been illegally produced inside Serbia. The production team would have remained inside the country. We already had everything worked out: technical stuff, safe apartments, secure communications. We counted on it as a seriously probable option.

'We worked out wireless communications among all our illegal production premises in Belgrade. Our broadcast server would have been managed by remote control, so in case of a police raid only technical equipment could have been "arrested". The plan was to produce some programmes in discretely rented apartments. A reporter would edit a programme on his PC by himself in an apartment, then send it via the Internet to our server. Then it would be broadcast.'

The election had been reduced to a simple referendum: were you for or against change? In Vojislav Koštunica's final campaign speech, he offered voters relief from conflict, a route back into the global community – and a life more ordinary: 'Tranquillity is what we need,' he said. 'We need a way of life where all the excitement will happen on a personal level and the political life will be monotonous, even boring. We need a state where authority is afraid of the people; not the people of authority. Only DOS and I can offer you that kind of state. A state without blood rivers for borders, a state where we are no one's slaves, nor servants, not to internal conquerors, nor to foreign ones.'[9]

Milošević's final words in the campaign, on the other hand, presented a stark choice between national autonomy under the Socialists or a lifetime of servility to foreign powers with the opposition: 'Other so-called political parties are responsible for urging criminal behaviour and terrorism, for spreading chauvinism, and also for producing anti-national feelings and for disturbing the lives of every family,' he explained. 'They are destroying the minds of the younger generation. They are abusing children and youth through sects, spy organisations, terrorist groups and drug-dealing mafia.'[10]

The election would be a monumental turning point for Serbia – and as the first results from polling stations emerged late on 24 September, all the evidence suggested that Koštunica had beaten Milošević soundly. Thousands gathered in the streets of Belgrade to begin the celebrations, believing change had finally come. The following day, DOS called a rally to toast its victory, although the Federal Election Commission was still silent on the poll's outcome and the Socialist Party was insisting that Milošević was in the lead.

The Socialists, meanwhile, staged their own rally, with pro-Milošević singers serenading his faithful. Only a few hundred turned up, while 20,000 came out on to the streets for the opposition. Chants of 'Save Serbia, kill yourself Slobodan' could be heard above the crooning.

'It was so pathetic, they couldn't even show it on television as some big show of support for Milošević,' says Duška Anasta-sijević. 'He had been a figure of mythical proportions. Even people who hated him respected his uncanny ability to turn everything in his favour and survive any situation. Then all of a sudden he was reduced to normal proportions. He was just a man.'

A day later, the Election Commission declared that Koštunica had captured 48 per cent of the vote – short of the 50 per cent minimum required to win outright victory and prevent a second round of voting. Milošević, it said, had won 40 per cent. DOS contested the results, saying that Koštunica had scored 55 per cent against Milošević's 34. Vuk Drašković's Serbian Renewal Movement had been decimated as its support collapsed.

Disputes over figures aside, the results showed that Milošević had grossly misread the public mood and miscalculated his strategy. 'The morning after the elections everybody knew that change had come,' says Dragan Ambrozić. 'The atmosphere had been transformed, there was still some tension, but the overall feeling was that something huge and beautiful was happening – and everybody wanted to participate in it.'

Insiders claim Milošević was shocked by the scale of his defeat, having been convinced he would win outright. A second round of voting was scheduled for 8 October. DOS refused to participate in the run-off, insisting on its own victory and claiming the Election Commission was acting fraudulently.

Hundreds of thousands packed central Belgrade to hear Koštunica speak. 'Dear, brave, fellow citizens, free people, we have won!' he announced. 'All of us on Sunday said what kind of Serbia we want to live in. They have once more tried to sneer at the will of the people, they have tried again to steal the elections; they have tried to bargain on the second round, but we are saying to them: there will be no second round, there is no bargaining. We are fighting for democracy and democracy is based on truth, not on lies. The truth is that we have won this election.

'Slobodan Milošević is a tyrant who has lost his strength,' he concluded.

Otpor activists were triumphant. 'We're just ignoring him now,' said one. 'It's a new psychological phenomenon that I have never seen before. He can do whatever he wants. He can say he's king of the earth – but nobody cares.'[11]

Some still feared that Milošević might annul the results and declare a state of emergency – a course of action favoured by some corrupt officials and supporters of his wife's JUL party – and that the only way the matter would be settled would be on the streets, violently – the Ceauçescu solution. DOS's campaign manager, Zoran Djindjić, stated that unless the opposition was allowed to audit the results, it would call a general strike. 'This will not be a protest meeting, but a blockade of the entire country,' he said. 'The world will see a different Serbia this time.'[12]

By Friday, civil disobedience had erupted all over the country. High school students walked out of classes. Factory workers, bus and taxi drivers joined them. Roads were blocked. In many cities, only essential services continued to operate. State radio and television workers and staff at the news agency Tanjug began to demand changes to their employers' pro-regime editorial policies and the institution of unbiased reporting of current events. Some reporters, silent through the Milošević years, even rebelled and went on strike – although many independent journalists saw this as the cynical, desperate act of people who were afraid of losing their jobs if a new order came to power. 'They are so pathetic and miserable, you can't even hate them,' says B2-92's Gordan Paunović of the new-born democrats who had finally dis- covered their voices. 'They should build a special towerblock for them in New Belgrade, give them all one-room flats and a pension of 200 Deutschmarks a month and see how they survive. And have special shops for them where they can queue for oil and sugar.' Nevertheless, even as its reporters protested, Radio Television Serbia ignored the strikes.

Thousands of miners at the Kolubara collieries, 30 miles south of Belgrade, which supplied half of Serbia's coal, downed tools, threatening to put the lights out all over the country. DOS confirmed that the general strike and boycott of all state institutions would begin at 5 a.m. on 2 October.

Milošević hit back in a televised presidential address: 'Ahead of the second round of presidential elections, members of the Democratic Opposition of Serbia are bribing, blackmailing and threatening the citizens of Serbia,' he said, explaining that Koštunica's party was fomenting anarchy on behalf of NATO, and that if he himself was not victorious, Yugoslavia would be occupied by the enemy. 'My wish is that the citizens do not receive confirmation of my warnings too late.'[13]

His broadcast was interpreted by many as a sign of weakness. 'He could have proclaimed a state of emergency, but when we saw he didn't do it in the first minute of his appearance, we knew he was finished, definitely,' says Dragan Ambrozić. 'Instead of being a distant, untouchable figure of power, he tried to explain things and he didn't have the words. When you have to explain so much, it's obvious how weak you are.

'With every sentence it was getting more absurd. It was like he was saying: "I gave you the chance to vote for me and you didn't. Don't you like me?" He was really hurt.

'Part of his speech was portraying the future of Serbia if the "NATO traitors" won. He was saying that Kosovo was not going to be Serbian any more, that the mafia would rule this country and that this small nation is not used to criminals. Didn't he know that all this had already happened? What a joke!'

The first fighting between protesters and riot police broke out when students attempted to march to the Belgrade suburb of Dedinje, where the president lived. In response, the government threatened severe reprisals against 'subversive activities'. A violent resolution was still distinctly possible.

But behind the scenes, the powers which had guaranteed Milošević's power were beginning to abandon him. The loyalty of the 120,000-strong police force was wavering, and the head of the Yugoslav Army, General Nebojša Pavković, stated that he would respect the will of the electorate and was not prepared to crack down on any popular uprising. The Serbian Orthodox Church recognised Koštunica as president, as did Vojislav Šešelj, leader of the Radicals, and the Serbian Renewal Movement's Vuk Drăskovié. A few leading figures in the business community, whose fortunes had been ensured by Milošević's regime, deserted their provider. Even Russia, for years an ally in the cause of Orthodox and Slavic brotherhood, was preparing to ditch him. The opposition, some reports suggested, was already making secret contacts with senior military figures to ensure the safe transfer of power.

Milošević was playing for time, desperate for a way out. Speculation mounted that he might flee the country – to Russia, where he might be offered immunity from prosecution for war crimes, or to some other friendly state like China, Belarus, Iraq or Libya, where he could claim asylum to avoid arrest, assassination, or the possibility of being sent to face the UN tribunal in The Hague. None of the rumours could be confirmed, but they indicated that belief in Milošević's ability to endure was crumbling as fast as his support. Nevertheless, many Belgraders would claim one minute that his rule was over, and the next that he would, as ever, find some ruse to survive.

By Wednesday 4 October, as tension heightened and neither side showed signs that it was prepared to capitulate, power cuts commenced, with the authorities blaming the striking Kolubara miners. But when the police threw up a cordon around the colliery complex to contain the uprising, they were driven back by the swelling ranks of protesters who had arrived to support the strikers. The miners declared that Kolubara was 'Serbia's Gdansk', a reference to the shipyard whose strikers hastened the fall of Communism in Poland.

Buoyed by the miners' triumph, the opposition called a national rally in Belgrade for the next day, and gave Milošević a deadline of 3 p.m. to concede defeat. It was a high-risk strategy: the president could still call on his paramilitary police, and the demonstration could be crushed, or turn into a blood-bath. Serbia was on the verge of meltdown.

As dawn broke on 5 October, convoys began streaming towards Belgrade from all corners of the country. Police road-blocks were erected, blocking all roads into the city, where the rally was due to commence at 3 p.m. But they were overwhelmed by the sheer number of vehicles moving pur-posefully from the provinces – cars, buses and lorries from the towns and villages of the north, the south, the east and west – all heading for a showdown in the capital. Patrol vehicles were shoved aside with bulldozers; lorries barring roads were pushed off the highway; a police car was tipped into a ditch. Reports reaching Belgrade increased the anticipation, although few really realised that this, finally, would be the day. All routes approaching the city were gridlocked, and many protesters walked the last few miles on foot, chanting and blowing whistles.

'Nothing was normal that day. Everything stopped,' says Dragan Ambrozić. 'When we heard that people coming to Belgrade were just pushing the blockades aside, we knew something was going to happen. People were just pouring into the city, for hours. One mass of people would be walking along, chanting: "Here comes Niš, here comes Niš!" Then from another direction, another mass, chanting: "Here comes Kruševac, here comes Kruševac!" If you were pro-Milošević, this must have been a terrifying experience.'

From early morning onwards, the crowds in downtown Belgrade grew. Hundreds of thousands – perhaps the largest ever demonstration seen in the city – gathered in front of the federal parliament. At noon, some attempted to rush the doors and break into the building; the police forced them back, setting off a fog of tear gas.

To an uninformed onlooker, the demonstrators resembled

a chaotic rabble. But Velimir Ilić, the mayor of the provincial town of Čačak and a key opposition instigator, claims that the assault on Belgrade had been meticulously planned months in advance, like a military operation. Ilić had forged a secret coalition with disaffected soldiers, Bosnian war veterans, state security agents and police from the special forces who had changed sides; they were armed with guns, sticks and, most significantly, an earth-mover. 'Each demonstrator was allocated a specific task,' he said afterwards. 'We knew which group was in charge for each part of the city and what they had to do.'[14] Neither Koštunica nor DOS was fully briefed about his plans, Ilić said.

Before his convoy of followers left the southern town, he told them: 'Today, we will be free or die.'[15] These were determined men, many of them battle-hardened, who felt they had little to lose. Some said final farewells to their families before departing. 'We dared not return home without completing the job, because the police would have beaten us and put us into jail on the way back,' one explained later.[16]

The demonstrators did not just represent Belgrade, where the political opposition had always been strong, but the entire country. Their mood was not festive, but tenacious and resolute. 'There were no follies like there were in 1996 and 1997, people dressing up in crazy costumes – it was much more serious,' says Duška Anastasijević. 'It wasn't a carnival, it was more like: "This is serious stuff now, we don't have the time for that any more. We had fun before, now it's not funny any longer."'

A few hours later, they tried to storm the parliament again, hurling petrol bombs at the police who were guarding the building, setting parts of it ablaze. This time they proved too strong to resist. Zlatko Josić, who worked as tour manager for B2–92 on the 'Vreme je' concerts, recognised some of them as security guards who had staffed the Čačak gig, and joined them as they burst through the doors. 'The parliament was locked and the police were inside, throwing gas through the windows. The only way to get them out was with fire,' he says. 'They were confused, they expected reinforcements, but lots of policemen didn't want to get involved and just refused to come. They were asking for help and more gas, and their chiefs were telling them to be patient and that help would arrive. When we got inside, some people started to destroy things while the others were trying to stop them. I was very happy, I felt proud, but I was afraid because I knew that Milošević's people did not care about human lives.'

Outnumbered, the police fled, discarding their flak jackets and helmets and joining the protesters. Some pleaded for mercy, begging not to be beaten. Only a handful fought back. Chairs were carried out by demonstrators who took turns sitting and having their photographs taken by their friends. Pictures of Milošević were thrown out of the windows, while men waved flags from the balconies. The Serbian revolution had begun.

Amidst the smoke, gas and confusion, many did not realise exactly what had happened. 'I didn't know what was going on, I didn't know parliament had fallen,' says Otpor activist Marija Baralić. 'I just heard detonations and saw smoke in the sky and military helicopters flying overhead. I thought: "This is it, we finally got to this stage." I was planning how to hide, to run away, to find something hard to hit anybody who attacked me. I was scared. But we knew this might happen, this was why we came here, so we had to stay and finish the job.'

Tear gas was fired into the crowd again and people retreated, gasping, choking and vomiting, only to cover their faces and surge forward once more. 'The closer I got, the more I was sure that this was going to be it. These were people I had never seen before in Belgrade on demonstrations. They were going: "Oh come on, it's only tear gas! Wimps!"' says Duška Anastasijević. Gangs of football fans were in the thick of the fighting, keen to wreak revenge on the police. They took up their terrace chant once again: 'Save Serbia, kill yourself, Slobodan!'

The police were in disarray. As barricades were thrown up around the city centre, all they could do was look on while the revolutionaries brandished captured truncheons and riot shields – or throw away their riot gear and join the revolution themselves, as many did. A central police station was occupied, and law and order effectively broke down. Although sporadic gunshots could be heard, the special armoured police units retreated; tanks which had been spotted in the suburbs of Dedinje and Banjica did not enter the city centre, and soldiers remained in their barracks. Milošević had called on the army to intervene, but his pleas had been rejected. There were no orders left to obey. Belgrade was an autonomous zone.

'In those few hours it was possible to do anything,' says B2–92 programme director Milivoje Čalija. 'The system totally disintegrated. Because the whole system was attached to the Socialist Party, when that started to decompose, every-thing else went with it. The chain of command was broken down totally.'

Just past 5 p.m., in a storm of tear gas and gunfire, protesters used the Čačak bulldozer to charge the Radio Television Serbia building, then set it alight. Some of the most hated editors were beaten up and thrown out into the street; others had already run away. Computers were trashed and equipment looted as smoke billowed out and young men danced around the blaze, while others hurled stones into the inferno. Three storeys of the building were gutted; all of RTS's channels went dead. The Bastille had fallen.

Not long afterwards, RTS returned to the air with the message: 'This is the new Radio Television Serbia. Please be patient until we start the transmission.' The message was clear: Milošević's political and cultural propaganda machine had col-lapsed. Glitzy entertainment channel TV Pink and Marija Milošević's TV Košava went off the air, while the state news agency Tanjug and the ultra-loyalist daily newspaper *Politika* switched sides (the next day *Politika*'s, headline would read, almost unbelievably after years of branding the democratic opposition as traitors: 'Serbia on the road to democracy').

Marko Milošević's cosmetics shop was looted and destroyed, and its bottles of expensive perfume smashed, leaving a heavy, sickly scent hanging in the air. (Marko himself was rumoured to be hiding out in the family's underground bunker, a secret complex deep in the forests of eastern Serbia; he later fled to Moscow under a false name and his Madona nightclub was taken over by a youth radio station.) The headquarters of Milošević's Socialist Party and his wife's Yugoslav United Left were ransacked – as they were in over 20 towns nationwide. The symbols of the past decade, once potent, now stood emasculated.

The night before, Veran Matić of B2–92 had been told by one of his staff that Otpor was planning to liberate the old B92 studios in the city-centre House of Youth. It was rumoured that technical equipment was already being evacuated. On the afternoon of 5 October, B2–92 presenter Srdjan Andjelić was one of the first on the scene after the offices were occupied by the protesters. 'They had just climbed up to the fifth floor and after a short negotiation with some policemen who agreed to put down their pistols and leave the building, they entered the radio,' he says. 'Several technicians were beaten up. Nikačević [the regime loyalist who had taken over the station's management] and the other bad guys had already escaped.'

When Andjelić arrived, two young men carrying police batons stopped him with the question: 'Where do you think you're going?' Once they realised he was one of the original B92 staff, they left him pass, and a technician got the station back on the air on its original frequency, 92.5 FM.

'I grabbed the mic and reminded people of our *real* name, which is not B2–92, but B92,' says Andjelić. 'And I invited the listeners to join us in the crowded streets on one of the most beautiful nights in the history of our country.'

The impostors had departed in haste, taking little with them. 'Our managing director Saša Mirković said when he came back to his office, which had been used by Nikačević, there was still a bunch of business cards, some condoms and an unfinished cup of coffee on his desk because he left so fast,' says Dragan Ambrozić. 'Saša told me: "It felt like somebody had been wearing my underpants. We're going to need some powerful disinfectant in here."' The courts rapidly recognised the original B92 management as legitimate.

Nevertheless, B92's position was still fragile, even though the country had new political masters. 'We still have to survive in a market that has no rules nor any conditions for normal operations. There is no security, there are no rules,' says Veran Matić. 'We will remain independent, so we will not have to depend on the mercy of the new authorities. It is much easier for them to take over state-run media which will obey them and be loyal, just like they were loyal to the previous government. Independence has a price tag on it. We are well aware of the fact.'

That evening, victorious, people drank, danced and sang in the streets, as brass bands played, firecrackers exploded and cars raced around blaring their horns; a cacophonic fiesta of liberation to mark the long-awaited triumph of people power. During the day's turmoil, only two people had died, one of them accidentally. And in less than 13 hours, 13 years of fear had been banished, at least temporarily.

President Koštunica addressed the rapturous crowd from the balcony of the city hall, hailing the country's new era. 'Good evening, liberated Serbia,' he said. 'What we are doing is making history.' When people clamoured for Milošević to be arrested, Koštunica stated: 'He doesn't need to be arrested. He arrested himself long ago.'[17]

Fears were still rife that Milošević might yet regroup, summon his paramilitary police and strike back. 'There was a lot of tension that night. Nobody knew whether they would get their act together and mobilise some armoured units. It was very emotional, the feeling was very good, but it was a very dangerous moment,' says Dragan Ambrozić.

And some were already looking to the future and the inevitably traumatic transition period ahead. So many questions were still unanswered in this unstable country: how could Serbia construct a genuinely equitable society, repair its shattered economy, reform its corrupt civic institutions, reconcile itself to its bloody past and peacefully resolve its disputes in Kosovo and Montenegro? Could the opposition alliance hold together after its common enemy was vanquished? And there remained the issue of Slobodan Milošević: would he ever face trial for his crimes?

'I was not celebrating, I was not in the mood. I wanted to go home and sleep,' says Duška Anastasijević. 'It was over, you know. The job was done, but there was still another job unfinished.'

But others simply gave in to the moment – the ultimate realisation of long years of hoping. Petar Luković, a pessimist finally allowing himself to embrace optimism, was breathless with joy: 'That which I have been dreaming about for years has happened: everything, literally, everything is possible in Serbia! We have won!

'The streets of Belgrade are brimming with people, sitting, drinking, kissing each other, uncontrolled,' he wrote that night. 'The necessary wine, mineral water and cigarettes are brought. I am happy. I believed that I would turn into dust and ash before Milošević disappeared.

'To live without Milošević is a feeling that spreads slowly, that enters the veins slowly, very slowly . . . Tired, I salute the Revolution and devote myself to a bottle of 1997 Chardonnay. I officially close the chapter of my life of these 13 years and try to begin to be normal.'[18]

The next morning there was no more bloodshed or looting. The revolution was won. The European Union and United

States asserted that sanctions would soon be lifted and economic aid would follow.

Following a meeting with Koštunica at which he was forced, finally and unhappily, to admit defeat, Slobodan Milošević addressed the country before retreating to a villa in Dedinje with his wife and daughter, effectively under house arrest. After days of denial, lies and threats, Milošević stood next to the national flag, faced the camera and announced: 'Respected citizens, I have just received the official information that Vojislav Koštunica has won the presidential election.' He explained that he felt relief at no longer having the responsibility of leadership which had burdened him for a decade. He would now 'rest a little more', and spend time with his family.

The president who had sustained his regime through his control of the media ended his reign, fittingly, on national television. 'I congratulate Mr Koštunica on his electoral victory and I wish much success to all citizens of Yugoslavia,' he concluded.[19]

He was finished.

# appendix 1
# timeline of events

## 1989

June 28: After two years of mass rallies against Communist 'bureaucracy', Slobodan Milošević, president of Serbia, delivers a keynote nationalist speech at a mass meeting in Kosovo – a prelude to the break-up of Yugoslavia.

## 1990

May 13: Violent clashes between Serbian and Croatian football hooligans at the Dinamo Zagreb vs Red Star Belgrade match in Zagreb hints at the ferocity of the coming Serb–Croat war. Armed skirmishes break out between Serbs and Croats in Croatia shortly afterwards.

June 13: 70,000 demonstrate in Belgrade, the capital of Serbia and of Yugoslavia, for multi-party democracy. Later there are clashes with police outside the Belgrade Television building.

July: Following a referendum on multi-party elections, Serbia declares itself a democratic state. The Socialist Party of Serbia is founded; its president is Slobodan Milošević.

October: Željko Ražnatović, alias Arkan, founds the Serbian Volunteer Guard paramilitary group. Its nucleus comes from FC Red Star football hooligans.

December: First multi-party elections in Serbia. Slobodan Milošević wins a landslide victory and becomes president.

## 1991

March 9: 40,000 rally in Belgrade for liberalisation of the media. The demonstrators are attacked by riot police and Yugoslav Army occupies the city. Radio B92 is temporarily taken off the air.

June 25: Slovenia and Croatia declare independence from Yugoslavia. This is followed by a ten-day war in Slovenia and an escalation of conflict in Croatia between Croat police and the Serb-dominated Yugoslav Army, assisted by paramilitary groups.

November: After a lengthy siege, the town of Vukovar in Croatia falls to the Yugoslav Army and paramilitaries including Arkan's Tigers. The Croatian resort of Dubrovnik is also besieged.

## 1992

February: A petition calling on Slobodan Milošević to resign is circulated in Serbia. It attracts 840,000 signatures.

March 3: The Bosnian government declares independence from Yugoslavia.

April 6: Bosnia is recognised as an independent state by the European Community and the United States. Fighting had already broken out around Sarajevo. The city would be under siege from the Bosnian Serbs for three years and four months.

May: The United Nations Security Council imposes sanctions on Yugoslavia (which now consists of Serbia and Montenegro) as the war in Bosnia continues.

December: Milošević beats the independent candidate Milan Panić in a strongly contested Serbian election.

## 1993

January 6: Radio Television Serbia purges its staff to ensure loyalty to the Milošević regime.

February: A period of hyperinflation begins in Serbia. At its peak, the monthly rate of inflation reaches 313,563,558 per cent.

March: The Jugoskandik and Dafiment 'banks' collapse. Both are pyramid schemes which have impoverished tens of thousands of Serbs.

April: The UN steps up sanctions on Yugoslavia after the Vance–Owen plan for peace in Bosnia is rejected.

December: Milošević's Socialist Party wins another election.

## 1994

January: A programme of fiscal stabilisation leads to the end of hyperinflation.

August: In a move towards conciliation with the West, Milošević cuts his ties with Radovan Karadžić's Bosnian Serb statelet, Republika Srpska.

December: The Belgrade independent daily paper *Borba* is shut down by the authorities and relaunched under the control of the Socialists.

## 1995

February 19: Arkan marries 'turbo-folk' singing star Svetlana Veličković ('Ceca').

March: Mirjana Marković, Milošević's wife, launches her own United Yugoslav Left party, which will operate in partnership with his Socialists.

July: The UN-designated 'safe area' of Srebrenica falls to the Bosnian Serbs. An estimated 8,000 Muslims are massacred.

August: The Croatian army retakes the Serb-majority Krajina region of Croatia. Tens of thousands of refugees, almost the entire population, flee to Serbia.

August 30: NATO launches air strikes on the Bosnian Serbs after the shelling of Sarajevo's market square.

November 1: Negotiations begin between Serb, Croat and Bosnian leaders at the Wright-Patterson air force base in

Dayton, Ohio. The Dayton Agreement concludes the war in Bosnia.

## 1996

February 15: The independent Studio B television station is returned to public control under the Socialist Party-dominated Belgrade city assembly.

September 2: Zajedno ('Together'), a coalition of opposition parties including Vuk Drašković's Serbian Renewal Movement and Zoran Djindjić's Democratic Party, is formed.

November 17: Local elections in Serbia lead to wins for Zajedno victories in Belgrade, Novi Sad, Kragujevac, Niš and elsewhere. The election results are annulled by the authorities. Huge street protests erupt, continuing for eighty-four days. The number of protesters in Belgrade peaks at 500,000.

November 22: The Student Protest Committee is formed, calling for recognition of election victories and beginning its own street demonstrations.

December 3: Radio B92 is shut down, but after international pressure it begins broadcasting just over two days later.

December 24: The Socialist Party organises a counter-rally in support of Milošević in Belgrade. Scuffles break out with opposition protesters.

## 1997

February 4: Milošević asks the Yugoslav prime minister to frame a law to recognise the Zajedno victories.

February 21: A rally to celebrate Zajedno taking power in Belgrade attracts 150,000.

June: The Zajedno coalition disintegrates in acrimony.

July 15: Milošević, formerly president of Serbia, becomes president of Yugoslavia.

September 21: Elections leave Milošević's Socialists with no overall majority. There are large gains for Vojislav Šešelj's far-right Serbian Radical Party.

## 1998

February: Fights break out in Kosovo between Serb police and the ethnic Albanian guerrillas of the Kosovo Liberation Army.

March 9: The international community sets a deadline of ten days for Milošević to withdraw his brutal special police units from Kosovo, threatening economic sanctions. The deadline is later extended.

March 24: A new Socialist/Yugoslav United Left/Serbian Radical Party coalition government is formed. Vojislav Šešelj becomes deputy prime minister.

April 23: In a referendum, voters reject 'the participation of foreign representatives in resolving the Kosovo problem'.

October 6: Deputy prime minister Vojislav Šešelj threatens Serbian independent journalists, labelling them spies and traitors.

October 20: An Information Law, with the capacity to impose huge fines on dissident media, is passed. Alongside the similarly Draconian Universities Law, it inspires the formation of the student movement Otpor ('Resistance').

## 1999

January: Vuk Drašković joins Milošević government as Yugoslav deputy prime minister, leaving Serbia without an effective opposition. He is kicked out of office in April after he turns against Milošević's war policy.

March 24: NATO begins bombing Serbia after Milošević defies the latest 'final warning' to quit his military campaign in Kosovo. Radio B92 is shut down for the third time soon afterwards.

April 11: Opposition publisher Slavko Ćuruvija is shot dead outside his apartment in central Belgrade.

May: Milošević is indicted for war crimes by the United Nations.

June 9: NATO bombing ends as troops enter Kosovo.

July 27: Protests against the Milošević regime begin again shortly afterwards as Serbia's economic crisis continues. B92 returns to the Belgrade airwaves as B2–92, on an unused frequency owned by Studio B.

October 3: Vuk Drašković escapes death in a car crash that kills four colleagues. He claims it was an attempted assassination.

## 2000

January 15: Indicted war criminal Arkan is shot dead in the lobby of Belgrade's Hotel Intercontinental. His murder is followed shortly afterwards by the killing of defence minister Pavle Bulatović.

May 27: The Serbian Renewal Movement-controlled Studio B TV and radio station is taken over by the regime; B2–92, which is based in the same premises, is also shut down again. Violent demonstrations follow in Belgrade.

September 24: A coalition of opposition parties, the Democratic Opposition of Serbia, unites to contest elections. Its candidate, Vojislav Koštunica, beats Milošević in the poll for president. But the Election Commission says Koštunica has not gathered enough votes to win outright and declares a second round of voting. Street protests erupt all over Serbia.

October 2: DOS, claiming victory and refusing to participate in a second round of voting, launches a nationwide general strike.

October 5: A rally in Belgrade turns into a revolution. The federal parliament, Radio Television Serbia and the offices of Milošević's Socialist Party are stormed. Half a million protesters control the streets and Koštunica addresses a victory rally. B92's original premises are liberated and the station returns to the air.

October 6: Milošević admits defeat on national television and congratulates new president Koštunica.

# appendix 2
# soundtrack to the
# resistance

The top ten albums of the year from 1991 to 1999 as chosen by B92/B2–92's music department.

## 1991

1. Nirvana: *Nevermind*
2. REM: *Out of Time*
3. Teenage Fanclub: *Bandwagonesque*
4. Primal Scream: *Screamadelica*
5. Massive Attack: *Blue Lines*
6. Metallica: *Metallica*
7. Electronic: *Electronic*
8. Urban Dance Squad: *Life 'N' Perspectives Of A Genuine Crossover*
9. Prince: *Diamonds And Pearls*
10. PM Dawn: *Of The Heart, Of The Soul And Of The Cross: The Utopian Experience*

## 1992

1. REM: *Automatic For The People*
2. Sugar: *Copper Blue*
3. Nick Cave: *Henry's Dream*
4. Arrested Development: *3 Years, 5 Months And 2 Days In The Life Of...*
5. kd lang: *Ingenue*
6. Tom Waits: *Bone Machine*
7. The Black Crowes: *Southern Harmony*
8. Lou Reed: *Magic And Loss*
9. Sonic Youth: *Dirty*
10. Buffalo Tom: *Let Me Come Over*

## 1993

1. Dinousaur Jr: *Where You Been*
2. Lemonheads: *Come On Feel The Lemonheads*
3. Rage Against The Machine: *Rage Against The Machine*
4. The The: *Dusk*
5. Smashing Pumpkins: *Siamese Dream*
6. New Order: *Republic*
7. Pet Shop Boys: *Very*
8. Teenage Fanclub: *Thirteen*
9. Cypress Hill: *Black Sunday*
10. Björk: *Debut*

## 1994

1.= Portishead: *Dummy*
1.= Beastie Boys: *Ill Communication*
2. Oasis: *Definitely Maybe*
3. Massive Attack: *Protection*
4. Pavement: *Crooked Rain, Crooked Rain*

5. Prodigy: *Music For The Jilted Generation*
6. Nirvana: *Unplugged*
7. Morphine: *Cure For Pain*
8. Neil Young & Crazy Horse: *Sleeps With Rust*
9. The Stone Roses: *The Second Coming*
10. Blur: *Parklife*

## 1995

1. Tricky: *Maxinquaye*
2. Goldie: *Timeless*
3. St Germain: *Boulevard*
4. Chemical Brothers: *Exit Planet Dust*
5. Oasis: *What's The Story (Morning Glory)*
6. Boo Radleys: *Wake Up!*
7. PJ Harvey: *To Bring You My Love*
8. Teenage Fanclub: *Grand Prix*
9. Jon Spencer Blues Explosion: *Experimental Remixes*
10. Method Man: *Tical*

## 1996

1. Beck: *Odelay*
2. DJ Shadow: *Endtroducing*
3. Everything But The Girl: *Walking Wounded*
4. Manic Street Preachers: *Everything Must Go*
5. A Tribe Called Quest: *Beats, Rhymes And Life*
6. Fugees: *The Score*
7. Dr Octagon: *Dr Octagon*
8. Underworld: *Second Toughest In The Infants*
9. Barry Adamson: *Oedipus Schmoedipus*
10. REM: *New Adventures In Hi-fi*

# 1997

1. Roni Size Reprazent: *New Forms*
2. Cornershop: *When I Was Born For The Seventh Time*
3. Bjork: *Homogenic*
4. Ballistic Brothers: *Rude System*
5. Stereolab: *Dots And Loops*
6. Daft Punk: *Homework*
7. Spiritualized: *Ladies And Gentlemen We Are Floating In Space*
8. Wilco: *Being There*
9. The Verve: *Urban Hymns*
10. Bob Dylan: *Time Out Of Mind*

# 1998

1. Lauryn Hill: *The Miseducation*
2. Mercury Rev: *Deserter's Songs*
3. Massive Attack: *Mezzanine*
4. Air: *Moon Safari*
5. Beastie Boys: *Hello Nasty*
6. Terry Callier: *Timepeace*
7. Billy Bragg & Wilco: *Mermaid Avenue*
8. Beck: *Mutations*
9. Belle & Sebastian: *The Boy With The Arab Strap*
10. REM: *Up*

# 1999

1. Flaming Lips: *Soft Bulletin*
2. Roots: *Things Fall Apart*
3. Beck: *Midnite Vultures*
4. Bassment Jaxx: *Remedy*
5. Super Furry Animals: *Guerilla*

6. Mos Def: *Black On Both Sides*
7. Bonnie 'Prince' Billy: *I See A Darkness*
8. Tricky: *Juxtapose*
9. Pavement: *Terror Twilight*
10. Suba: *Sao Paulo Confessions*

# notes

## chapter one

1. Slavenka Drakulić, *Café Europa*, Abacus, London, 1996.
2. Predrag Delibasić, *Uzurlikzurli* website, December 1996.
3. Tim Judah, *The Serbs*, Yale University Press, London, 1997.
4. *The Guardian*, April 24th, 1999.
5. *The Guardian*, February 26th, 2000.
6. Peter M. Lewis and Jerry Booth, *The Invisible Medium*, Macmillan, London, 1989.
7. Speech by Veran Matić to the International Studies Association Conference, February 1999.
8. Dragoš Ivanović, *Plot Against the Public*, Republika, Belgrade, 1999.

## chapter two

1. Misha Glenny, *The Fall of Yugoslavia*, Penguin, London, 1996.
2. Ibid.
3. Ibid.
4. Ibid.
5. Slavenka Drakulić, *How We Survived Communism and Even Laughed*, HarperPerennial, New York, 1993.
6. Dragoš Ivanović, *Plot Against the Public*, Republika, Belgrade, 1999.
7. *Vukovar 1991*, B92 documentary.
8. Ivanović, *Plot Against the Public*.

9. Ibid.

10. Daniel Sunter, Institute for War and Peace Reporting, Balkan Crisis Report, date unknown.

11. Bojana Šušak, *An Alternative to War*, in Nebojša Popov (ed), *The Road to War in Serbia*, CEU Press, Budapest, 2000.

12. Timothy Garton Ash, *We The People*, Penguin, London, 1999.

13. Eric D. Gordy, *The Culture of Power in Serbia*, Penn State Press, Pennsylvania, 1999.

## chapter three

1. Eric D. Gordy, *The Culture of Power in Serbia*, Penn State Press, Pennsylvania, 1999.

2. Ibid.

3. Gene Greva, *The Albanian Experience*, Nettime e-mailing list, September 30th, 1998.

4. Tim Judah, *The Serbs*, Yale University Press, London, 1997.

5. Ibid.

6. *The Crime That Changed Serbia*, B92 documentary.

7. *Chicago Tribune*, December 17th, 1997.

8. Ivan Čolović, *Football, Hooligans and War*, in Nebojša Popov (ed), *The Road to War in Serbia*, CEU Press, Budapest, 2000.

9. Ibid.

10. Ibid.

11. *The Telegraph*, March 30th, 1999.

12. *The Sunday Telegraph*, May 24th, 1998.

13. Gordy, *The Culture of Power in Serbia*.

14. Ibid.

15. Slavenka Drakulić, *Café Europa*, Abacus, London, 1996.

16. Global Information Network, February 2nd, 1999.

17. Gordy, *The Culture of Power in Serbia*.

18. Free B92 news, April 26th, 2000.

19. Gordy, *The Culture of Power in Serbia*.

20. *Geto*, B92 documentary.

21. Bill Drummond, *45*, Little, Brown, London, 2000.

22. Ibid.

23. Matthew Collin, *Altered State*, Serpent's Tail, London, 1997.
24. *Vreme*, March 9th, 1996.
25. OGD annual report, 1997.


## chapter four

1. Eric D. Gordy, *The Culture of Power in Serbia*, Penn State Press, Pennsylvania, 1999.
2. Mladen Lazić, *The Emergence of a Democratic Order in Serbia*, in Mladen Lazić (ed), *Protest in Belgrade*, CEU Press, Budapest, 1999.
3. Underground Resistance, from sleevenotes to the album *A Revolution for Change*, 1992.
4. Lazar Džamić, *Of Midget and Giants*, in *Walking on the Spot*, B92, Belgrade, 1997.
5. Jovan Čekić, *No Comment*, in *Walking on the Spot*.
6. *Sunday Times*, December 1st, 1996.
7. Robert Thomas, *Serbia Under Milošević*, Hurst and Company, London, 1999.
8. *Wired*, April 1997.
9. *Sydney Morning Herald*, April 29th, 2000.
10. Reuters, December 17th, 1996.
11. Stevan Vuković, *Personal Experiment in Art*, Samizdat, Belgrade, 1998.
12. Gordy, *The Culture of Power in Serbia*.
13. Transcript from interview for the documentary *Collateral Damage*, 2000.
14. *The Independent*, January 8th, 1997.
15. Ivica Dolenc, *Walking on the Spot*, in *Walking on the Spot*.
16. Ivan Čolović, *Reading a Handful of Serbian Palms*, in *Walking on the Spot*.

## chapter five

1. Robert Thomas, *Serbia Under Milošević*, Hurst and Company, London, 1999.
2. Ibid.
3. Ibid.
4. *The Independent*, October 8th, 1998.
5. Dragoš Ivanović, *Plot Against the Public*, Republika, Belgrade, 1999.
6. Petar Luković, Institute for War and Peace Reporting, Balkan Crisis Report, March 13th, 1999.
7. *The Guardian*, March 25th, 2000.
8. Diary of Slobodan Marković, April 25th, 1999.
9. *The Guardian*, April 5th, 1999.
10. *The New York Times*, March 30th, 1999.
11. 'Insomnia', *Serbian Diary*, Nettime e-mailing list, March 30th, 1999.
12. Diary of Jasmina Tesanović, published via Internet, March 26th, 1999.
13. *Moral Combat*, BBC2, March 12th, 2000.
14. Petar Luković, Institute for War and Peace Reporting, Balkan Crisis Report, March 28th, 1999.
15. Veran Matić, *Where Did We Go Wrong?*, private paper, 1999.
16. Ibid.
17. Interview on FreeB92 website, October 11th, 1999.
18. Ibid.
19. Anon, Institute for War and Peace Reporting, Balkan Crisis Report, May 21st, 1999.
20. Diary of Jasmina Tesanović, published via Internet, April 9th, 1999.
21. Petar Luković, Institute for War and Peace Reporting, Balkan Crisis Report, March 28th, 1999.
22. 'Insomnia', *Serbian Diary*, Nettime e-mailing list, March 30th, 1999.
23. *The Big Issue*, April 19th, 1999.
24. 'Baža', *Bastard Special Edition*, 1999.
25. Geert Lovinck, *Bastard Special Edition*, 1999.
26. Nettime e-mailing list, April 5th, 1999.

27. *Washington Post*, April 17th, 1999.
28. *Washington Post*, November 8th, 1999.
29. Petar Luković, Institute for War and Peace Reporting, Balkan Crisis Report, June 1999.


## chapter six

1. Petar Luković, Institute for War and Peace Reporting, Balkan Crisis Report, August 1999.
2. *The Guardian*, July 31st, 1999.
3. Institute for War and Peace Reporting, Balkan Crisis Report, August 1999.
4. Institute for War and Peace Reporting, Balkan Crisis Report, October 1999.
5. Radio B2–92, February 10th, 2000.
6. Nettime e-mailing list, March 14th, 1999.
7. Petar Luković, Institute for War and Peace Reporting, Balkan Crisis Report, April 28th, 2000.
8. Veran Matić, *Truths, Responsibilities and Reconciliations*, April 2000.
9. Petar Luković, Institute for War and Peace Reporting, Balkan Crisis Report, August 1999.


## chapter seven

1. FreeB92 News, September 15th, 2000.
2. *The Independent*, September 24th, 2000.
3. Institute for War and Peace Reporting, Balkan Crisis Report, August 25th, 2000.
4. Dejan Anastasijević with Anthony Borden (eds), *Out of Time*, Beta News Agency, Belgrade, and Institute for War and Peace Reporting, London, 2000.
5. *The Times*, October 16th, 2000.
6. Institute for War and Peace Reporting, Balkan Crisis Report, September 22th, 2000.

7. Institute for War and Peace Reporting, Balkan Crisis Report, September 8th, 2000.

8. *The Independent*, September 24th, 2000.

9. FreeB92 website, September 2000.

10. Ibid.

11. *The Guardian*, September 28th, 2000.

12. FreeB92 News, September 27th, 2000.

13. FreeB92 News, October 2nd, 2000.

14. Institute for War and Peace Reporting, Balkan Crisis Report, October 13th, 2000.

15. *The Guardian*, November 3rd, 2000.

16. Institute for War and Peace Reporting, Balkan Crisis Report, October 13th, 2000.

17. *The Guardian*, October 6th, 2000.

18. Institute for War and Peace Reporting, Balkan Crisis Report, October 6th, 2000.

19. FreeB92 News, October 6th, 2000.

# acknowledgements

This book is dedicated to Gordan Paunović and Stephanie Collin for inspiration and support. Thanks for research materials, advice, hospitality and encouragement are due to Dragan Ambrozić, Doug Aubrey, Chris Bohn, Audrey Collin, Lisa Eveleigh, Miomir Grujić (Fleka), Tomislav Grujić, Vladimir Janjić, Veran Matić, Laurence O'Toole, Susanne Simon and Jelena Subotić; to my *Big Issue* colleagues, particularly Sally Stainton, Andrew Davies, Tina Jackson, Gibby Zobel and Adam Macqueen, to Marija Milosavljević and Goran Dimitrijević for translation, and to all at Serpent's Tail.

Thanks to all those who gave up their time to be interviewed for this book. I am also indebted to the fine work of the authors and journalists who have reported on Yugoslav politics and culture over the past decade, particularly Ivan Čolović, Steve Crawshaw, Slavenka Drakulić, Robert Fisk, Timothy Garton-Ash, Misha Glenny, Eric D. Gordy, Dragoš Ivanović, Tim Judah, Alan Little, Petar Luković, Laura Silber, Robert Thomas, Mark Thompson and Vesna Perić Zimonjić, and to the websites and publications of Article 19, Free B92, Free Serbia, the Institute for War and Peace Reporting, Nettime, Press Now and Vreme.

All interviews were conducted between December 1996 and November 2000. Some comments are unattributed where the interviewees requested anonymity.